Novel Bodies

TRANSITS:
LITERATURE, THOUGHT & CULTURE 1650–1850

Series Editors
Greg Clingham, Bucknell University
Kathryn Parker, University of Wisconsin—La Crosse
Miriam Wallace, New College of Florida

Transits is a series of scholarly monographs and edited volumes publishing beautiful and surprising work. Without ideological bias the series seeks transformative readings of the literary, artistic, cultural, and historical interconnections between Britain, Europe, the Far East, Oceania, and the Americas during the years 1650 and 1850, and as their implications extend down to the present time. In addition to literature, art, and history, such "global" perspectives might entail considerations of time, space, nature, economics, politics, environment, gender, sex, race, bodies, and material culture, and might necessitate the development of new modes of critical imagination. At the same time, the series welcomes considerations of the local and the national, for original new work on particular writers and readers in particular places in time continues to be foundational to the discipline.

Since 2011, sixty-five *Transits* titles have been published or are in production.

Recent Titles in the Series

Fire on the Water: Sailors, Slaves, and Insurrection in Early American Literature, 1789–1886
Lenora Warren

Community and Solitude: New Essays on Johnson's Circle
Anthony W. Lee, ed.

The Global Wordsworth: Romanticism Out of Place
Katherine Bergren

Cultivating Peace: The Virgilian Georgic in English, 1650–1750
Melissa Schoenberger

Intelligent Souls? Feminist Orientalism in Eighteenth-Century English Literature
Samara Anne Cahill

Jane Austen and Comedy
Erin M. Goss, ed.

The Printed Reader: Gender, Quixotism, and Textual Bodies in Eighteenth-Century Britain
Amelia Dale

For a full list of *Transits* titles go to https://www.bucknell.edu/script/upress/series.asp?id=33

TRANSITS

Novel Bodies

DISABILITY AND SEXUALITY
IN EIGHTEENTH-CENTURY
BRITISH LITERATURE

JASON S. FARR

LEWISBURG, PENNSYLVANIA

Library of Congress Cataloging in Publication Number: 2019012863

A British Cataloging-in-Publication record for this book is available from the British Library.

Copyright © 2019 by Jason S. Farr

All rights reserved

No part of this book may be reproduced or utilized in any form or by any means, electronic or mechanical, or by any information storage and retrieval system, without written permission from the publisher. Please contact Bucknell University Press, Hildreth-Mirza Hall, Bucknell University, Lewisburg, PA 17837-2005. The only exception to this prohibition is "fair use" as defined by U.S. copyright law.

♾ The paper used in this publication meets the requirements of the American National Standard for Information Sciences—Permanence of Paper for Printed Library Materials, ANSI Z39.48-1992.

www.bucknell.edu/UniversityPress

Distributed worldwide by Rutgers University Press

Manufactured in the United States of America

For Alan

CONTENTS

Introduction: Disability and the Literary History of Sexuality   1

1 Deaf Education and Queerness in the Duncan Campbell Compendium (1720–1732)   36

2 The Reforming Bodies of Samuel Richardson's *Pamela* (1740) and Sarah Scott's Fiction (1754–1766)   71

3 Chronic Illness, Medicine, and the Healthy Marriages of Tobias Smollett's *The Expedition of Humphry Clinker* (1771)   103

4 Gendered Disfigurement and Queer Ocular Relations in Frances Burney's *Camilla* (1796) and Maria Edgeworth's *Belinda* (1801)   131

Coda: Hypochondria and the Implausibility of Heterosexual Romance in Jane Austen's *Sanditon* (1817)   164

Acknowledgments   171

Bibliography   175

Index   185

Novel Bodies

INTRODUCTION

Disability and the Literary
History of Sexuality

THE EIGHTEENTH CENTURY IS OFTEN regarded as a period in which the idea of the individual undergoes significant developments and, relatedly, in which nascent codes of modern embodiment that feel to us at once familiar and foreign proliferate in a variety of cultural forms.[1] From their variable representations of gender and sexuality, to their malleable ideas about race, eighteenth-century writers demonstrate an elasticity of thought about what makes bodies appear and act as they do.[2] *Novel Bodies: Disability and Sexuality in Eighteenth-Century British Literature* argues that early novelists depict corporeal and sexual difference in capacious and flexible ways, often to reconfigure the political and social landscapes of the Georgian period. Throughout the eighteenth century, authors often portray the lived experience of disability as analogous to—and as informed by—queer genders and sexualities.[3] In the process, they expose able-bodiedness and heterosexuality as imbricated systems that sustain dominant models of reproductive futurity.[4] However, the authors featured in this book do not just relegate bodily difference to the peripheries of their narratives; rather, they use intersections of disability and queerness to stage an array of eighteenth-century debates covering contemporaneous topics as diverse as education, feminism, kinship, medicine, and plantation life. *Novel Bodies* examines the fiction of Horace Walpole, Eliza Haywood, Samuel Richardson, Sarah Scott, Tobias Smollett, Frances Burney, Maria Edgeworth, and Jane Austen, whose representations of embodiment offer a diverse spectrum of bodies and desires.[5] In grappling with prevailing norms that would appear to privilege nascent models of heterosexuality and able-bodiedness, these writers imagine impaired bodies as defining and exceeding the bounds of gender and sexual normativity. In this way, they establish queer, disabled embodiment as an ambivalent experience marked by the exquisite pleasure of transgression and the enduring social and physical pain of disability. In doing so, I argue, these works make clear that the British literary history of sexuality is thoroughly reliant on impaired bodies for its discursive contours.

Given its critical emphasis on the interplay between disability and sexuality in British literature of the eighteenth century, *Novel Bodies* intervenes in the robust wealth of scholarship that engages Michel Foucault's foundational three-volume work *The History of Sexuality*.[6] In *Volume 1: An Introduction*, Foucault argues against the "repressive hypothesis" by making the case that a repressive model of sexuality does not adequately account for the "discursive explosion" about sex in the West, which may be traced back to the seventeenth century.[7] Foucault ties this proliferation of sexual discourse to mechanisms of power that produce knowledge and meaning. The eighteenth century serves as a key period for Foucault in his contestation of the repressive hypothesis. He argues, for instance, "Rather than a massive censorship, beginning with the verbal proprieties imposed by the Age of Reason, what was involved was a regulated and polymorphous incitement to discourse."[8] Foucault accounts for how models of "decency"—such as what one might observe in the culture of sensibility—facilitate, rather than stymy, discourses of sex, which get channeled through decorous language, sentiment, and prescriptive sexual conduct campaigns (among other things). Concurrently, a number of "peripheral sexualities" emerged as scrutiny of the heterosexual couple intensified.[9] *Novel Bodies* argues that these marginal sexualities are often bound to impairment and that this affiliation helped to create the conditions for modern sexual categories to emerge. Representations of physical and sensory impairment often anchor heterosexuality to emergent notions of health and ability, relegating its doubles, homosexuality and disability, to the role of unnatural supplement. Yet, I will show how these representations also destabilize the ostensible naturalness of heteronormativity by revealing its ideological inconsistencies. Impaired bodies are thus fundamental to the cultural constructions of homo- and heterosexuality, and the novels examined in this study reflect this eighteenth-century discursive phenomenon.[10]

Pioneering titles in disability studies have elucidated the centrality of deformity and disability in the long eighteenth century.[11] Helen Deutsch demonstrates the expansive part that deformity plays in the writings and biographies of the eighteenth-century luminaries Alexander Pope and Samuel Johnson.[12] According to Deutsch, *deformity*—a commodious term that encompasses various kinds of physical deviation from the status quo—"reigned supreme" in the eighteenth century, before the institution of scientific norms defined our "modern conceptions" of disability in the following century.[13] Lennard Davis conceives of the eighteenth century as a time in which social constructions of physical difference undergo a transition marked by "the contradiction of an earlier sense in which disability per se did not exist and of a later one in which disability is a modality used to explain a great deal."[14] For Davis, the literature of the period reflects this transformation. In a more recent study, David Turner emphasizes the significance of gender and class for understanding how disability was represented and for how disabled people saw themselves in relation to their communities.[15] *Novel Bodies* is

INTRODUCTION

indebted to these and other trenchant studies of the cultural history of disability, but it brings its own objective to the fore, which is to deepen our understanding of the centrality of physical and sexual variance for early British novels. This book assumes that eighteenth-century British novels are a particularly fertile venue for conceptualizing disabled and queer pasts. My readings of novels reveal that these facets of embodiment have defined and mutually sustained one another as far back as the early modern period, and that the points of convergence between variable bodies and queer desires serve crucial narrative functions.

To attend to representations of embodiment, I focus my analysis on the characters of these narratives, who are often described in decidedly physical ways. Such physicality, as Aileen Douglas has observed, is typical of early British novels, in which characters' bodies betray empiricist philosophies that emphasize sensory perception as a conduit to knowledge. Corporeality, according to Douglas, "is one of the problems that the early novel mediates."[16] Douglas regards novels as addressing questions that determine the "definition, legibility and control of the body."[17] Douglas thereby examines the body as the product of social forces. Such an approach has also been an objective of disability studies scholars, who have argued that to attend only to the material form of the body reproduces hierarchies of ableist oppression by distracting attention away from the social forces that render impairment a stigmatized experience.[18] *Novel Bodies* attends to both the physical and the social facets of embodiment, arguing for a relational approach to disability, whose meaning changes according to historical and geographic contexts.[19] I argue, for instance, that characters' bodies grant vital insights into lived experience but that authors also use these characters to mediate the social conditions that inform their narratives. Blakey Vermeule claims that authors (and readers) use literary characters "to sort out basic moral problems or to practice new emotional situations."[20] In the case of the novels under scrutiny in this book, authors may have represented variable embodiment for an array of moral or emotional situations, but my focus in the coming pages is to discern how they employ disability and queerness in their fiction to critique and rework the social fabric—to imagine "novel" social orders that rearrange widespread assumptions, principles, and social practices. In this introduction, I investigate the ableism of John Locke to position disability theory as an urgent critical intervention for eighteenth-century literary studies, and I explore the expansive consequence of deformity in the eighteenth century. I follow this with an overview of the interlocking attributes of queerness and disability. I then historicize queer and disabled affiliations through my close reading of Horace Walpole's *The Castle of Otranto* (1764) before situating this project within existing scholarship in eighteenth-century novel studies. Finally, I give a chapter-by-chapter overview of the book as a whole.

[3]

LOCKE'S ABLEISM, DEFORMITY, AND DISABILITY THEORY

Scholars often discuss the enormous impact of John Locke's ideas about education and individual subjectivity on the novel form, but what is customarily overlooked in these studies is Locke's ableism, which relegates people with impairments of various kinds to non-subjecthood. During the long eighteenth century, in large part because of Locke, evolving conceptions of the *individual*—a feeling, intuiting subject that is capable of experiencing the world in an autonomous manner—emerge in the midst of social and political shifts that cast modernity as a clean break from an earlier, dark Medieval period. As Raymond Williams argues, the etymological forebear of *individual* is *individuus*, which in the Medieval period referred to a collective "unity or spirit" that was indivisible (such as the holy trinity).[21] Williams shows that the emergence of our modern usage of *individual* was a consequence of political and economic developments that occurred over the course of many centuries. During that period, there was an increased emphasis on the "personal existence" of man that gradually supplanted rank or status in the rigidly stratified system of feudalism.[22] The modern individual did not emerge suddenly at the end of the seventeenth century, when Locke wrote his influential theories of mind and political philosophy, but we may observe in Locke, and in many of the eighteenth-century novels that follow him, an emphasis on the subjective experience of the individual. Novels often exploit the tension between old and new social orders, with the body functioning as a key representational player in the social turn that Williams identifies. For Nancy Armstrong, novels "gave tangible form to a desire that set the body on a collision course with limits that the old society had placed on the individual's options for self-fulfillment, transforming the body from an indicator of rank to the container of a unique subjectivity."[23] As Armstrong indicates, British novels of the eighteenth century encompass Lockean thought about the role that sensation plays in constituting the individual body and mind. How the "container" of the body comes to indicate one's "unique subjectivity," for Locke, occurs through education.[24] Locke argues that, through the senses, young children "furnish" their minds—which he compares to "empty cabinets" and "white paper"—with "particular ideas."[25] In time, "the mind abstracts" these ideas, and, through word association, children learn language.[26] Eventually, they experience the growth of reason and the facility to manage the self. This includes an ability to "govern his passions . . . for what he can do before a prince, or a great man, he can do alone, or in the presence of God, if he will."[27] To be capable of reason is tantamount to exercising self-control, making the absolutist rule of a monarch superfluous. In this way, individuals are, in effect, constituted through their keen sensory perception of the external world. They are objects, "touched" by sources exterior to the self.[28] Over time and with suitable guidance, individuals become subjects, capable of rational thought.

Locke's understanding of the making of the individual reinforced already existing educational barriers for many disabled people. For one thing, Locke neglects to take into account how people with sensory impairments figure into the educational process he meticulously outlines. When he does write about sensory impairment, as he does in *An Essay Concerning Human Understanding*, he focuses on the limitations that it is thought to betoken: "The fewer senses any man (or other creature) has, the fewer and duller the impressions are that his senses make; and the duller the faculties are that he brings to bear on them, the more remote he is from having the sort of knowledge that is to be found in some men."[29] Since humans are formed entirely through their capacity to perceive the world around them through their five senses, impairment in one of the senses reduces the impression's ability to engrain itself in the mind. Such thinking has a marginalizing effect on the deaf and blind, who are considered to be "remote" from the "knowledge that is to be found in some men." Given the historical context in which Locke wrote, a century before the formation of academies for the deaf and blind in Britain, his perspective is hardly surprising. He does, however, engage in ongoing discussions about signed language, which natural philosophers preceding him often conflated with gesture: "Men who through some physical defect can't utter words still manage to express their universal ideas by signs that they use instead of general words: and we see that non-human organisms can't do that."[30] Despite this caveat, which allows for some communicative aptitude in deaf and nonverbal peoples, there is clearly an ableist hierarchy at work in Locke's thinking that forecloses the possibility that sensory-impaired people could match sighted and hearing peers in their intellectual development. In this way, Locke disqualifies a considerable part of the population from the most elevated kinds of education available.

Beyond excluding people with sensory impairments, Locke's entire basis for conceptualizing education and the development of reason relies on suppositions about normative bodies and minds that reflect Cartesian dualism. The opening lines of *Some Thoughts Concerning Education* elucidate this: "A sound mind in a sound body, is a short but full description of a happy state in this world: he that has these two, has little more to wish for; and he that wants either of them, will be but little the better for any thing else. Men's happiness or misery is most part of their own making. He whose mind directs not wisely, will never take the right way; and he whose body is crazy and feeble, will never be able to advance in it."[31] To begin his treatise, Locke invokes Juvenal's "mens sana in corpore sano"—the maxim that a healthy body serves as the repository of a sound mind. *Sound*, according to the *Oxford English Dictionary*, denotes a constitution that is "free from disease, infirmity, or injury" and is characterized by "bodily health" and robustness.[32] In this instance, *sound* functions as an antonym for *deformity*, which in the long eighteenth century denotes ugliness, physical disfigurement, and "abnormal formation of the body or of some bodily member."[33] In order to receive a proper education—to fill the "empty cabinet of the mind," per Locke—one must possess a mind and body devoid of physical and intellectual impairment. To be *unsound*—to be found lacking in either mind or body—is to want the necessary conditions for cultivation of the intellect, depriving the individual of "a happy state in this world." Locke elsewhere reinforces the connection between impaired body and mind in *An Essay Concerning Human Understanding*, where, as Nancy J. Hirschmann points out, Locke suggests that both the physically and cognitively disabled lack *freedom*, a necessary state in which to live for one to count as human. Hirschmann reveals that, according to Locke, the physically disabled experience a kind of mental atrophy when unable to work: "Insofar as the physically disabled cannot participate in labor, the key to gaining property, their rationality will likely decline unless they find some other way to be useful and productive."[34] The cognitively impaired, meanwhile, "are similarly unfree because they lack the ability to reason altogether."[35] As Locke proposes in both *An Essay Concerning Human Understanding* and *Some Thoughts Concerning Education*, men must create their own experience of happiness, but those who are deemed "crazy" or "feeble" are left out of his equation for leading a fulfilling life. As he proposes, the soundness of the body is a gauge of the mind's capacity to be educated, or to develop reason. Through such ableist ideas about the relationship between body and mind, Locke expels the physically and intellectually impaired from the proper channels of education and thus from the attaining of happiness.

Locke's inability to account for a diverse spectrum of bodies and minds is indicative of what Tobin Siebers calls "the ideology of ability"—a profound "preference for able-bodiedness" that masquerades as one of our most deeply engrained cultural truths.[36] Siebers defines the ideology of ability as that which "simultaneously banishes disability and turns it into a principle of exclusion."[37] Siebers notes that, despite the vulnerability of our bodies, efforts to perfect the body and to live in a constant state of health and able-bodiedness are symptomatic of ideological conditions that are often invisible to us. Locke betrays a philosophical orientation immersed in the ideology of ability when he argues that impairment necessarily precludes proper cultivation of the intellect, and when he posits that the state of the body is a sure reflection of the state of the mind (and vice versa). Through Locke's invocation of Juvenal, one observes a long history of the exclusionary principles that inhere in the ideology of ability. According to Siebers, disability provides a necessary counterpoint to this system, for it potentially stands in critical opposition to such untenable assumptions about the body.[38] To refute such thinking, according to Siebers, we must recast "disability as a form of human variation."[39] Throughout *Novel Bodies*, I understand disability as a natural life course given the diverse spectrum of bodies and minds that inhabited eighteenth-century Britain. A number of novels from this period represent impaired characters as what Siebers would call "complexly embodied"—that is, as disabled by social, educational, and architectural barriers, and as impacted by the physical and social pain of impairment.[40] Now, to be sure, my use of *disability* here—and throughout *Novel Bodies*—requires some explanation and historical nuance. When I use *disability*, I refer to our modern-day understanding of the term: a social category in which people with impairments encounter institutional, social, or physical barriers that impede them from unfettered access to a given community or society. In the eighteenth century, however, *disabled* refers specifically to military men and male laborers who are unable to serve or toil due to bodily impairment. Thus, in Enlightenment Britain, *disability* is a gendered and class-based term with somewhat limited usage.[41]

Conversely, *deformity* was used in an array of contexts. As it was understood throughout the long eighteenth century, *deformity* could be any visible deviation from standards of beauty or bodily form, including that which results from physical disfigurement. *Deformity* differs in crucial ways from how we conceptualize *disability* today, especially with regard to how it encompasses appearance but not necessarily bodily function. Essaka Joshua rightly argues that deformity in the eighteenth century is to be "understood in aesthetic terms, without specifically referencing function."[42] Indeed, as Joshua shows, deformity entails a visual peculiarity in an individual's physical constitution—that which would be understood as a deviation from corporeal standards but which would not necessarily encompass function impairments. In addition, while deformity was often the punch line of malicious jokes in the unsentimental tradition, as Simon Dickie has indicated, it could also be construed as a mark and enabler of literary genius, as Helen Deutsch's work on Pope and Johnson demonstrates.[43] Deformity was also profoundly embedded in the intellectual imagination and at the core of the most influential of eighteenth-century philosophy. Paul Kelleher reveals that "the rhetoric of deformity not only pervades the discourse of eighteenth-century moral philosophy, but more importantly, it makes possible the articulation of moral systems as such."[44] Moreover, in his astute reading of Adam Smith's *The Theory of Moral Sentiments*, Kelleher argues for the centrality of deformity in Smith's understanding of how an individual cultivates sympathy: "Smithean civil society is underwritten, from first to last, by an ideological dispensation that divides the beautiful from the deformed."[45] As Kelleher attests, deformity functions as both potent rhetorical device and embodied experience, and is the means by which Enlightenment philosophers conceptualize everything from morality, to sympathy, to the formation of civil society. As Dickie, Deutsch, Joshua, and Kelleher each show in their unique ways, deformity is an utterly indispensable part of eighteenth-century British culture. Given the diversity of their objects of inquiry, methods, and findings, one surmises that there is still much to be written about how extensively deformity undergirds Enlightenment thought.

Novel Bodies intervenes in this vibrant conversation by showing that deformity is also linked to queer genders and sexualities in the literary imagination of the eighteenth century. Deformity and other forms of bodily difference—including deafness, chronic disease, and chronic illness—serve as vital tools for British novelists, who imagine physical variability and queer desire as interrelated, consequential literary devices. By attending to the nuance of fictional narrative, this book shows that literary representations of bodily difference sometimes adhere to, but sometimes are not in standing with, Locke's ableist conceptions of rationality. *Novel Bodies* draws on disability theory to scrutinize the connection that Locke and others have imagined to exist between embodiment and rationality, and to generate new understandings of the dynamic role that variable bodies play in British novels of the eighteenth century. Moreover, this book aims to enrich disability theory by extending its critical reach to the eighteenth century.

One of the more radical interventions in disability theory for which *Novel Bodies* accounts is crip theory. A shortened version of the traditionally pejorative term *cripple*, *crip* has been adopted in recent years by disability activists and scholars whose intentions are, among other things, to defy able-bodied presumptions about disability, to protest the architectural and institutional barriers that discriminate against variable minds and bodies, and to eschew the myth of the perfectibility of the body. In a strategic move that is reminiscent of LGBTQ activists and scholars who adopt the term *queer* to challenge assimilation, mainstream politics, and taken-for-granted gender and sexual categories, disability activists have found in *crip* a rallying point from which to "stare back" at the probing able-bodied gaze that demands conformity, or failing that, imposes alienation, judgment, pity, and condescension.[46] As Carrie Sandahl has argued, *crip* denotes "a radical stance towards concepts of normalcy."[47] Crip can also be used as a verb. Robert McRuer argues that *to crip* is to take "a sledgehammer to that which has been concretized."[48] Here, McRuer establishes an apt analogy between the creation of critical frameworks that imagine society in radically different terms and the guerilla activism of disability rights advocates who demolish inaccessible curbs with sledgehammers. Alison Kafer discusses crip futures in which impairment—typically viewed as a corporeal or intellectual state that has no future—is regarded "as political, as valuable, as integral."[49] By recasting disability as a potentially desirable state of mind and/or body, Kafer contests long-standing social assumptions that alienate so many individuals. I draw my critical approach from these and other scholars who theorize disability as facilitating accessible futures, but I would add that the tenets of crip theory are relevant not only for the recent past, present, and future; they can also allow us to think differently about the discursive underpinnings of cultural production and the lived realities of people with impairments from earlier periods.

To crip the literature of the Georgian period, then—to "take a sledgehammer to that which has been concretized" in relation to how we interpret cultural production—is one of the primary objectives of this book.[50] The eighteenth century is a time in which the idea of rationality itself became "concretized" in British print culture, in part through a widespread endorsement of certain bodies and desires and a disavowal of others. To crip the eighteenth century is to interrogate the ideological fissures in those exclusionary discursive formations. To crip the Enlightenment also entails finding new ways to conceptualize the period: to identify stereotypical representations of impairment-as-deprivation, to be sure, but also to draw attention to portrayals of crip futurity. Eighteenth-century novels serve as the object of inquiry for this study because they oscillate between archaic stereotypes and innovative thinking about impairment, and because they offer a rich and varied tapestry of bodies and desires. Throughout this book, I conceive of eighteenth-century fiction in crip terms to critique the enduring trope of the individual who overcomes physical impairment, and social challenges generally, alone. *Novel Bodies* contests the notion that impairment is inevitably a manifestation of limitation or pain in the eighteenth century; it critiques that which is taken-for-granted in how the body is constituted by examining novels that generate new, socially transformative avenues of expression through queer and disabled characters; and finally, it contemplates the significance of narrative moments in which atypical bodies and desires come into contact with one another.

AFFILIATIONS OF DISABILITY AND QUEERNESS

Disability is absolutely central for the emergence of modern systems of sexuality, in which homo- and heterosexuality form two of the foremost categories of sexual identity in the West. We can note in the eighteenth century the establishment of sexual morphologies that rely upon impaired bodies for their formation. Like other recent titles in disability studies that theorize identity categories as interconnected and mutually constitutive, *Novel Bodies* considers disability as inseparable from other forms of identity.[51] This latest stage of disability inquiry, for Michael Davidson, consists of an "intersectional turn" in which scholarship from recent years challenges the notion of disability as social construction, now widely considered an ineffective tool for theorizing chronic pain and the "lived reality" of people with disabilities.[52] As Davidson argues, recent works in disability studies reflect "alliances and intersections across disciplines and methodologies."[53]

Black feminist thought has played an indispensable role in the growth of this latest phase of disability studies, in which *intersectionality* has been adopted as a key method. In her groundbreaking essay, "Mapping the Margins: Intersectionality, Identity Politics, and Violence against Women of Color," Kimberlé Crenshaw argues that women of color's political, legal, and social devaluations are the product of not racism *or* sexism, but racism *and* sexism. Crenshaw claims that not only do women of color experience heightened forms of oppression, but that progressive movements often do not capture this complexity due to the narrow scope of identity politics: "The problem with identity politics," Crenshaw writes, "is not that it fails to transcend difference, as some critics charge, but rather the opposite—that it frequently conflates or ignores intragroup differences."[54] Crenshaw's foundational work has opened the door for scholars to consider intersectionality in relation to other identity categories. For instance, Nirmala Erevelles and Andrea Minear draw on theories of intersectionality and Critical Race Feminism to argue that disabled people of color are harmed by the very institutions meant to grant them agency and security in a social order that is hostile to their existence.[55] Other disability theorists have likewise adopted intersectionality as a key term, but as some feminists of color have recently pointed out, intersectionality is flattened out when we lose sight of the contributions of scholars of color, or when we forget that women of color feel structures of oppression in particularly violent ways. As Nikol G. Alexander-Floyd argues, "Other research on white women or other groups can, of course, be usefully informed by intersectionality. But in order to avoid further (neo)colonization of this term, intersectionality research must be properly understood as the purview of researchers investigating women of color."[56] In heeding Alexander-Floyd's critique, I would acknowledge that this book is not "intersectional" because it does not explicitly consider the work or experience of women of color. However, methodologically, *Novel Bodies* owes much to the insights of feminists of color who have established intersectionality as a critical framework for analyzing how power and oppression operate in relation to clusters of identity categories.

Following these principles, I examine how deafness, deformity, and chronic disease and illness shape sexuality and gender in novels of the eighteenth century. It must be noted, however, that I am far from the first to claim that the categories of *disability* and *queerness* are intricately bound to one another.[57] As identities that share pathologized histories, and that potentially disrupt normative formulations of embodiment and desire in our present moment, disability and queerness share political, cultural, and social orientations. Robert McRuer uses Adrienne Rich's critique of "compulsory heterosexuality"—the seemingly unassailable truth that cross-sex marriage and procreation are the expected life course for women, even as lesbian existence functions as a necessary complement and distorted mirror-image to heterosexuality—to frame his argument that heterosexuality and able-bodiedness rely upon one another for their logic: "The system of compulsory able-bodiedness that produces disability is thoroughly interwoven with the system of compulsory heterosexuality that produces queerness."[58] Compulsory able-bodiedness—the taken-for-granted truth that one ought to be, or, failing that, must *desire* to be, of able body and mind—is a discursive strategy through which heterosexuality asserts its supremacy over homosexuality. As McRuer argues, heterosexual subjects are often represented as able-bodied. McRuer, Alison Kafer, David T. Mitchell, Sharon L. Snyder, and other scholars that study contemporary cultures consider the forging of *queer* with *crip* as a potentially insurgent affiliation that undermines the systemic consolidation of heterosexuality and able-bodiedness. Because they are aligned with queerness in this way, crip bodies contest the logic of heteronormativity.

As disability scholars have argued, disability is, like sexuality, fluid, and perhaps even more so than sexuality: one may become disabled at any point, temporarily or permanently, and the likelihood of one's becoming impaired only increases as one ages.[59] Such marked mutability establishes disability as an ever-shifting identity category in which the boundary between able-bodied self and disabled other is often blurry. While disability scholars today understand that binary thinking regarding disability and able-bodiedness simultaneously promotes and hinders rights advocacy, in eighteenth-century Britain, the idea of health as a distinctive, desirable, and attainable state, was only just emerging.[60] Thus, the boundary between what we would think of today as ability and disability is likewise unstable and incoherent in the Enlightenment but in ways that are strikingly distinct from our current moment. This book will trace the resonances between the present and the eighteenth century, while accounting for such significant departures.[61]

The notion that disability is tinged with sexual or gender transgression may be traced as far back as Francis Bacon's essay *Of Deformity* (1612), in which Bacon imagines the figure of the eunuch as the quintessential example of deformity. To begin his essay, Bacon argues that "deformed persons" possess "unnatural affections": "For as nature hath done ill by them, so do they by nature; being for the most part (as the Scripture saith) void of natural affection; and so they have their revenge of nature."[62] As Deutsch remarks, Bacon's essay is unclear about what such an absence of "natural affection" entails, exactly: whether he means to say that deformed persons are lacking in sympathetic will toward their peers, or whether they are accustomed to the privation of sympathy from others, or perhaps some combination of the two.[63]

What is especially striking to me about Bacon's essay is the way in which it imbues deformity with an exotic form of gender and sexuality when it discusses the Turkish royalty's habit of placing eunuchs in positions of authority. Bacon writes, "Kings in ancient times (and at this present in some countries) were wont to put great trust in eunuchs; because they that are envious towards all are obnoxious and officious, towards one. But yet their trust towards them, hath rather been as to good spials, and good whisperers, than good magistrates and officers."[64] Bacon suggests that eunuchs are capable of wielding substantial political power due to their loyalty, an effect of their deformity. Moreover, as this excerpt indicates, eunuchs are believed to be empowered by their castration. In stark contrast to our modern, post-Freud conceptions of castration, Bacon posits the eunuch's loss as strength. In early modern England, the eunuch was often viewed as an asexual individual who embodies a foreign or outdated gender position.[65] However, in certain contexts, eunuchs wielded political power that derived from the loss of their anatomy. "For certain specialized purposes," writes Gary Taylor, "the eunuch was not a defective man but an improved one."[66] Eunuchs played integral roles within courts in Ancient Eurasia, where they were entrusted with control over harems. Later on, within a European, Christian context, eunuchs were exemplary members of the church fold, as their wounded anatomy carried currency within a religious system that values martyrs and those who undergo physical suffering.[67] In an early modern context, eunuchs occupy a distinct gender category, and they are strengthened in crucial ways by their physical variance. Thus, while Bacon is unclear about what deformity might signify or cause among deformed persons, he argues that deformity of the sort that eunuchs are subject to increases their social and political power. Moreover, Bacon's employment of eunuchism as the epitome of physical difference suggests that deformity is aligned with gender mobility, an affiliation that we might understand today as *queer*. Bacon's essay is a touchstone for the long history of disabled and queer association, in that it establishes involuntary disfigurement as antecedent to queer ways of being that are still contained within dominant social and political paradigms. In fact, disfigurement and queerness, as Bacon's essay suggests, enable such political frameworks to sustain themselves.

Given its attention to such disabled and queer affiliations, *Novel Bodies* intervenes in an array of ongoing critical conversations in the fields of disability studies, sexuality studies, and eighteenth-century British literary studies. One of the aims of this book is to bring disability theory to bear on the literature and archival materials of the Georgian period. To date, there has been little exploration of how disability and sexuality inform the literature of eighteenth-century Britain.[68] For McRuer and Kafer, the connections among queerness and disability may be found in more recent modes of cultural production, and David T. Mitchell and Sharon Snyder identify the consolidation of queer and disabled affiliations as occurring in the later nineteenth century, as a consequence of sexual prohibition and as a symptom of biopolitics.[69] However, as I argue in this book, heterosexuality has long relied upon disabled bodies to establish its healthy appearance. This study, then, strengthens our understanding of queer and disabled association by showing its literary precursors. A disability methodology, when supplemented by close reading, theory, and archival materials, makes visible nascent configurations of heteronormativity and ablebodiedness. Eighteenth-century authors imagine bodily orientations which challenge these emerging systems as key features of their novels. By bringing bodily and sexual difference to the center of their narratives, these authors establish innovative approaches for managing social and political impasses. In other words, through the queer and disabled characters that they imagine, novelists of the eighteenth century envision reform.

Disability is a version of embodiment whose discursive formations repeat themselves over time. In the Georgian period, for example, authors imagine capacious, flexible renderings of sexuality through representations of impairment—deafness, physical difference, disfigurement, and chronic illness—and in this, we may observe reverberations, and of course significant differences, between Georgian Britain and our current moment. What seems true of both then and now is that depictions of queer and disabled embodiment often manifest new critical vistas and are suggestive of unanticipated ways of being in the world. In the novels featured in this study, disability and queerness are linked together in the bodies of characters that indicate a change of direction for British society. Duncan Campbell, the deaf soothsayer who is the focus of chapter 1, foretells the future through his possession of the second sight, and more generally indicates a future in which deaf people receive an education. In chapter 2, I consider how the ladies of *Millenium Hall*, sapphically oriented and physically marked by the vicissitudes of life, right the wrongs of patriarchal society through their utopian economy, thereby yielding more humane futures. In chapter 3, we see how Tabitha Bramble and Obadiah Lismahago, characters from Smollett's *The Expedition of Humphry Clinker*, who are also marked in their physical constitutions by age, unsettle the centrality of youth for heterosexual reproductive futurity in their union. Finally, as chapter 4 reveals, Eugenia Tyrold from Burney's *Camilla* becomes the bellwether for feminist achievement in the typically male realm of classical education, even while

Harriet Freke from Edgeworth's *Belinda* disrupts heterosexual domesticity in spectacularly visible ways. Taken together, these characters, and the novels they populate, mediate the troubles of British society, opening up remarkable avenues of expression and being for generations of readers. These novels show that queer and disabled representations mark narrative moments in which authors reimagine British society, for their characters often function as agents of reform. What is *novel* about the bodies imagined in these works is that they herald a new world order for eighteenth-century Britain.

AFFILIATIONS OF DISABILITY AND QUEERNESS: HORACE WALPOLE'S *THE CASTLE OF OTRANTO* (1764)

In my reading of Horace Walpole's *The Castle of Otranto*, I model the methodology that I use throughout *Novel Bodies*: through close reading, attention to the tenets of disability and queer theories, and engagement with secondary criticism in eighteenth-century studies and contemporaneous archival materials, I regard queer and disabled embodiment as a persistent source of narrative conflict. In many ways, *The Castle of Otranto* is an ideal text through which to introduce this methodology because of how it imagines deformity and queerness as sources of unresolvable tension. *The Castle of Otranto* in particular relies upon three discursive formations through which we may perceive emerging constructions of heteronormativity and able-bodiedness in the Enlightenment: the system of primogeniture, early theories of degeneracy, and the culture of libertinism. Walpole exploits cultural anxieties tied to these systems through key plot developments that lead to the novel's climactic "catastrophe," in which father murders daughter, a family's unjust dynasty collapses, and order seems to be restored to the many unruly excesses that appear throughout the narrative.[70] Beyond his prosthetic use of queerness and disability, Walpole also levels a critique at the very systems that rely upon normative embodiment and desire. In this sense, Walpole's gothic tale is not only amenable to queer subject formation, as George Haggerty has argued; we might also think about the novel as *crip* for the way that it depicts impairment as the critical, resilient center of narrative that haunts healthy, able bodies.[71]

The System of Primogeniture

The system of primogeniture, or patrilineal succession, plays an absolutely vital role in constituting the family drama in *The Castle of Otranto*. This system, in which the eldest son inherits a landed family's estate unencumbered, depends entirely upon the notion of healthy young men and women who merge family interests through alliance marriage, socially sanctioned sexual practice, reproduction, and effective child-rearing, all so that the next generation can repeat this well-trodden pattern. Through these seemingly inviolable principles, elite, landed families could sustain their interests from generation to generation. In later novels such as *Sense and Sensibility* (1811) and *Pride and Prejudice* (1813), Jane Austen portrays the difficulties of such a legal framework for young women, who are vulnerable in this exacting, male-centered system. However, the Jane Bennets and Fanny Prices of Austen's fiction are not the only characters exposed to the precarious conditions of patrilineal succession. Walpole and the other novelists featured in this study also explore the demanding social pressures of reproductive futurity by imagining queer, disabled bodies within an emergent two-sex system. Their works often complicate the social imperative to facilitate succession and property inheritance through the compulsory heterosexuality that is inherent in the system of primogeniture.

Throughout Walpole's novel—widely considered the first in the British gothic tradition—queerness and disability haunt the tyrant Manfred, who ultimately cannot sustain his lineage due to their very persistence. In the narrative's first pages, Manfred's only son, Conrad, is bound to marry Isabella, the daughter of a rival aristocrat, to consolidate Manfred's already precarious status as ruler of Otranto. However, young Conrad—"a homely youth, sickly, and of no promising disposition"—suffers from an unnamed chronic illness, and the impending nuptials are delayed until his "infirm state of health would permit" the ceremony (17). Despite Manfred's wife Hippolita's anxieties pertaining to their son Conrad's various bodily impairments, Manfred is eager to establish the union because he is consumed by an obsessive desire to preserve his reign through the reproductive extension of his family line, and to live down the ancient prophesy "that the castle and lordship of Otranto should pass from the present family, whenever the real owner should be grown too large to inhabit it" (17). When the much-anticipated marriage is about to occur, however, Conrad is found "dashed to pieces" by a mysterious, "enormous" knight's helmet, an overdetermined symbol of archaic male virility that crushes him beneath its unbearable weight (18). It is soon revealed by an unknown peasant (who turns out to be Theodore, the rightful prince) that the helmet belongs to the statue of a prince from former times, Alfonso the Good, whose massive, armored resemblance is housed nearby at the Church of St. Nicolas. The helmet's "miraculous" decimation of Conrad is suggestive of the illegitimacy of Manfred's claim to the principality, driving Manfred into a frenzied set of senseless, despotic actions to uphold his status as sovereign (20). Conrad is a central figure for the British gothic genre generally. His "disfigured corpse," Haggerty argues, becomes "central to the formation of subjectivity in gothic fiction" for the way that it connotes an "erotics of loss."[72] I would add that, in addition to the loss connoted by Conrad's queerness, Conrad's impairment is at the center of Walpole's work. Conrad is, after all, chronically ill, and his bloody annihilation under the weight of the armor's monstrous masculinity sets in motion Manfred's tyranny, including his incestuous lusting after, and sexual violence toward, Isabella. Conrad is not just a peripheral character who is eradicated on the very first pages of the novel; he is the queer, disabled catalyst of the plot, and by extension, of the early British gothic genre.

Conrad's untimely death creates the major conflict of the narrative: with no male heirs to whom he can pass his ancestor Ricardo's ill-gotten monarchical claim, Manfred decides to divorce Hippolita and marry Isabella himself. As Manfred makes his case to Isabella for their union, he urges her to forget her now deceased fiancé Conrad in the following terms:

> He was a sickly, puny child, and Heaven has perhaps taken him away, that I might not trust the honours of my house on so frail a foundation. The line of Manfred calls for numerous supports. My foolish fondness for that boy blinded the eyes of my prudence—but it is better as it is. I hope, in a few years, to have reason to rejoice at the death of Conrad . . . Instead of a sickly boy, you shall have a husband in the prime of his age, who will know how to value your beauties, and who may expect a numerous offspring. (23–24)

Through Manfred's audacious and heartless justification for marriage to Isabella, Walpole elucidates a deeply engrained system of thought that stigmatizes disabled people as weak, as anomalous, as *lesser than*. Manfred assumes here the status of *normate*. A term coined by Rosemarie Garland-Thomson, normate is a social identity in which an able-bodied man assumes a place of privilege and power based on his blatant marginalization of physical, sensory, or intellectual difference.[73] In identifying his "fondness" for Conrad as that which "blinded his eyes," Manfred articulates his baseness through ableist language meant to capture his own temporary inability to see the truth of his stymied lineage (23). It might seem as though Walpole affirms normate values by eliminating Conrad so early on in the narrative, excluding forever the possibility that Manfred's succession might be passed down through his son. However, through Manfred's delirious and desperate attempts to secure authoritarian rule, Walpole exposes the normate's condition as contradictory and injurious. By establishing Manfred's partiality for able-bodiedness, even at the expense of the memory of a recently deceased and beloved son, Walpole shows that such values contaminate familial relations.

Within this framework, the likes of Conrad are perceived to be better dead than alive because impairment is thought of as a fate worse than death. Death, however, cannot and does not eradicate the specter of disability in the narrative.

The above passage also reveals that Conrad is sexually suspect. Because, as Manfred implies, Conrad does not know how to "value" the "beauties" of Isabella, he has no place in the courtship drama. The "frail foundation" that Manfred identifies refers to Conrad's incapacity to produce a healthy male heir to continue the family line. In other words, it is because he is chronically ill that Conrad is also queer; he stands outside of the normative frameworks of heterosexual desire and patrilineal succession due to his "sickly" constitution. Manfred's invoking of Conrad's infertility as he attempts to exercise authority over Isabella's body indicates that heteronormativity and ableism are his foremost rhetorical strategies to enact unbridled patriarchal domination. Manfred's belief that male health is a vital factor for successful procreation indicates a moment of rhetorical clarity in the midst of the unhinged disorder to which he has succumbed in the wake of his son's demise. Questions would of course surround Manfred's own "foundation": after all, he and Hippolita have only given birth to two children, one of whom is chronically ill. Through the characterization of Conrad's queerness, and the desperate measures that Manfred takes as a result of his own reproductive ineptitude, Walpole draws attention to the consternation surrounding variably-embodied male heirs who bear the burden of continuing the family line. Though Conrad's debilitating illness might seem to serve as an intergenerational reflection of his father's moral deformity and the family's fragile, unjust claim, it becomes the means by which Walpole reveals Manfred's hard-heartedness and vicious inclinations. The system of primogeniture, which operates under the coordinates of health and heterosexuality, is thus shown to perpetuate violence when its narrow script is unsettled. This disruption of heterosexual reproduction is also the narrative tension that Walpole dramatizes to heighten the horror of the narrative.

The plot tension of Walpole's gothic tale inheres not only in the impaired body of Conrad but also in a system that prescribes normative embodiment and heterosexual desire as buttressing authority across generations. During the eighteenth century in Britain, the shift away from an emphasis on monarchical rule to that of a parliamentary one might seem to entail a move away from the fundamental practice of primogeniture for elite families. However, the Glorious Revolution of 1688, a key moment that would appear to mark such a shift (in which Parliament opted for James II's daughter over his eldest son as ruler) did not eradicate the public's obsession with the procreative practices of its rulers.[74] Though they generally consolidate the cultural values of emergent middle classes, eighteenth-century novels also participate in a "panoptical conception" of domesticity that sustains the principles of primogeniture, and include representations of aristocratic privilege such as that depicted in *The Castle of Otranto*.[75] In fact, one of the novel's greatest mysteries, which is not revealed until the final pages, is that the apprehensions provoked by Conrad's compromised virility are intensified by Manfred's frantic but ultimately futile attempts to avoid the fulfillment of an ancient prophecy, that his ancestor Ricardo's "posterity should reign in Otranto . . . as long as issue male from Ricardo's loins should remain to enjoy it" (104). The prophecy only heightens the urgency of reproduction, and in his absolutist adherence to this social obligation, Manfred becomes the basest of villains: he seeks to divorce Hippolita; he offers his daughter, Matilda, to Frederic in exchange for union with Isabella; and finally, when his temper reaches its zenith, he murders his only remaining child, Matilda, in cold blood in the Church of St. Nicolas. At the heart of these narrative conflicts is the inherent problem of compulsory heterosexuality and health that undergirds the system of primogeniture. It is because of the absolutely entrenched nature of primogeniture that Manfred seeks in vain to step in as able-bodied replacement for Conrad's heterosexual failure. Conrad's body is a threat to the established order of the castle, but as we finally discover at the end of the narrative, his fate had already been sealed long before his birth. Disability and queerness thus pose serious threats to the continuity of the state, according to Walpole's narrative.

Despite the spectacular way that he is decimated by the oversized rendering of Alfred the Good's masculinity, Conrad's presence is never eradicated from the plot, and in this we observe his crip haunting of heteronormativity. Given Conrad's demise, a yawning chasm would seem to divide him from the other male characters in the novel. While Manfred, "in the prime of his age" and seemingly of a vigorous body, discourses at length about his rule, and Theodore—valiant, robust, and handsome—articulates his righteous resistance to Manfred, Conrad never actually speaks (24). However, Conrad haunts the present tense of the narrative until the ending, when Theodore finally becomes the rightful prince of Otranto. At two points in the novel especially, Conrad's crip hauntings disrupt exchanges between Theodore and his potential romantic interests, Isabella and Matilda, who believe that the eerie sounds and visions they confront are attributable to Conrad's ghost. In Matilda's case, unfamiliar noises interrupt a conversation between her and her servant, Bianca, about her romantic prospects with Theodore:

"Blessed Mary!" said Bianca, starting, "there it is again! Dear Madam, do you hear nothing? this castle is certainly haunted!"
"Peace!" said Matilda, "and listen! I did think I heard a voice—but it must be fancy: your terrors, I suppose, have infected me."

"Indeed! indeed! Madam," said Bianca, half-weeping with agony, "I am sure I heard a voice."

"Does anybody lie in the chamber beneath?" said the Princess.

"Nobody has dared to lie there," answered Bianca, "since the great astrologer, that was your brother's tutor, drowned himself. For certain, Madam, his ghost and the young Prince's are now met in the chamber below—for Heaven's sake let us fly to your mother's apartment!" (39–40)

In this stilted conversation between Matilda and Bianca, terror is couched as infection, which Matilda imagines to have passed from Bianca to herself. The source of said infectious terror is initially attributed to Conrad, whose ghost, Bianca supposes, mingles with that of his deceased tutor. Their ghostly cohabitation in the chamber below is suggestive of a pederastic relationship that haunts Bianca's heteronormative fantasy and disrupts her attempts to instigate a romance between Matilda and Theodore. In the end, the noises stem not from homophile ghosts, but from Theodore. Bianca and Matilda's conflation of Conrad with Theodore suggests that Conrad is Theodore's ghostly double.

A very similar misunderstanding occurs as Isabella flees Manfred and encounters Theodore in the castle's underground passages. When she initially senses Theodore's presence, Isabella wrongly supposes that he is "the ghost of her betrothed Conrad," only to soon be disabused of her misperception (28). During her frightening escape from Manfred, Isabella is haunted by the injunction to marry someone that she does not love. Once again, Conrad's ghost functions as a double to Theodore, in the way that the doppelganger, for Freud, represents the projection of repressed desires and traumatic fears imposed by social taboos.[76] Conrad and Theodore seem far from one another in terms of their physical constitutions, but their proximity to one another in these passages reveals something about the temporary nature of corporeal vigor. By portraying this uncanny crip troubling of the masculine ideal, Walpole implies that, despite what measures might be taken, disability inevitably endures in the context of heterosexual, ablebodied courtship. Walpole's narrative reveals that ongoing preoccupations with chronic illness, physical difference, and sexual dysfunction are the stuff of recurring heteronormative nightmares.

And indeed, this is the case if we look to the ending of *The Castle of Otranto* as a circular culmination of the narrative. In the final pages, Theodore, previously the intrepid hero, has become permanently depressive. He finds in his new wife, Isabella, "one with whom he could forever indulge the melancholy that had taken possession of his soul" due to his beloved Matilda's death at the hands of Manfred (105). Given Conrad's lingering presence, physical disability is not eliminated until novel's end, only to be supplanted by the psychological variance of Theodore, who will never come to terms with Matilda's untimely demise. In this sense, Alfred the Good's past haunts the present tense of Manfred's unjust rule in the same way that Conrad's chronically sick body troubles the masculine vigor of Manfred and Theodore. There is no "happily ever after," as the gothic teaches us, even for the likes of Theodore, who would seem to have it all in a corporeal sense. Disability becomes one of the persistent and circular elements of Walpole's narrative—evident from the very start, and despite a number of events which would seem to subdue it, still evident at the end. Melancholia is, admittedly, a very different discursive and lived experience from the chronic illness that Conrad possesses, but in a parallel fashion, these two forms of impairment function as symptomatic markers of the system of primogeniture. Far from offering resolutions for embodied and psychological variability, *The Castle of Otranto* implies that these states are inevitable qualities of the human experience, that they accompany the just and the unjust in equally insistent ways. The reader is left to imagine what the future might hold for Theodore and Isabella: will their marriage, like that of Manfred and Hippolita, be disturbed by the difficulties of negotiating the narrow demands of primogeniture for the extension of their family line? And just what does impairment signify in the context of procreation in this period?

Degeneracy in the Eighteenth Century

Besides exposing the central significance of heteronormativity and able-bodiedness for the system of primogeniture, Walpole's excision of Conrad from the first pages of *The Castle of Otranto* belies an enduring cultural assumption: that disability is thought to render one incapable of engaging in procreative heterosexuality. When Manfred tells Isabella that his line "calls for numerous supports" he may as well be talking about heterosexuality itself, which relies on an array of ideological stakes—ranging from courtship rituals, to gender normativity, and from sentiment to standard sexual intercourse—to sustain itself as the ultimate source of moral excellence.[77] In the eighteenth century, disability complicates heterosexuality, for, as theories of degeneracy stipulated, it raises the possibility that the propagation of future generations might be compromised. As *The Castle of Otranto* makes clear, Enlightenment-era apprehensions surrounding variably-embodied people sometimes involved their ability to bear healthy children. Fears about disabled people engaging in procreative sexual intercourse—the idea, especially, that this would bring about degeneracy in future generations—underscore the indissoluble character of disability and sexuality in eighteenth-century Britain, a full century before Francis Galton coined the term *eugenics*. Michel Foucault identifies the emergence of eugenics and psychoanalysis as two "innovations in the technology of sex" in the latter half of the nineteenth century, which together, helped to forge modern sexuality:

> The theory of "degenerescence" made it possible for [psychoanalysis and eugenics] to perpetually refer back to one another; it explained how a heredity that was burdened with various maladies (it made little difference whether these were organic, functional, or psychical) ended by producing a sexual pervert (look into the genealogy of an exhibitionist or a homosexual: you will find a hemiplegic ancestor, a phthisic parent, or an uncle afflicted with senile dementia); but it went on to explain how a sexual perversion resulted in the depletion of one's line of descent—rickets in the children, the sterility of future generations. The series composed of perversion-heredity-degenerescence formed the solid nucleus of the new technologies of sex.[78]

As Foucault argues here, the linkage between bodies and desires coalesce around emerging theories of eugenics and psychoanalysis, for "perverse" sexual practices were perceived to result in the degeneration of a family's lineage. If perversity occurs, degeneracy follows; if people with physical or cognitive disabilities reproduce, they give birth to "perverts," or so scientists argued. Foucault establishes this causal relationship as central to what he terms "the deployment of sexuality," a system of sexuality which gradually supplants the "deployment of alliance" from the eighteenth century onward. He characterizes this shift as one in which laws and customs that prohibit certain sexual practices (the deployment of alliance) are supplanted by an "intensification of the body—with its exploitation as an object of knowledge and an element in relations of power."[79] For Foucault, the establishment of eugenics and psychoanalysis epitomize this new approach to the body, in which science links perversion with degeneracy. In this way, heterosexuality is established discursively as a system that is, in its ideal form, devoid of physical or cognitive impairment.

Theories of degeneracy, however, did not emerge suddenly with Freud or Galton. We may look back to the eighteenth century to see evidence of its prehistory. One mid-eighteenth-century tract, for example, allows us to envision contemporaneous ideas about sex and degeneracy. *Advice to New-Married Persons: Or, The Art of Having Beautiful Children* (1750), an English translation from a 1655 advice book called *Callipedie* by the French doctor and poet Claude Quillet, imagines a future free of deformity and illness. Quillet counsels newlyweds on how to have "healthy and beautiful Offspring," which he argues "is not only the highest Pleasure and Honour to Parents, but of great Importance to Mankind in general."[80] In the opening lines, Quillet comments upon the importance of the rites and customs of the marital bed for establishing this perfect future:

> The muse instructive shall their Offspring grace,
> And form the future Honours of their Race:
> Beauty the long successive Line shall crown,
> And no deform'd unsightly Birth be known.[81]

The imperative of heterosexual reproductive futurity that is apparent in these lines speaks to the legal custom of patrilineal succession. Quillet explains to young husbands and wives how to avoid giving birth to the "misshapen breed" that would dilute the "purity" of their lineage.[82] While beauty is adorned with a crown, the ultimate symbol of triumph and rule, the "unsightly Birth" is, like Conrad, eliminated and thereby deemed a non-subject. Thus, any "deformed" birth becomes a manifestation of procreative failure. With such an investment in certain forms of embodiment and health made manifest, Quillet imagines a future in which disability has disappeared due to the wholesome reproductive practices of young, beautiful couples. This tract advances the notion that the "race" of families could be perfected if the young people of those families avoid "unsightly" spouses as partners. To do heterosexuality correctly, in other words, is to eradicate deformity. This line of thought, as Foucault would argue, is indicative of larger cultural forces that policed sex, "that is, not through the rigor of a taboo, but the necessity of regulating sex through useful and public discourses."[83] Ann Stoler claims that the sort of thinking embedded in this tract foreshadows modern forms of racism, in that it merges middle-class domesticity, sexuality, and "regular" forms of embodiment into a productive discourse that would eventually culminate in a scientific vision that "undesirables," in terms of race and/or disability, could be eradicated from human populations.[84] Such a strict, exclusionary framing of heterosexuality and reproduction inspires Manfred's urgent maneuvering to secure his rule. Walpole uses this urgency to heighten the drama of his narrative.

Libertinism and Disability

Beyond encompassing the system of primogeniture and emergent theories of degeneracy, *The Castle of Otranto* also critiques the culture of libertinism, another system that brings together disability and sexuality in the eighteenth century. While earlier novels and literary works examine the libertine's reform—perhaps most notably, Samuel Richardson's *Pamela* (1740)—Walpole's work capitalizes on the notion of the unreformed aristocratic man who gives way to his animal spirits and

INTRODUCTION

uses his sexuality as a tool to dominate and exploit those beneath him. Manfred's base villainy and lurid desire establish him as such a memorable monster. One may examine this in his unabashed pursuit of Isabella, whom he sexually terrorizes for the purposes of strengthening his political power. As I have argued elsewhere, libertine sexuality is marked by a mobilization of political and sexual ascendancy through the complex negotiation of corporeal vigor.[85] In this milieu, there is often a dismissal of physically disabled women as sexually impenetrable and an emasculation of disabled men due to the perception that they are incapable of active sexual penetration. In the context of libertine embodiment, able-bodiedness serves as linchpin for the dominant sexual posturing of men, but also renders them vulnerable to sexual dysfunction, a kind of temporary disability that muddles the boundary between masculinity and emasculation, ability and disability. This is observable in John Wilmot, Earl of Rochester's "The Imperfect Enjoyment," in which the male speaker is forced to confront the question of his own virility. After prematurely ejaculating with his lover Corrina, the speaker is thereafter unable to get an erection. Sexual dysfunction defines the poem and serves as a reminder of the vulnerability of not only the libertine's sexual dominance but of his political ascendancy, for the two are resolutely conjoined in the culture of libertinism.[86] This is the case until the very end of the poem, at which point the speaker concedes that there are "ten thousand abler pricks" that could potentially make up for his shortcoming.[87] The notion that an unnamed substitute penis will please Corrina, who remains unfulfilled, frustrated, and subordinate, ultimately restores the order of male dominance that the poem comes so close to undermining.

Such negotiation of desire and embodiment are at work in another Restoration text, William Wycherley's *The Country Wife* (1675). Horner, the play's rake-hero, is driven to cuckold men, which, as Eve Sedgwick argues, is his primary motive, establishing the significance of male homosocial bonding for perpetuating the "traffic in women" and generating the play's plot.[88] He is aided in these endeavors by feigning a case of the syphilis that he is supposed to have contracted while gallivanting about in France. Once the physician Quack's reports spread of Horner's impotence—that he is "as bad as a eunuch"—Horner hopes to have free access to the women of the town.[89] His scheme ends up working. Horner has a dalliance with Lady Fidget, whose husband Sir Jasper seems utterly unconcerned about the sexual threat posed by a man who has contracted a sexually transmitted infection, during the memorable China scene. When Sir Jasper walks in on Lady Fidget and Horner with their arms about each other, Lady Fidget is able to pass it off as an innocent game of tickling. What is more, Horner and Lady Fidget continue their sexual frolicking in Sir Jasper's presence, behind a closed bedroom door.[90] Through his successful performance of disease, Horner becomes the virile

[23]

rake-hero of the play, and true to Restoration court culture, enjoys his sexuality without having to marry in the end. In this case, the performance of disease—which gets coded as "eunuchism"—grants the libertine the gratification of his animal spirits. Thus, libertinism is defined in part by one's negotiation of ability and disability, or of health and illness, in the context of sexuality, further reinforcing how absolutely interconnected disability and sexuality are in the Restoration and in the century to follow. Walpole, writing nearly one hundred years later, imagines a very different kind of male sexual dominance, in which politically ascendant men come to embody the horrific impulses of unrestrained libido and appetite for power. Walpole is able to capitalize on cultural apprehensions about procreation, succession, and sexual excess—all through the ideology of ability—in order to establish a tale of horror that struck a chord with eighteenth-century readers and that set the tone for a new generation of writers such as Ann Radcliffe, Matthew G. Lewis, and Charlotte Dacre.

THE NOVEL FORM, INDIVIDUALISM, AND DISABILITY

Having established some of the ways in which disability defines heterosexuality and reproduction in *The Castle of Otranto*—through the system of primogeniture, early theories of degeneracy, and libertinism—I turn now to the novel form, in which we may examine the discursive mediation of a variety of ableist conditions that depend upon Enlightenment configurations of queer, disabled bodies. By identifying assumptions about embodiment in these narratives, I hope to draw attention to how novels at once establish and destabilize developing forms of disabled subjectivity. For instance, eighteenth-century British novels often represent the tribulations of individual characters, regardless of impairment status, as they make their way through challenging social environments. In these narratives, significant conflicts habitually involve characters struggling for subjectivity as they overcome challenges of diverse sorts. Such narrative conflict draws our attention to the uneven relationship between *individual* and *society* that novels theorize and universalize. The emphasis on the individual who meets society's demands—no matter the cost—is precisely the type of culturally engrained "truth" that disability scholars and activists have sought to reconceptualize through the social model of disability, in which inaccessible built environments and institutions, as well as restrictive prejudices, are charged with creating disability. According to this social model, *disability* refers to the ways in which societies organize impairment, while *impairment* denotes the physical or cognitive condition of the body.[91] In establishing this division, scholars and activists have argued that disability is not in the body per se but in ableist communities and institutions.[92] Eighteenth-century novels function as a testing ground for such modern theorizations of disability. In their foregrounding of individual characters against social backdrops that are inaccessible for a variety of reasons (in terms of class, race, gender, and embodiment) novels often stage a fraught relationship between self and society that would pose unique difficulties for people with impairments. Like the heroine of a Radcliffe novel, disabled people are expected to demonstrate pluckiness by overcoming hardship, to surmount their particular impairment through sheer willpower. Such a paradigm perpetuates the quandary that beleaguers disabled people, who are pitied for their ostensible lack but who often do not receive respect until they have risen above their impairment to become "normal," or some semblance thereof.[93] The notion of character triumphing over adversity likewise serves as blueprint for many eighteenth-century novels. In Daniel Defoe's *Moll Flanders* (1722), Richardson's *Pamela* (1740), and Burney's *Evelina* (1778), for instance, each of the eponymous protagonists withstand affliction, prove themselves worthy of accolade, and achieve admission to polite society. Significantly, the characters from these works must create access for themselves—through their ingenuity, their virtue, their persistence, and so forth. Hence, British novels' emphasis on the determination of the individual to rise above conflict correlates with one of the fundamental social difficulties that disabled people face today: the expectation that they should strive for acceptance—that society does not need to change by becoming more accessible, but that they themselves must surmount obstacles that *seem* natural but are actually implemented and maintained by social forces.

Eighteenth-century novelists imagined such individualized complications in a way that was meant to feel real to readers. Defoe and Haywood, for example, often framed their narratives as histories, and their works were received by the reading public as such. These and other authors exploited the convoluted relationship between fiction and nonfiction, revealing in turn the promiscuous generic makeup of novels in their early form. Later in the century, as more novels saturated the market and the form appears to have consolidated somewhat, writers attempted to define the novel's features by contrasting it with what they perceived to be discrete forms, especially romance. Clara Reeve in *The Progress of Romance* (1785) argues that novels diverge from the prose romances that dominated earlier periods in their representation of the "probable" and quotidian:

> The Romance is an heroic fable, which treats of fabulous persons and things. The Novel is a picture of real life and manners, and of the times in which it is written. The Romance in lofty and elevated language, describes what never happened nor is likely to happen. The Novel gives a

familiar relation of such things, as pass every day before our eyes, such as may happen to our friend, or to ourselves; and the perfection of it, is to represent every scene, in so easy and natural a manner, and to make them appear so probable, as to deceive us into a persuasion (at least while we are reading) that all is real, until we are affected by the joys or distresses, or the persons in the story, as if they were our own.[94]

Reeve draws clear distinctions between the novel, which she deems "real," "familiar," and "natural," and prose romance, which is "fabulous," "lofty," and ultimately treats of the impossible. For Reeve, novels resonate because of the intense emotional connection that readers develop with characters that are three-dimensional—that seem so *real*. Ian Watt, writing in the mid-twentieth century, argues that romances "had reflected the general tendency of their cultures to make conformity to traditional practice the major test of truth," while the novel (for Watt, an Enlightenment English invention) challenges this tradition in its emphasis on "individual experience which is always unique and therefore true."[95] For Reeve and Watt, then, novels offer realistic plot complications which deceive readers into believing their veracity. In this way, the reader takes on the distresses of the main character through the cultivation of a sympathetic imagination. When examined through such a lens, eighteenth-century novels may be understood to resonate with readers due to their capacity to depict an individual character's tribulations within a social order that values individuality but, paradoxically, demands conformity.

Watt's influential study has engendered generations of critique, some of which are aimed at exposing Watt's assumptions regarding the degree to which eighteenth-century novels incorporate realism, or which interrogate the term *realism* itself. Michael McKeon, for example, takes issue with Watt's thesis for making too fine a distinction between romance and realism, so that, though the fiction of Defoe, Henry Fielding, and Richardson (Watt's triumvirate of novel innovators) "subvert the idea and ethos of romance, they nonetheless draw upon its stock situations and conventions."[96] McKeon reminds us of the impracticality of binary distinctions between what gets deemed "real" in the novel and what is construed as "impossible" in romance. Ros Ballaster concurs, arguing that Watt "underplays the continuing potency of the language and plots of romance for, and the diversity of narrative forms available to, the eighteenth-century writer and reader."[97] Ballaster identifies the ample variety of novel genres in eighteenth-century Britain (including the amatory genre, the subject of her own learned study) and argues that we should not examine the novel as an unvarying form. Finally, William Warner challenges "the novel's realist claims," arguing that novels, after all, represent a mediated form that "no matter how earnest its aspirations to facticity or truth, can bear a mark in its own language that verifies its relation to something outside itself."[98] Warner argues against the notion that novel writers and readers have truly accepted the claims of literary critics that realism is the foremost organizing principle of the form. As these scholars persuasively demonstrate, the extent to which eighteenth-century novels could be read as a mimetic reproduction of the day-to-day life of individuals is restricted by the hybridity of the form, the flexibility of the form, and the self-referential, mediated character of the form.

Existing scholarship for the most part overlooks the ways in which the novel form makes disability a key part of narrative structure.[99] The novels in this study, for instance, grapple with ableist thinking in varied ways. In fact, given their vivid and complex portrayals of embodiment, eighteenth-century novels provide substantive commentary about a spectrum of lived reality that both incorporates and challenges Cartesian and Lockean thinking about the duality of the body and mind. I read these novels not merely as vehicles for ableist thinking but also as thought experiments that construe various kinds of disability as vital to the social, physical, and psychological makeup of Georgian Britain. The novels in this study suggest that, far from simply serving as an indication of irregularity in nature, disability is in fact often considered part of the regular course of life, something that cannot be fixed, but which can be managed given the right circumstances. These novels draw attention to the relationship between the individual, an integral part of novel writing, and the settings that the individual navigates. They all argue, to varying degrees, for more accessibility. In the case of *The History of the Life and Adventures of Mr. Duncan Campbell*, this manifests itself in a convincing case for educating deaf people. In *Millenium Hall*, disabled inhabitants of an estate work together to accommodate each other. In Smollett's *The Expedition of Humphry Clinker*, Bramble complains about the inaccessibility of the streets in Bath. In *Camilla*, Eugenia Tyrold accesses a classical education, typically reserved for men, due to her various physical disabilities.

The novelists considered in this study write disabled people into subjectivity through their narratives about disability, in which they situate codes about queer and disabled embodiment among a host of social issues. As representations, novels shaped perceptions about disability by implicitly or explicitly transmitting codes that eighteenth-century readers could generally understand as shared cultural "truths."[100] In fact, there are a variety of perspectives and overlapping codes at work in and across the novels under examination in the following pages. These novelists imagine multivalent experiences of disabled embodiment through their narratives, and the various codes which they transmit help to constitute a shared understanding about the struggles and pleasures of people with impairments during the period. These codes, I will show, map disability as an embodied manifestation of queer desire. The crossing of queerness with disability is one that is situated on the cusp of compulsory reproductive futurity and social reform. The novels of this study highlight the significant roles of queerness and disability in mediating some of the significant cultural and historical shifts that characterize the Georgian period. Through my exploration of these novels' codes of embodiment, I argue that queer and disabled characters function, in part, as agents of social change, as harbingers of reformist impulses.

OVERVIEW OF THE BOOK

Chapter 1 examines a series of fictional works about a real-life deaf man who was widely considered a prophet for his possession of the "second sight" and for the miraculous deeds that he supposedly wrought on behalf of paying clients. An array of print sources detailing the life of this man, Duncan Campbell, appeared between the years 1720 and 1732 and mark a significant moment in the history of deaf education, and in the growth of deaf subjectivity in Britain. *The History of the Life and Adventures of Duncan Campbell* (1720), Eliza Haywood's *A Spy on the Conjurer* (1724), and other narratives about Campbell mediate deafness through the period's *audism*—a system of auditory norms that uphold the primacy of vocal speech in casual, day-to-day interaction among hearing people. These narratives both assert and call into question the prevailing wisdom of audism through their engagement with writing and gesture, modes of communication which extended the possibility that deaf people could be integrated into mainstream, hearing society. In these works, Campbell embodies competing discourses of deafness that both justify deaf education and draw on long-standing stereotypes about the miraculous orientation of nonhearing, nonspeaking people. In this way, Campbell seems to straddle archaic and future models of disability. However, his oscillation between queer and normative masculinities throughout these works challenges the idea that the eighteenth century is a transitional period for disability. At some points in the narrative, he appears out of time, as an angelic being that I identify as *cosmically queer* due to his radiant, boyish otherworldliness. Campbell also experiences sound in queer ways due to his unconventional phenomenological relationship with stringed instruments. And yet at other points in the narratives about him, Campbell is normatively masculine—sometimes acting as paternal guide, and sometimes as libertine or reformed libertine. Such conflicting depictions of Campbell's gender and sexuality reveal that deafness at this point in Britain is a flexible form of embodiment that authors used to suit the aims of the genre in which they wrote.

In the works about Campbell, the prospect of queerness and disability emerge at intervals, challenging damning perceptions about deaf people and expanding the possibilities for their inclusion in society through education. In chapter 2, I consider widely divergent narratives about heterosexuality, sapphism, and physical disability within the context of sensibility. In *Pamela* (1740), Richardson asserts a new model of heterosexual domesticity, prompted in the first place by Pamela's resistance to rape and libertine domination, and followed by Mr. B.'s development of sensibility. Richardson also frames this new classed version of marriage through Mrs. Jewkes, housekeeper and prison warden to Pamela. Mrs. Jewkes possesses a variable body and queer desire, which, as I argue, are meant to align her with the base immorality of Mr. B. Richardson uses Mrs. Jewkes as a form of "narrative prosthesis" to establish the contours of Pamela and Mr. B.'s marriage.[101] In stark contrast to Richardson, Sarah Scott conceives of physical and sexual difference as central to narrative, rather than as a peripheral device to consolidate heterosexuality. Throughout her literary works, Scott imagines queer and disabled bodies as foundational for reform. Scott's envisioning of the body undergoes critical transformations throughout her writing career. In *A Journey through Every Stage of Life* (1754), physical vitality and gender mobility are necessary for young women who dare to inhabit the public sphere, while aging and disabled female characters serve as cautionary tales. Later, in *Millenium Hall* (1762), the aged, the disabled, and the queer are imbued with the moral excellence, vision, and diligence necessary to transform British society. Finally, in *The History of Sir George Ellison* (1766), Scott's reformist vision becomes global in scope, as she turns her critical eye to plantation life and the horrors of chattel slavery in Jamaica. The enslaved characters that she imagines, however, reproduce racist assumptions about white paternalism and the perfectibility of black male bodies as physical tools for the expansion of capital. As a whole, Scott's novels critique the multivalent manner in which the emergent model of bourgeois heterosexuality that Richardson imagines relies upon specific renderings of gender, class, and race for its moral authority.

While Scott accepts disability as a natural physical state and disregards altogether the potential of medicine to ameliorate or cure impairment, Tobias Smollett's *The Expedition of Humphry Clinker* (1771) represents the body in pain as a source of consternation which men of means seek to cure through medical intervention. In this way, chapter 3 places the cultural study of medicine in conversation with that of disability. These two modes of inquiry are often regarded as competing (rather than as complementary) critical projects. As this chapter demonstrates, however, when brought together, they shed light on the interconnectedness of disability and chronic disease in the Georgian period. The last of Smollett's novels, *Humphry Clinker* offers a fantasy of healthy closure for its central character, Matthew Bramble, who overcomes the painful symptoms of gout and rheumatism through dietary changes, country living, personal restraint, and travel. As Bramble and his fellow family members tour the south of Britain, Scotland, and Wales, they try out a variety of medical treatments for their various ailments. They gradually learn to regulate their bodies, and concurrently, a number of heterosexual courtships develop among the group's members. The narrative's eventual establishment of marriage and health among young characters conveys the notion that, in its ideal state, heterosexuality is imbued with physical well-being and reproductive futurity. But Smollett also represents other kinds of intimate connections, including a marriage between Tabitha Bramble and Obadiah Lismahago, aging partners who challenge the novel's otherwise stout argument for health and reproductive futurity in marriage. Through Tabitha and Lismahago, Smollett allows that aging and variable bodies are an inevitable state of corporeal being, and registers the body in pain as disruption to healthy heterosexual union. *Humphry Clinker* thus provides a medical component for this book's examination of the joint cultural histories of heteronormativity and able-bodiedness.

Representations of impairment also facilitate insights into women's education at the turn of the nineteenth century. In chapter 4, I examine the contours of what I call *queer ocular relationships*—intimate connections that are based on wonder, astonishment, and mutual consent between starer and staree—as critical for feminist thought. Frances Burney's *Camilla* (1796) critiques the one-way optics of the male gaze, which contrasts with the queer intimacy that develops between Lady Delacour and Harriet Freke in Maria Edgeworth's *Belinda* (1801). Both novels insinuate that disability serves as a critical site for debates over feminism and education. *Camilla* aims to apply to women the Georgian cultural construction of the monster-genius, in which physically disabled men (including luminaries such as Alexander Pope and Samuel Johnson) are imagined as being brilliant precisely because of their physical difference. *Camilla* extends this trope to women through Camilla's sister, Eugenia, a lame, hunchbacked young woman who becomes a classical philosopher as a direct consequence of her physical disabilities. The men that stare at Eugenia's physical difference do so without her consent, but by the end of the novel, when she begins her feminist autobiography, she critiques the male gaze that has caused her so much distress. A few years after *Camilla*'s publication, Edgeworth would represent a relationship that is utterly innovative for the history of the English language: her use of the term *staree* is on record as being the first use of its kind. In the starer-staree relationship that develops between Lady Delacour and Harriet Freke, Edgeworth offers a mutually sustaining, consensual queer relationship that leads to new ways of being, but that has embodied consequences for both characters, culminating in Harriet's crural maiming and dismissal from the plot. However, *Belinda* also reveals that kinship and domesticity are performed, granting legibility to Harriet's transgender embodiment. Despite these remarkable differences, *Camilla* and *Belinda* both establish a link between education and corporeality, revealing an anti-Cartesian philosophy that marks women's disabled bodies as cultivating conventionally male forms of intelligence.

And finally, in the coda, I briefly consider one of the most canonical of authors in the British literary tradition, Jane Austen. Austen's novels typically represent health as an imperative for marriage, but in the unfinished *Sanditon* Austen shifts her focus from the urgency of heterosexual romance to an exploration of *aromantic* relationships that are centered around newly constituted doctor-patient dynamics in the Romantic period. Given its fragmentary state, *Sanditon* is the queerest of Austen's works. Because Austen could not complete the novel, the marriage plot never takes hold, leaving ill and hypochondriac characters unregulated. *Sanditon* thus becomes a story in which non-normative bodies exist for their own sake and are not beholden to the eradicating inclinations of heteronormative plot development.

These novels represent impairment as both an embodied, lived reality and as a problem that is difficult to resolve given the unfavorable conditions of a social order that was learning to map disability on the individual's body. At the heart of these stories is the imagining of an individual's embodied subjectivity as it gets tested by an array of social pressures and constraints. To not overcome these barriers is tantamount to losing out on the prize of subjectivity; however, the novels that I investigate in this book also probe the logics of ableism though variably-embodied characters that signal social change. Through them, authors imagine novel social orders that redress an array of injustices.

NOTES

1. George Haggerty and Lennard Davis view the eighteenth century as a transitional period, in which modern gender and sexual categories coalesce (Haggerty), and in which representations of physical difference are marked by earlier models of monstrosity and future conceptualizations of disability as an embodied, epistemological problem to be solved (Davis). Novels help to bring to life such liminal codes of embodiment and individualism. Nancy Armstrong argues, "Written representations of the self allowed the modern individual to become an economic and psychological reality." For Armstrong, the novel helps to establish modern individualism, and the modern individual is "first and foremost a woman." See Armstrong, *Desire and Domestic Fiction*, 8; Davis, "Dr. Johnson, Amelia, and the Discourse of Disability," 56; and Haggerty, *Men in Love*.
2. Roxann Wheeler argues that in eighteenth-century Britain "understanding of complexion, the body, and identity were far more fluid than ours is today." Wheeler, *The Complexion of Race*, 5–6.
3. The term *queer* figures prominently throughout this book. As Susan Lanser has shown, queerness denotes a "resistance to all categories" and "an attack on rational epistemologies and classificatory systems in favor of the disorder, or the different logic, of desire" (21). Lanser makes a compelling case for understanding *queer* as an early modern term for the emerging sapphist—or "women whose erotic desires are oriented primarily to

women"—demonstrates "that the Enlightenment project of fixing sexual categories was from the start an unstable and self-contradicting enterprise" (22). Lanser describes Anne Lister's early nineteenth-century use of *queer* as a euphemism for vagina in her sexual encounters with other women, giving queer a sexual connotation. See Lanser, "'Queer to Queer'," 21–46. The label *queer* suits the aims of this project, which is to identify literary and archival registers in which disabled bodies are aligned with same-sex or non-procreative erotic desire and alternative kinship structures. To read more about how reproduction and the figure of the child sustain the primacy of heterosexual identity at the expense of queer rights, see Edelman, *No Future*.
4. Lauren Berlant and Michael Warner argue that heteronormativity is a set of "institutions, structures of understanding, and practical orientations" that champion heterosexuality as the ultimate source of "social belonging." They claim that in the eighteenth century, the hierarchical systems of property ownership and decorum help to facilitate the formation of national identities. Moreover, David Turner shows that able-bodiedness has a long history and that the eighteenth century plays a fundamental role in its emergence as modern ideology. See Berlant and Warner, "Sex in Public" 547–566; and Turner, *Disability in Eighteenth-Century England*, 18–22.
5. Disability scholars have argued that embodiment should not be understood in binary terms, such as *disability* and *able-bodied*. Chris Mounsey's use of the term *variability* or *variable bodies* and Tobin Siebers's "theory of complex embodiment" both account for the ways in which embodiment is best understood as existing along a spectrum. See Mounsey, "Introduction: Variability: Beyond Sameness and Difference," 1–27; and Siebers, *Disability Theory*.
6. Since the publication of *The History of Sexuality*, a number of scholars have used Foucault's framework to understand "the interplay of truth and sex" that we have inherited from the Enlightenment. *Novel Bodies* is the product of years of ongoing conversations with scholars who work in queer studies. As in the following works, I investigate the multivalent manner in which our modern categories of sexuality and gender have been forged through literary and philosophical production from the long eighteenth century: Kelleher, *Making Love*; Lanser, *The Sexuality of History*; Brideoake, *The Ladies of Llangollen*; Haggerty, *Men in Love*; Kavanagh, *Effeminate Years*; King, *The Gendering of Men, 1600–1750*; and Moore, *Dangerous Intimacies*.
7. Foucault, *The History of Sexuality, Volume 1*, 10, 17.
8. Ibid., 34.
9. Ibid., 42–43.
10. Paul Kelleher addresses the question of how heterosexuality becomes a site of moral goodness at the expense of queer desires and practices, which consequently become stigmatized as immoral and narcissistic. I contribute to this conversation by arguing that the growth of the idea of able-bodiedness is another discursive apparatus that aids in the gradual implementation of heterosexuality as a dominant identity category. See Kelleher, *Making Love*.
11. The long eighteenth century generally refers to the period encompassing 1660–1830s. For book titles and essay collections that examine disability in the long eighteenth century, see Davis, *Enforcing Normalcy*; Deutsch, *Loving Dr. Johnson* and *Resemblance and Disgrace*; Deutsch and Nussbaum, "*Defects*"; Mounsey, *The Idea of Disability in the Eighteenth Century*; Nussbaum, *Limits of the Human*; Stanback, *The Wordsworth-Coleridge Circle and the Aesthetics of Disability*; and Turner, *Disability in Eighteenth-Century England*.
12. Deutsch, *Loving Dr. Johnson* and *Resemblance and Disgrace*.
13. Deutsch, "Deformity," 52.
14. Davis, "Dr. Johnson, Amelia, and the Discourse of Disability," 56.
15. Turner, *Disability in Eighteenth-Century England*, 9–10.
16. Douglas, *Uneasy Sensations*, xvi.

17. Ibid., xvii.
18. See, for instance, Davis, "Introduction: Disability, Normality, and Power," 1–17.
19. In thinking relationally about disability, I take a cue from Alison Kafer, who argues for a "political/relational model" that draws from "social and minority model frameworks but reads them through feminist and queer critiques of identity." See Kafer, *Feminist, Queer, Crip*, 4.
20. Vermeule, *Why Do We Care about Literary Characters?*, xii.
21. Williams, "Individual" from *Keywords*, 161–165. Scholars have argued that the roots of our modern day understanding of the individual may be found as far back as the thirteenth century. See, for example, McKeon, *The Origins of the English Novel, 1600–1740*.
22. Williams, "Individual," 163.
23. Armstrong, *How Novels Think*, 4.
24. Locke, *An Essay Concerning Human Understanding*, 13.
25. Ibid., 13.
26. Ibid., 13.
27. Ibid., 172.
28. Powell and Swenson, "Introduction: Subject Theory and the Sensational Subject," 146.
29. Locke, *An Essay Concerning Human Understanding*, 85.
30. Ibid., 93.
31. Locke, *Some Thoughts Concerning Education*, 25.
32. "Sound," *Oxford English Dictionary Online*.
33. "Deformity," *Oxford English Dictionary Online*.
34. Hirschmann, "Freedom and (Dis)Ability in Early Modern Political Thought," 181.
35. Ibid., 181.
36. Siebers, *Disability Theory*, 8.
37. Ibid., 10.
38. Ibid., 8.
39. Ibid., 25.
40. Ibid., 22–27.
41. Turner, *Disability in Eighteenth-Century England*, 18–29.
42. Joshua, "Disability and Deformity," 47. For more from Joshua on deformity, see "Picturesque Aesthetics," 29–48.
43. Dickie, *Cruelty and Laughter* and Deutsch, *Loving Dr. Johnson* and *Resemblance and Disgrace*. For more from these scholars on the subject of deformity, see Deutsch, "The Body's Moments," 11–26; and Dickie, "Deformity Poems and Other Nasties," 197–230.
44. Kelleher, "Defections from Nature: The Rhetoric of Deformity in Shaftesbury's *Characteristics*," 72.
45. Kelleher, "The Man Within the Breast," 48, 56.
46. I draw the term *staring back* from Rosemarie Garland-Thomson, who considers the means by which disabled artists reject the stare from able-bodied people that typically accompanies the question, "What happened to you?" Garland-Thomson, "Staring Back," 334–338.
47. Sandahl, "Queering the Crip or Cripping the Queer?," 26.
48. McRuer, *Crip Theory*, 35.
49. Kafer, *Feminist, Queer, Crip*, 3.
50. McRuer, *Crip Theory*, 35.
51. Recent studies, including Bell, *Blackness and Disability*; Chen, *Animacies*; Kafer, *Feminist, Queer, Crip*; McRuer, *Crip Theory*; and Samuel, *Fantasies of Identification*. According to Davidson, these titles indicate new directions for disability studies due to the way that they consider disability as linked to other forms of identity. Davidson, "Cripping Consensus," 433–453.

52. Davidson, "Cripping Consensus," 451.
53. Ibid., 434.
54. Crenshaw, "Mapping the Margins," 1242.
55. Erevelles and Minear, "Unspeakable Offenses," 127–145.
56. Alexander-Floyd, "Disappearing Acts," 19.
57. Robert McRuer argues that compulsory hetero-ablebodiedness aligns disability with queerness while affirming the cultural success which typically attends normative bodies and desires; Alison Kafer posits the scholarly and political productivity of aligning "queer" with "crip" and feminism; and Tobin Siebers demonstrates how disability facilitates conversations about intersectionality in the way that queer theory opens vital critical perspectives for disability studies. See McRuer, *Crip Theory*; Kafer, *Feminist, Queer, Crip*; and Siebers, *Disability Theory*.
58. McRuer, "Compulsory Able-Bodiedness and Queer/Disabled Existence," 370.
59. Davis, "Introduction: Disability, Normality, and Power."
60. Porter, "Spreading Medical Enlightenment," 215–231.
61. Valerie Traub refers to "cycles of salience" as marked repetitions of sexual ideologies that serve as "manifestation of ongoing synchronic tensions in conceptualizations about bodies and desires (and their relations to the gender system)." Ula Klein has helped me to think through Traub's theory in relation to queer embodiment in the eighteenth century. Traub, *The Renaissance of Lesbianism in Early Modern England*, 359; and Klein, "Eighteenth-Century Female Cross-Dressers and Their Beards," 119–143.
62. Bacon, *Essays or Counsels, Civil and Moral*, 74.
63. Deutsch, "Deformity," 52.
64. Bacon, *Essays*, 74.
65. Taylor, *Castration: An Abbreviated History of Western Manhood*, 149.
66. Ibid., 38.
67. Castrated males were also esteemed as singers, as Farinelli and other Italian castrati would demonstrate with their wild popularity in England in the eighteenth century.
68. Jarred Wiehe and I have explored these intersections in recent essay publications. See Farr, "Libertine Sexuality and Queer-Crip Embodiment in Eighteenth-Century Britain," 96–118; and Wiehe, "No Penis? No Problem," 177–194.
69. Mitchell and Snyder, *The Biopolitics of Disability*, 3.
70. Walpole, *The Castle of Otranto*, 6. All future references to the novel will appear in parenthetical citations.
71. Haggerty, *Queer Gothic*.
72. Ibid., 24.
73. Rosemarie Garland-Thomson coined the term *normate* to examine how able-bodied hierarchies function. For more on normate, see Garland-Thomson, *Extraordinary Bodies*, 8–9.
74. Even after the Glorious Revolution of 1688, which seemed to bring about a new era of Lockean political reason that triumphed over the primacy of bloodlines, the familial and procreative practices of British rulers continued to occupy public discourse, and, as we can see in *The Castle of Otranto*, literature. For more about the centrality of reproduction for conceiving of the British nation, see Cody, *Birthing the Nation*, 6.
75. Armstrong, *Desire and Domestic Fiction*, 130.
76. Freud, "The 'Uncanny,'" 219–253.
77. Paul Kelleher discusses sentiment's role in constituting heterosexual love as moral imperative. See Kelleher, *Making Love*.
78. Foucault, *The History of Sexuality*, 118.
79. Ibid., 107.
80. Quillet, *Advice to New-Married Persons*, preface.

81. Ibid., 2.
82. Ibid., 34.
83. Foucault, *The History of Sexuality*, 25.
84. Stoler, *Race and the Education of Desire*, 125.
85. Farr, "Libertine Sexuality."
86. For more on the sexuality and politics of Restoration-era libertinism, see Sanchez, "Libertinism and Romance in Rochester's Poetry," 441–459; and Weber, *The Restoration Rake-Hero*.
87. John Wilmot, Earl of Rochester, "The Imperfect Enjoyment," in *Selected Works*, 15–17.
88. Sedgwick, *Between Men*, 49–66.
89. Wycherley, *The Country Wife*, 4.
90. Ibid., 56.
91. See for instance Shakespeare, "The Social Model of Disability," 9–28.
92. The social model of disability has been critiqued, and rightly so, for ignoring the physical pain and suffering that disabled people often feel on account of their particular embodiment. See, for example, Wendell, "Unhealthy Disabled," 161–176.
93. Shapiro, *No Pity*, 12–40.
94. Reeve, *The Progress of Romance*, 111.
95. Watt, *The Rise of the Novel*, 13.
96. McKeon, *The Origins of the English Novel, 1600–1740*, 2.
97. Ballaster, *Seductive Forms*, 10.
98. Warner, *Licensing Entertainment*, 32–33.
99. Lennard Davis considers the role that disability plays in constituting the novel form as part of an argument that problematizes modern identity categories. See Davis, "Who Put the 'The' in 'the Novel'?," 317–334.
100. Stuart Hall argues that cultural production is a "representational" or "signifying system" that produces meaning so that members of any given society may come to an accord about what it means to be part of that society. For Hall, *codes* play a foundational role in this process as they "fix the relationships between concepts and signs" and "stabilize meaning within different languages and cultures. See Hall, "The Work of Representation," 21.
101. Mitchell and Snyder, *Narrative Prosthesis*.

1
DEAF EDUCATION AND QUEERNESS IN THE DUNCAN CAMPBELL COMPENDIUM (1720-1732)

IN THE EARLY EIGHTEENTH CENTURY, Duncan Campbell, who came to be widely known as a deaf prophet, moved from the Scottish Highlands to London in search of fame and fortune. In short order, he became a celebrity. He ran around with major authors of the day, including Susannah Centlivre, Martha Fowke, Eliza Haywood, and Richard Steele, and his house drew members of high society seeking diversion, often in the form of a foretelling of their futures.[1] Occasionally depicted as an attractive, athletic man who could rain fire down from heaven with his sword if need be, Campbell seems to have earned his keep by accurately guessing names and predicting future romances upon first meeting people. In addition to parlor tricks and excellent swordsmanship, he was reportedly able to heal disfigurements caused by witchcraft and to restore sanity to those confined at Bedlam. He was both admired and reviled for his possession of the gift of prophecy, referred to as the "second sight" and regularly attributed to Scottish Highlanders. Campbell became famous for the many forms of exoticism he embodied, from his deafness to his foreign origins, which lent him an enigmatic aura and magnified his sensational deeds. In the burgeoning print-cultural scene of early eighteenth-century London, authors capitalized on Campbell's immense popularity by penning fantastic tales of his marvelous feats. In perhaps the earliest print reference to Campbell, an excerpt from *The Tatler No. 14* (1709), Campbell is described as a "dumb Fortune-teller" who receives "visitants . . . full of expectations" that "pay his own rate for the interpretations they put upon his shrugs and nods."[2] Campbell, as this entry attests, attracted masses of people through his gestural pronouncements of the future.

We have today at our disposal a wealth of writings about Campbell.[3] In periodicals, pamphlets, poems, novels, and a supposed memoir (published between 1709 and 1732), Campbell's fame spread at a time when what we now know as *novels* were often involved in the business of histories. The frequency with which Campbell was written about suggests that he was no mere flash-in-the-pan celebrity. He captivated the interest and imagination of Londoners for a prolonged period of time, no small feat when one considers, for example, how fickle theatergoers could be, or the sheer quantity of print materials available to readers. In their exhaustive exploration of Campbell's deafness and second sight, the authors of what I call *The Duncan Campbell Compendium* chronicle the biography of the famed soothsayer, including his coming-of-age, marital life, and various intrigues.[4]

Campbell serves as a crucial touchstone for the cultural history of deafness in Britain. For Christopher Krentz, *The History of the Life and Adventures of Mr. Duncan Campbell* (1720) has a significant impact on the emergence of deaf education in Britain because it challenges disparaging discourses of deaf people as "savage" and "mad"—even if "Campbell himself seems impossible to know."[5] This is certainly the case: pinning down who Campbell was, and what exactly was the degree of his deafness, would be virtually impossible given the abundance of *fictional* sources about him. The supernatural character of the stories about Campbell may be why researchers of deafness sometimes overlook or outright dismiss these works.[6] But as a literary scholar, I am interested in the role that these narratives play as *representations*, and in this I follow the model of Stuart Hall, who argues for a constructivist approach to conceptualizing representation. Language and other representational systems, for Hall, offer us a common "conceptual map" that frames our ability to communicate with one another through shared cultural values.[7] As representations of a real-life deaf man, the fictional works about Campbell offer a conceptual map that orients our understanding of the gradual development of deaf subjectivity in Enlightenment Britain.

As Krentz also suggests, the works about Campbell portray in remarkable ways the possibility that a deaf gentleman could be educated just as readily as his hearing counterparts. These works about Campbell, I would add, imagine a future in which deaf people could be assimilated into the hearing order. They reveal a capacious understanding of the variability of human embodiment and language, even if the marvels that accompany Campbell fall in line with stereotypical depictions of deaf people as supernatural beings.[8] As a whole, these works mark a watershed moment in British deaf cultural history due to their extended engagement with the biography of a profoundly deaf character who was both literate and heroic, making their content utterly unique and unprecedented in Britain.

In this chapter, I examine Campbell's deafness in relation to the period's deeply embedded *audism*—a social system in which deaf people are oppressed due to the primacy of vocal interaction, which successfully masquerades as the most natural mode of casual, day-to-day communication. Audist codes relegate deafness and signing to the realms of the unnatural and anomalous. But like any system, audism is rife with contradiction, and so depictions of deafness and signing provide a potential critique of the hearing order. Though the works about Campbell were written long before the widespread establishment of Deaf or disabled identities, I argue that they both disturb and reinforce audism through their complex engagement with contemporaneous debates about signing, and through their employment of the very forms of epistolary and fictional writing that could be silently and effectively transmitted to a reading audience.[9] These soundless forms of communication raised the possibility that the deaf could be integrated into mainstream society. With integration, though, would eventually come containment and medicalization. Campbell is situated within these overlapping discourses of deafness. He encapsulates at once the past and future for deaf people in the Enlightenment: the past because he is aligned with marvels and miracles, as deaf people had been during the early modern period, and the future because, due to his refined literacy, he heralds the establishment of formalized deaf education in late eighteenth-century Britain.[10] However, Campbell's vacillation between queer and normative masculinities, and his education through already existing methods proposed by seventeenth-century natural philosophers, complicate our understanding of this historical trajectory. The incongruous set of representations about Campbell in these literary texts—oscillating between the exotic and the familiar, the queer and the customary, the old and the new—substantiate deaf education even as they contain deafness within the dominant audist social order.

DUNCAN CAMPBELL'S COSMIC QUEERNESS

The first extended narratives about Campbell, *The History of the Life and Adventures of Mr. Duncan Campbell* (1720) and Eliza Haywood's *A Spy on the Conjurer* (1724), convey preoccupations about the nature of language and rationality by familiarizing their audience with what would have been radical ideas for the time: namely, that a deaf man could be educated and that he could therefore communicate rational thought with interlocutors.[11] The authors of these narratives go about this in varied ways, but what both share is a commitment to mapping the cultural significance of deafness upon Campbell's gendered, queered, and exoticized body. *The History of the Life and Adventures of Mr. Duncan Campbell* portrays the deaf prophet as an exotic figure who brings his rare gifts from Lapland, where he is born to a Scottish gentleman and Laplandish mother, and the Scottish Highlands, where he lives as a child, to London. The narrative's geographical orientation reflects one of its most prominent features—to bring the peripheral (a deaf Laplandish-Highlander capable of supernatural feats) to the cultural and rational center of Britain. In this account, Campbell is living proof of relatively recent ideas about deaf education that had yet to materialize in Britain. In straddling the past and future, Campbell appears out of time and occupies a liminal position that I examine as *cosmically queer*. Campbell's ostensible ability to tap into the unknown, his birth among the pygmies of Lapland, and his communication skillset that flies in the face of accepted audist wisdom set him apart as an otherworldly entity that is, in significant ways, not beholden to conventional temporalities.

The queerness that Campbell embodies in this narrative is encapsulated in an extraordinarily vivid passage in which he is described as angelic. At this point in the story, Campbell, an adolescent, has recently arrived in London. The third-person, male narrator, who identifies himself as a friend of Campbell's family and as knowledgeable of Campbell's upbringing, describes the peculiar prophet as "the most beautiful Boy of his Age I ever knew," and as a "heavenly Youth, with the most winning comeliness of Aspect that ever pleased the Sight of any Beholder of either Sex."[12] The narrator further describes Campbell as seated in the midst of an "angelic tribe" of female attendants (128). Campbell's face is "divinely Fair, and ting'd only with such a sprightly Blush, as a Painter would use to Colour the Picture of Health with, and the Complexion was varnish'd over by a Blooming, like that of a flourishing Fruit, which had not yet felt the first Nippings of an unkind and an uncivil Air" (128). Campbell appears spry and fair, a blushing innocent who has not yet been tainted by city life and who hardly participates in the cares and sorrows of the world. His eyes are "large, full of Lustre, Majestick, well set, and the Soul shone so in them, as told the Spectators plainly, how great was the inward Vivacity of his Genius" (128). These physiognomic descriptions are meant to manifest Campbell's inward genius. He radiates an ethereal magnetism that attracts everyone, regardless of their gender. The captivated narrator further describes Campbell's perfect hair as "thick and reclin'd far below his Shoulders . . . a fine Silver Colour . . . in Ringlets like the curling Tendrils of a copious Vine" (128). The narrator's homoerotic encomium of Campbell establishes the queer contours of the narrative and suggests that the young prophet is inhabitant of the material and spiritual worlds. Campbell's otherworldly aura evokes a luminous otherness which captures the narrative's paradoxical representation of auditory difference: while Campbell is in this passage youthful, resolutely docile, and to some degree feminized—a most unconventional rendering of aristocratic maleness in light of contemporaneous representations of libertine sexual dominance—he also possesses the gift of the second sight to transform lives, and narrative, for that matter, through his signing, lip reading, and writing. Campbell is therefore at once passive and active, and his gender and sexual mobility is suggestive of the capaciousness of deaf representation at this time. Given that this novel was written more than forty years before the first deaf academy would open in Britain and almost eighty years before the first asylum, the author could draw from the generic tendencies of travel narratives to fill in the blank space of deaf identity in the popular imagination, for deafness at this point has not yet hardened into a medicalized category as it would in the following century.

And yet despite the future medicalization of disability and deafness, which would tie impairment to homosexuality, Campbell's deafness in this early context is bound up with a queerness that exceeds the bounds of the natural world. The narrative's portrayal of Campbell as an angelic being that brings knowledge of the unknown realms of prophecy and deaf literacy to Londoners invokes Milton's depiction of Raphael in *Paradise Lost*. Like Campbell, Raphael is a cosmic, angelic being with an important mission. He travels, at God's behest, to Eden, where he instructs Adam about God's magnificent heavenly and earthly creations. In Book 5 of *Paradise Lost*, Raphael journeys from the heavens to earth on his six "gorgeous wings" which he wears "to shade / his lineaments divine."[13] Adam sees Raphael's "glorious shape" and instantly recognizes that this must be a visitor from heaven.[14] The two soon break bread. In his representation of this earthly activity, Milton dispenses with the notion that angels do not need sustenance: "For know, whatever was created, needs / to be sustained and fed."[15] The ensuing fellowship that characterizes the budding relationship between Adam and Raphael, fully formed corporeal angel that he is, becomes the "the best kind of relationship possible," according to Stephen Guy-Bray, who argues that Milton's use of angelic bodies such as Raphael's indicates the ways in which all life forms fall short of a prelapsarian ideal.[16] However, in the exchange between Raphael and Adam, homoeroticism becomes the most ideal form of connection. The meeting between Raphael and Adam in Eden is both "friendly and sexual" and marks "the highest form of masculine friendship."[17] For Guy-Bray, Milton offers in Raphael "a nonreproductive and ultimately ungendered sexuality that we can only call queer."[18] Mortals such as Adam may access the elevated radiance of queer angelic bodies but never quite replicate it themselves. Milton's version of queerness inevitably eludes humankind, and perhaps its elusiveness is the point. In *The History of the Life and Adventures of Mr. Duncan Campbell*, the deaf prophet embodies such mysterious, queer radiance. Like Raphael, he is a prophet with a specific purpose: to teach Londoners about their love lives, but also to transmit knowledge regarding the literacy capabilities of deaf people. Campbell's celestial appeal transcends the thinkable boundaries of rationality and sexuality, and in the same spirit as

Raphael and Adam, he is surrounded by those that would seek his heavenly knowledge on terra firma.

The relationship between Adam and Raphael functions as a possible touchstone in the narrator's account, for, like Adam, the adoring women that sit in Campbell's presence tap into the celestial realm as they make contact with his body. In their attending to Campbell, these women express a communal desire for the prophet's cosmic form that reveals the expansiveness of early eighteenth-century gender and sexual codes. Campbell is clearly depicted as the center of the scene, a monarchical figure who reigns supreme. If Campbell is the king, then the women are a harem of admirers, as Felicity Nussbaum observes, with Campbell a passive recipient of their "angelic" caresses.[19] One woman holds a basin of water while her lovely companion washes Campbell's body. Still another woman dries Campbell with a towel, "while a Fourth was disposing into order his Silver Hairs with an Ivory Comb, in an Hand as White, and which a Monarch might have been proud to have had so employ'd in adjusting the Crown upon his Head" (129). A lady fixes Campbell's cravat, while another "stole a Kiss, and blush'd at the innocent Pleasure, and mistook her own Thoughts as if she kiss'd the Angel and not the Man" (129). The conflation of angel and man in this passage should by now be unsurprising: Campbell's variable embodiment establishes his simultaneous hypervisibility and illegibility. The attendants seem rather "to adore than to love him, as if they had taken him not for a Person that enjoy'd the frequent Gift of the Second Sight, but as if he had been some little Prophet peculiarly inspired, and while they all thus admired and wonder'd they all consulted him as an Oracle" (128–129). The women freely express a collective sexual desire toward the oracle that would guide them to self-knowledge. Rather than contend for his attention, as so many female characters in Restoration plays and early eighteenth-century fiction do, they join together in a harmonious expression of piety, love, and devotion. This description of Campbell and his harem certainly impedes any coherent reading of his masculinity, as Nussbaum points out.[20] I would add that this incoherence is facilitated by the angelic portrayal of his body. Such a communal vision of angelic sexuality subverts typical outlets for women's sexual expression in the period, for these women revel in their willing service to the young prophet.[21] The women in this passage experience an eroticism that is not often granted female characters, and it is no accident that the object of their admiration is a young, deaf man, whose atemporal queerness underscores the exoticism of the scene.

Moreover, Campbell's cosmic queerness illuminates his role as conduit between the nonhearing and hearing worlds. Figure 1.1 captures Campbell's prophetic qualities. It depicts a cherub and an angel hoisting a portrait of Campbell into the heavens, where Campbell hovers above the terrestrial world as a shining beacon of piety and knowledge, "to be known in the whole world" as the Latin phrase inscribed in the banner ("toto notus in orbe Campbellus") indicates. The other phrase at the bottom of the engraving, "Est Deus in nobis"—or "God among us"—is suggestive of his deification. The bell-wielding figure in the foreground is his genius, a celestial, silver-haired lad who gets Campbell's attention by ringing a bell, which sends vibrations to Campbell's inner ear. This visitor supplies Campbell with prophecies through signed language and by writing to him (as evidenced by his paper and quill). Like Raphael, who has a valuable message for Adam regarding the creation of heavens and earth, the war in heaven, and the fallibility of earthly sexuality, Campbell has his own message for all those willing to receive it.[22] In this way, Campbell becomes a totem for hearing people to conceptualize deafness as marvel and wonder, even as his sexual charisma highlights the allure of his extraordinary message. The narrative "universalizes" Campbell's marginality in order to contain it, as Davis would argue.[23] But while Campbell is to some degree "contained" by the stereotypical representation of exotic hypersexual appeal that is sometimes attached to deaf subjects, his queer embodiment is precisely what makes him narratable as harbinger of a new linguistic order.

Another likely touchstone for this passage is the widely discussed organization of Turkish courtly life, in which deaf people served as emissaries to the sultan in his harem. Even the sultans themselves were said to know the signed language used among his deaf attendants.[24] Campbell is sultan, the women his harem, and the exotic appeal of the scene invokes the strangeness of foreign cultures as often displayed in British travel literature. Campbell's cosmically queer embodiment is metaphorically reliant upon Britain's fraught relationship with the Ottoman Empire, a boundless source of the strange and marvelous to British writers. The introduction to the novel makes this point abundantly clear. After broaching the idea that there is a deaf man "now living" that teaches other deaf people to "Read, Write, and Converse with the Talking and Hearing Part of Mankind," the narrator anticipates that readers will "very religiously conclude" that

Figure 1.1. *Opposite:* Duncan Campbell as angelic messenger. A portrait of Campbell—with an accompanying banner that states "Toto notus in orbe Campbellus" (or "Campbell is known in all the world")—is being hoisted into the heavens by winged angels. In the foreground, Campbell's silver-haired genius rings a bell and is accompanied by a lamb. In the foreground, a quote from Ovid, "Est deus in nobis," or "God is with us," in reference to Campbell's godlike capabilities. Illustration from *The Supernatural Philosopher: or, the mysteries of magick, All exemplified in the history of the life and surprizing adventures of Mr. Duncan Campbell* (1728). Courtesy of the Huntington Library.

Est Deus in nobis ———— Ovid. p.129.

Campbell is "some strange new Miracle-Monger and Impostor into the World" heralding a "Sect of Antichristinism, as formidable as that of the Brahmans" (6). Here, the author anticipates that readers would consider Campbell in a similar light as the Brahmins, a religious group in India whom the British thought of as superstitious, idolatrous, and powerful. Campbell's iconoclastic posture is not tied to his second sight; rather, as the passage makes clear, his extraordinary communication skills and expansive literacy are what make him appear exotic to a British reading audience. Perhaps in an effort to engage an audience accustomed to reading of the wonders of travel narratives that comment upon the extraordinary flora, fauna, and peoples of foreign climes, the author makes these foreign references. But as the introduction to the novel suggests, Campbell is a liminal figure: he is enigmatic and foreign, as the Brahmins are, but at the same time he is not to be feared, for he actively participates in the public sphere like so many gentlemen of the time.

The narrative's allusion to the East further signals a widely held belief that deaf people, regardless of their geographical origins, form one nation, that they constitute their own tribe. In 1648, John Bulwer dedicates *Philocophus: Or, the Deaf and Dumb Man's Friend* (1648) to his deaf patrons: "And the Grand Signiour, or Emperour of the Turks, would take it for no disparagement, to be called Great Master of the Deafe and Dumbe; with whom *fifty of your Tribe* are always in Delitis."[25] For Bulwer, the deaf belong to a tribe that extends as far east as the Ottoman Empire. In another passage, Bulwer, attempting to affirm the capabilities of deaf people, writes, "Great are the *Nation* of those (otherwise ingenious men) who have fallen under this unhappy accident."[26] Deaf people, as Bulwer insinuates, inhabit an imaginary nation that transcends established borders. Later accounts from the nineteenth century reveal that this discourse persisted and developed over time. When the French deaf educator Laurent Clerc met a group of signing deaf children at the Braidwood School for the Deaf in London, he is reported to have become "as agitated as a traveller of sensibility would be on meeting all of a sudden in distant regions, a colony of his own countrymen."[27] Clerc's Frenchness is viewed as no impediment to his innate ability to converse with British children, who would have a distinct set of signs to communicate with one another from what Clerc would be accustomed to. And finally, in a U.S. context, the deaf writer John J. Fluornoy proposed the creation of a "deaf state" in the western U.S. territories in 1855 based on the model of Liberia: "A deaf state is the manifest destiny of our people. . . . It is a political independence, a State Sovereignty, at which I aim. . . . We will have a small republic of our own, under our sovereignty, and independent of all hearing interference."[28] As these examples show, the gradual construction of deaf subjectivity from the seventeenth through the nineteenth centuries is in part a product of nation building. Because of their particular way of communicating with one another through sign, deaf people are racialized, and sometimes grouped together in a way that captures the aspirational myth of a monolingual nation. In aligning Campbell with foreigners, the narrative taps into this discursive phenomenon. A perpetual border-crosser, Campbell occupies a liminal, transnational subject position due to his national illegibility, a point further underscored by his upbringing in Lapland and Scotland and his various travels abroad. And yet he is also unmistakably British when he performs genteel masculinity. His various forms of mobility suggest that the emergence of deaf subjectivity is tied to racial, gender, and sexual categories, as well as the development of modern state identities.

Clearly, according to the narrative, Campbell is no ordinary gentleman, even when he tries to be. A later passage from *The History of the Life and Adventures of Mr. Duncan Campbell* portrays Campbell's failed attempt at standard genteel masculinity. Once he has been in London some time and has made a name for himself, Campbell loses the luster of his cosmic queerness, seeking out the life of the leisurely gentleman. He takes an extended break from fortune-telling to indulge in the pastimes of affluent men with time on their hands: "His genius led him to a very gallant way of life; in his lodgings, in his entertainments, in paying and receiving visits, in coffee-houses, in taverns, in fencing-schools, in balls, and other public assemblies, in all ways, in fine, both at home and abroad, Duncan Campbell was a well-comported and civil fine gentleman; he was a man of pleasure, and nothing of the man of business appeared about him" (210). Here, Campbell's strange and miraculous feats give way to the utterly conventional. No longer the angel that floats above the masses, dispensing divine wisdom and tapping into unknown realms, Campbell now pursues libertine indulgence, spurning the money-making orientation of his oracle trade. Perhaps predictably, Campbell lives beyond his means and goes into debt, a stock representation of gentlemen that can be found in several Restoration plays. By the end of this account, Campbell must return to soothsaying in order to restore his prospects. Campbell thus fails to properly execute genteel masculinity, both because he lacks the financial means and because he cannot escape his identity as a miracle-working prophet. In this, Campbell's mobile gender and sexuality are tethered as much to his class position as they are to his exoticism.

Despite Campbell's best efforts, in *The History of the Life and Adventures of Mr. Duncan Campbell* he cannot step out of the shadow cast by his deafness and extrasensory capabilities. These two readily identifiable facets of his identity intertwine to consolidate his cosmic queerness. Around the turn of the eighteenth century, deafness and the second sight function as kindred spirits, as unnatural conundrums that the keen observational skills of the enlightened man may decipher. In their writings, Robert Boyle, Robert Kirk, Samuel Pepys, and John Frazer invoke the intellectual and spiritual environment of the age, in which natural philosophers and virtuosos attempted to use scientific means to prove the existence of an afterlife. As Alex Sutherland notes, "If science could confirm that there were people gifted with prophetic powers as described in the Bible, this would, in turn, confirm the validity of the Good Book."[29] With this objective, authors attempted to demystify and rationalize the spiritual traditions of their day. Their studies often attempted to address the enigmatic existence of sensory deprivation. Besides Campbell, other Scots were discussed in relation to the second sight, and some (but not all) of these figures were also deaf, blind, or nonverbal. In 1707, Frazer writes about Janet Dowglas, a deaf woman who is "mute" until she beholds "a Vision in lively Images" and subsequently communicates "by Signs and Words" to foretell the future.[30] Like Campbell, Dowglas is a source of the miraculous, a conduit to a spirit world that is imperceptible to the majority of people. Frazer also relates the story of an elderly man whose "sight was much decayed" and who receives visits from deceased friends that drink before him and "yet are not so civil to give [him] a tasting of it."[31] For both Dowglas and the old man, sensory impairment informs their experience of the second sight. Such renderings of the hearing- and visually-impaired establish a cultural tradition from which *The History of the Life and Adventures of Mr. Duncan Campbell* draws. However, rather unlike those miracles in which sensory-impaired individuals suddenly gain their ability to speak, hear, see, or prophesize, Campbell undergoes a rigorous education at the hands of a tutor while young to learn how to communicate through writing and fingerspelling. Campbell's anomalous coming-of-age tale elucidates the interplay between language, nature, and reason, which had so interested and vexed natural philosophers from the previous century. This is to say that Campbell, the cosmic prophet that brings the gift of prophecy to wayward Londoners, also carries transformative ideas about deaf education that had already been discussed in the seventeenth century.

DEAF SOUNDSCAPES: BULWER'S COMMUNITY OF SENSES, QUEER PHENOMENOLOGY, AND EDUCATION

The preponderance of writings about Campbell in the 1720s signals a heightened interest in auditory impairment and its relationship to language. As Lennard Davis argues, the long eighteenth century is a period in which deafness became a topic of "cultural fascination and a compelling focus for philosophical reflection" due to ongoing debates from such thinkers as Rousseau and Locke over the nature of language, cognition, and reason.[32] Moreover, some of these same philosophers were skeptical about what deaf people could achieve, as Locke's audism suggests.[33] The writings about Campbell challenge such limiting assumptions by drawing from the work of John Bulwer who, in the century before Campbell's celebrity erupted in London, had argued for inclusive education through his trumpeting of a "community among the senses" model and through his upholding of gesture as a universal language that could overcome linguistic difference.[34] Bulwer is somewhat of an anomaly in the early history of British deaf education because he believed that signed language was a viable form of expression. He seems to have been inspired by an account from Kenelm Digby that depicted Charles I's astonishingly lucid encounter with a deaf Spanish boy during his visit to the Spanish court in 1623.[35] In his first publication, *Chirologia: or, the Natural Language of the Hand* (1644), Bulwer deems gesture a rich communicative form that is expertly practiced by deaf people, who thereby demonstrate rational thinking. For Bulwer, deaf people can "understand and express themselves in this language of gesture" to demonstrate "that capable they be not only of the inward discourse of Reason, but of the outward gift of utterance by gesture."[36] Bulwer's work on gesture led to his 1648 publication, *Philocophus: or, the Deaf and Dumb Man's Friend*, in which he proposed the establishment of an academy for deaf students. Unfortunately for Bulwer, as a Royalist, he lost support during the Interregnum. This may be why he was unable to establish his academy.[37] Bulwer's legacy, however, endured; his model of sensory perception from *Philocophus* is evident throughout the Duncan Campbell Compendium. Bulwer's model illuminates the unique sociability of deaf people and is suggestive of the queer orientation of deaf soundscapes.

In *The History of the Life and Adventures of Mr. Duncan Campbell*, the narrator depicts Campbell as able to perceive objects through the intermingling of his senses. Even before he arrives to London, Campbell, at this point just a boy, explains to the narrator that he receives knowledge for his prophecies from a bell-carrying, silver-haired lad who regularly appears to the young seer (as depicted in figure 1.1). This messenger writes notes to Campbell but usually speaks "with his Fingers" (72). Campbell offers a sensory-laden description of these visits: "[The boy] has a little Bell in his Hand, like that which my Mother makes me a Sign to shake, when she wants the Servants; with that he tickles my Brain strangely, and gives me an incredible Delight of Feeling in the Inside of my Head" (72). In joining the visual (bell) and aural (ringing) with the haptic (tickling), the narrator conceives of Campbell's ability to perceive the visitor's messages through the very model of sensory perception that Bulwer proposes, in which disparate sensory organs work in harmony.[38] Regarding the community of senses, Bulwer writes, "so careful is Nature like a good mother, to make amends for a fault, that none should accuse her to be a stepmother: for what she taketh away in some of the senses, she allows, and recompenseth in the rest."[39] Bulwer further describes his sensory model as "admirable" in that "the objects of one Sense may be known by another" and that "one Sense will oftentimes supply the office and want of another: for light may be felt, odours may be tasted, the relish of meates may be smelt, magnitude and figure may be heard, and sounds may be seen, felt, or tasted."[40] Bulwer argues that what we would now call synesthesia—the crossing of sense organs with unexpected stimuli—is commonplace among humankind. His theory suggests that deafness and blindness are not barriers to education since deaf and blind people can actively perceive sounds and sights through their other senses. While Bulwer seems to be arguing for a compensatory model of sensory perception, he is especially keen to observe that our five senses work together to perceive objects. As Elizabeth Bearden argues, Bulwer refutes the notion that deafness hinders communication and offers instead a scheme that is "inclusive and accepting" of auditory difference, and that upholds deaf people as important contributors to society.[41] Bulwer's stance, for Bearden, captures the enriching perspectives that deaf people offer due to their distinctive embodied language and phenomenological experience, referred to today as "Deaf-gain."[42] In representing various episodes in which Campbell's expansive awareness of space and visual cues raises hearing characters to new levels of self-knowledge, the Duncan Campbell Compendium likewise offers moments of Deaf-gain.

The frontispiece from *Philocophus* (figure 1.2) illustrates Bulwer's community of senses in action. There are three men portrayed in the foreground of the frontispiece. Their intimate connections to one another, and their collective sensory experience of sound and objects, invoke queer phenomenological relationships. On the right side of the engraving sits a man at a table. Before him, on the table itself (from left to right) lie a framed portrait of an individual, a canister of incense that perfumes the hall, and a plate of fruit. Dotted lines connect each of these objects to the seated man's sense organs, building unanticipated relationships among them. The portrait, for instance, is linked to his ear, indicating that he hears (rather than sees) the portrait. The canister of incense connects to his mouth, revealing that he tastes (rather than smells) the incense. He is also able to smell the fruit, the least surprising of the sensorial relationships indicated in the engraving. The illustration reveals how, in Bulwer's estimation, the five senses work in concert to perceive such objects. An impairment in one of the man's senses would not hinder his ability to process external signals one way or another. The illustration captures Bulwer's "Orphic" formulation of bodily and sensory variation, in which he shows respect for the mysteries of the natural world.[43] The frontispiece also elucidates in visual terms Bulwer's argument that deaf people could perceive external signals

Figure 1.2. Three figures participating in Bulwer's community of senses. To the left, a man plays a bass viol. In the center, a deaf man places his teeth over the scroll of the bass viol to hear the instrument through the vibrations of the instrument. On the right, a man sits at a table, and on that table, from left to right, rest a portrait, a canister of incense, and a bowl of fruit. Each of these objects connect via dotted lines to unexpected sense organs on the man. A dotted line along the top connects all of the men, with the statement "Ad motum labioru" ("the movement of lips"). Detail, frontispiece from John Bulwer's *Philocophus, or, the deafe and dumbe man's friend* (1648). Courtesy of the Huntington Library.

just as readily as their hearing counterparts and that they should therefore have access to education.

The two other figures in the engraving likewise illustrate the community of senses in action and serve as evidence of the relationship between deaf sensory perception and queerness. On the left side of the image there is a man playing a bass viol. The neck and head of the instrument that he plays extend into the air, and the body of the instrument rests between the man's legs. As a whole, the instrument's placement in relation to the player's body is reminiscent of an erect penis and testicles, an engorged vessel that supplies the hall with music. The other bodies that receive the music, however, do so in unexpected ways. To the right of the bass viol player is a kneeling deaf man, turned to the right, with his mouth over the right ear of the scroll, which is in the shape of a human head.[44] The deaf man is able to hear the bass viol through *bone conduction*, in which vibrations that emanate from the instrument are transmitted to the teeth, through the skull, and on to the inner ear. In this manner, the deaf man can hear the music through his mouth's unrestricted contact with the scroll.[45] The intimate relationship between bass viol player and deaf listener is nothing short of homoerotic given the deaf man's rapt, oral engagement with the player's instrument, which fills him with its sweet reverberations.

The queer orientation of the image is also evident in the coordination of written words, objects, men, and dotted lines. Along the top of the image, the declaration "Ad motum labioru!"—a Latin phrase that translates to "the movement of his lips"—brings the three men together in unison. The deaf man's positioning of his lips around the scroll of the bass viol makes visible atypical bodies' queer orientations toward objects. In *Queer Phenomenology*, Sara Ahmed theorizes embodied relationships "toward different objects, those that are 'less proximate' or even those that deviate or are deviant."[46] These objects operate as "orientation devices" for the queer bodies that seek them out.[47] In the frontispiece, the bass viol is a deviant object because the deaf man uses it "to find" his "way" and to "feel at home"—in this case, to hear the music from the instrument in an extraordinary manner.[48] The remarkable affiliation between deaf man and instrument is queer, not only for the oral orientation of the man toward the phallic instrument, but because of the way that the instrument enables the deaf man to process what would otherwise be inaccessible to him, short-circuiting the "natural" underpinnings of Baconian science as well as the logic of heterosexual desire.[49] Further, the player's lips (perhaps he is singing) and the deaf man's vibrating labial movements reach the eyes of the seated man on the right, as a dotted line indicates. So, while the man at the table perceives the mundane objects on the table before him, he also "hears" the melody from the bass viol through the community of his senses, which ties him to the deaf man and the bass violist. Together, the men experience a reciprocal three-way exchange of queer sensation.

Ahmed's discussion of desire lines in natural scenes is likewise useful for understanding the dotted lines that connect bodies to objects in the frontispiece. Ahmed posits desire lines as "unofficial paths" where "marks left on the ground . . . show everyday comings and goings, where people deviate from the paths they are expected to follow."[50] Ahmed argues that, as in such natural scenes, the non-normative body also "leaves its own marks on the ground, which can even help generate alternative lines, which cross the ground in unexpected ways. Such lines are indeed traces of desire; where people have taken different routes to get to this point or to that point."[51] The lines in the frontispiece of

Bulwer's *Philocophus* are indicative of such alternative forms of desire in that they expose less-trodden pathways between objects and sense organs. Perhaps the artist's decision to represent them through lines that are not solid, but dotted, indicate that while they are "unofficial" avenues, they are not unprecedented; the dotted lines prove to be of vital consequence for the sensational orientation of variable bodies.[52] The men depicted in the frontispiece demonstrate their queer phenomenological orientations by turning toward objects in unconventional ways. The image represents the community of senses as an alternative economy of desire in which atypical bodies process the outside world in atypical ways. In this way, it establishes the queer phenomenology of deafness that is also at the heart of Bulwer's sensory model.

The appendix of the anonymously authored *The Friendly Daemon: or, the Generous Apparition* (1726), also from the Duncan Campbell Compendium, likewise invokes Bulwer's community of senses as a spectacular phenomenological experience. In a description of Campbell's communicative capacities, the narrator reveals Campbell's alternative sensate pathways, from his reading of lips (which Bulwer also discusses at length in *Philocophus*) to the queer phenomenological relationship between Campbell and a stringed musical instrument:

> [h]e certainly had a wonderful Comprehension of what was said, if he fixed his Eyes on the Person who spoke, and observed the Motion of their Lips; and by the other he could distinguish Sounds, as was evident by putting the Neck of the Violin between his Teeth, and holding it there till he screwed the Pegs to what Pitch he thought fit.... There are Reasons both Chirurgical and Philosophical for the feeling of Sounds, as may be seen at large in several learned Treatises; and common Experience may inform us, that a deaf Person, when he sees an Instrument of Musick touched, will immediately clap the Drum of his Ear to one End of a Stick, and hold the other against a hollow Board, and this will enable him to beat Time with as just a Cadence, as if he had the Sense of Hearing in the utmost Perfection.[53]

Campbell's oral engagement with the neck of the violin enables him to adjust the pegs, and through bone conduction, he discovers the right pitch for playing the instrument. The narrator observes that deaf people experience sound through such haptic means, a "common Experience" that hearing people may readily observe in quotidian scenes. Just as Bulwer outlines in his treatises, Campbell and other deaf individuals are perfectly capable of feeling and processing soundscapes. The passage's reference to "many learned Treatises" that discuss the "feeling of Sounds" likely refers to Bulwer's work (among others). In this way, Campbell's queerness extends beyond his gender and sexual mobility and cosmic affect to encompass his oral and haptic experience of sound.

Queerness, as I have argued, informs the contours of Campbell's deafness. How Campbell comes to learn to think like a gentleman is not an entirely unrelated matter. *The History of the Life and Adventures of Mr. Duncan Campbell* registers the writings of another seventeenth-century natural philosopher who came after Bulwer, John Wallis, a founding member of the Royal Society. In his tutoring of a young, deaf aristocrat named Alexander Popham in the decades following Bulwer's publications, Wallis emphasized an oralist approach to deaf education, which would influence Thomas Braidwood in the following century.[54] Like the first Western European tutors for the deaf, Pedro Poncé de León and Juan Pablo Bonet of Spain, Wallis's foremost concern was to teach deaf, nonverbal aristocrats how to speak so that they could overcome the barriers imposed on them by inheritance law, which prohibited deaf children from becoming heirs to estates due to their inability to express themselves vocally.[55] This form of social death in aristocratic life, marked by the appearance of physical anomaly within a family, betokens anxieties surrounding degeneracy that would eventually materialize in public campaigns to rid deformity from reproducing couples because, like sodomitical activity, deafness could be a potential impediment to the passing down of land and the extension of the family line. To remedy this problem within one particular family, Wallis emphasized speech exercises and focused also on written literacy in his tutoring of Popham.[56] Wallis left behind letters and treatises that explain his method, and *The History of the Life and Adventures of Mr. Duncan Campbell* credits one of Wallis's letters as the blueprint for the teaching of young Campbell to read, write, read lips, and sign.[57] The narrative excerpts Wallis at length in a chapter titled "The Method of Teaching Deaf and Dumb Persons to Write, Read, and Understand a Language." While introducing Wallis's letter, the narrator asserts that deaf people are capable of lip reading:

> How are Children first taught a Language that can hear? Are they not taught by Sounds? And what are those Sounds, but Tokens and Signs to the Ear, importing and signifying such and such a Thing? If then there can be Signs made to the Eye, agreed by the Party teaching the Child, that they signify such and such a Thing; will not the Eye of the Child convey them to the Mind, *as well as* the Ear? They are indeed *different* Marks to different Senses; but *both* the one *and* the other do *equally* signify the same Things or Notions, according to the Will of the Teacher, and consequently, must have an *equal* Effect with the Person who is to be instructed: For tho' the Manners signifying are *different*, the Things signified are the *same*. (38–39, emphasis mine)

In the passage above, I have italicized the words that denote difference and equality. It is telling that *different* appears on only two occasions, both of which represent an acknowledgment that communicating via speech and finger talk are indeed discrete forms. However, the remainder of the passage contains words denoting equality: "as well as," "equally," "both . . . and," "equally," "equal," and "same." This outweighing of similitude over difference conveys that language can be spoken *and* signed with *equal* efficiency, in turn justifying educating deaf children by equating those "Tokens and Signs to the Ear" with "Signs made to the Eye." In turn, both the ear and the eye are "equally" efficient in their ability to "convey" meaning to the mind. It is up to the teacher, this passage implies, to understand and capitalize on the potential of the eye to capture meaning. The teacher must know that it is every bit as possible for the hands and eye to coordinate meaning as it is for the voice and ear. The author then goes on to reprint an epistle from Wallis, which outlines his method for teaching deaf people by grouping words according to type. Wallis's extended lists of individual words are included under titles such as "beasts," "plants," and "clothes." This interweaving of Wallis's instruction with descriptions of Campbell's second sightedness reveals the novel's dual aims to entertain and raise awareness about deaf education.

The History of the Life and Adventures of Mr. Duncan Campbell also includes a chart of Wallis's fingerspelling alphabet (see figure 1.3), which consists of a two-handed sign for each letter in the alphabet. Fingerspelling requires one to spell out words from a spoken language, a painstaking alternative to the fluidity of signed languages that capitalize on one's ability to establish meaning in a much more fluid and less labor-intensive manner. These methodical signs were invented by some hearing person or other (perhaps not Wallis himself) and were the means by which Wallis intended to teach deaf children the tenets of written and spoken language.[58] In the chart, there are squares with each letter of the alphabet and the sign which accompanies it. In the third edition of the novel, a 1739 publication, the chart is accompanied by a description: "A good Method to teach deaf & Dumb Persons to converse with one another, and with all who are willing to learn this Secret & Silent way of Conversation."[59] Wallis's fingerspelling chart is offered as a means by which the deaf could communicate with each other, but it also gives hearing readers an opportunity to learn to fingerspell so that they, too, could communicate with deaf people. The chart's location within a series of narratives about Campbell's extraordinary achievements draws attention to the novel's polarizing tendency, in which the narrative shifts between the familiar and the exotic, the normative and the queer. Through his queer phenomenology and supernatural achievements, Campbell becomes the occasion for significant revelations about deaf people, their abilities to reason, to be educated, and to communicate with

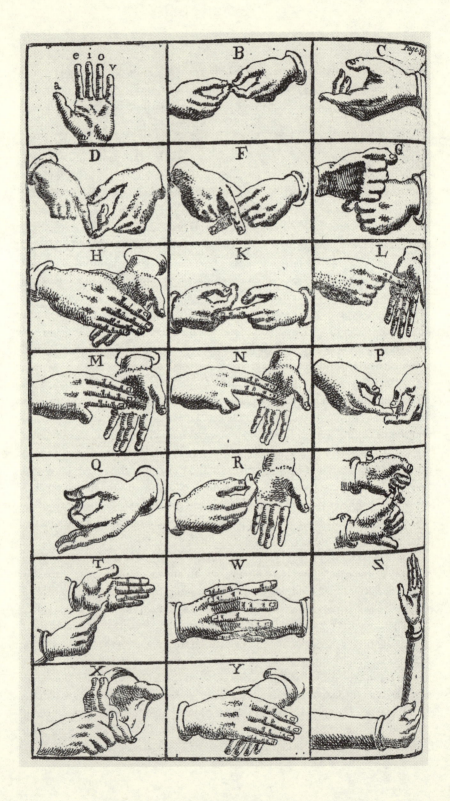

one another and with hearing people alike. In its entirety, *The History of the Life and Adventures of Mr. Duncan Campbell* suggests that the experience of deaf embodiment is tied to queer ways of being in the world.

CAMPBELL'S PATERNAL MASCULINITY IN HAYWOOD'S *A SPY ON THE CONJURER*

As I have argued to this point, *The History of the Life and Adventures of Mr. Duncan Campbell* establishes the deaf prophet as a queer, heroic harbinger of a new linguistic order. The narrative simultaneously celebrates and exoticizes Campbell's marvelous persona. In contrast, in *A Spy on the Conjurer*, printed four years later in 1724, Eliza Haywood uses Campbell as a narrative vehicle to explore the salacious scandals of the clientele that seek out his services. Perhaps because Haywood's novel appeared during the height of her market success, when her distinctive brand of amatory fiction was in style, Haywood depicts Campbell's literacy and communication skills as utterly unremarkable to clear up space for the secret sex lives of the characters that commission him. Through the narrator's incessant spying, Campbell becomes the occasion for Haywood's articulation of a woman-centered, heterosexual eroticism. As Ros Ballaster has shown, Haywood's scandal fiction focuses especially on women's desire: "Haywood was unequivocal in her address to a female audience, and her commitment to the discourse of love. Female desire is no longer a ruling metaphor in her fiction, but rather the subject and generating ground of its plot."[60] The secret histories which the novel's narrator, Justicia, explores consist in her tireless ferreting out of sexual intrigue. Campbell's deafness comes to play second fiddle to the governing principle of the amatory genre, which is women's sexual desire. This diminution of attention to Campbell's deafness is indicative of Haywood's integration of deafness into polite society, for it acts as the backdrop for that which especially resonates with Haywood's readership: the protagonist's empirical drive for the acquisition of knowledge, women's sexual experience and subjectivity, and the manner in which these and other facets of the narrative work together to facilitate one's coming-of-age.[61] Haywood transforms Campbell into a source of paternalistic masculine authority—a mature family man who is married with children—to teach Justicia to manage her excessive

Figure 1.3. *Opposite:* John Wallis's fingerspelling chart as it appears in the first edition of *The History of the Life and Adventures of Mr. Duncan Campbell*. The chart contains a number of boxes, and each box consists of a letter from the alphabet that is accompanied by the corresponding, appropriate sign.

desire. Due to these generic conventions, Haywood abandons entirely the youthful angelic queerness that underpins *The History of the Life and Adventures of Mr. Duncan Campbell*, offering in its stead a normatively masculine version of Campbell.

When considered in relation to *The History of the Life and Adventures of Mr. Duncan Campbell*, Haywood's account is striking because Justicia rarely remarks upon Campbell's deafness at all. In fact, she typically mentions it in passing, save for a few instances in the narrative in which she reveals other characters' ignorance about deaf people. In such passages, Justicia describes an erotically charged learning experience for women. For example, while awaiting Campbell's arrival in his home, a lady asks his wife, Mrs. Campbell, whom she sees as being "so fine a Woman," why she has chosen to marry a "Monster."[62] Here, the lady wrongly associates Campbell's deafness and prophetic abilities with physical disfigurement, but when Campbell finally arrives and the two meet, she refuses to believe that such a handsome man could in fact be the "Seer" of whom she has heard so much: "It was not without a great deal of Difficulty she was persuaded it was he, imagining, as she afterwards confess'd, she should have seen something very deform'd, and miserable in his Aspect" (154). The lady, now captivated by Campbell's handsome appearance, is disabused of her ignorant prejudices about deaf people. She soon becomes "so diligent in learning the Art of talking on her Fingers, that in a little Time she grew a perfect Mistress of it, and made use of it to invite Mr. Campbell to come to see her at her Lodgings by himself" (154–155). What transpires in Campbell's visit to the lady is left to the reader to imagine, but given the amatory orientation of the narrative, one may safely assume that the woman learns to sign in order to have sexual contact with Campbell's irresistible body. This passage serves as a microcosm of the "excitable imagination" that an early eighteenth-century reader of Haywood's experiences in reading about Campbell, who besides being something so extraordinary as a deaf soothsayer is also an erotic outlet for reading women.[63] As Kathleen Lubey argues, Haywood's fiction communicates an "erotic feeling" that "explicitly theorize[s] the imagination as a faculty whose pleasure can be both enjoyed and trained to serve instructive ends."[64] For her part, Justicia regards Campbell's deafness as an unremarkable characteristic, something that might be commented upon in passing, but that is not worth dwelling upon. What *is* remarkable is the degree to which the client becomes conversant in signed language due to her sexual desire for the deaf prophet. In this case, the lady's attraction to Campbell becomes the means by which she learns a secret language, which in turn grants her access to Campbell's body. Women readers, by extension, participate vicariously in the erotically charged exchange between the lady and Campbell; they gain insight into the eroticized textual body in which signing and prophecy are couched as means to both educational and (hetero)sexual ends.[65]

For Haywood, Campbell's charisma attracts large groups of people seeking direction for their futures. Campbell's rich social life flies in the face of established wisdom, in which deaf people were understood to be socially isolated and wretched. In a letter to Campbell, one woman expresses awe at the "Chearfulness" he exudes despite his deafness: "The Want of Hearing and Speaking would to another Person be an inconsolable Affliction; yet you, methinks, appear as gay and unconcerned as those who labour not under either of those Defects" (238). The lady wonders, "By what Reasons you strengthen yourself to live with any Tranquility in a Condition I should think justly deplorable?" (239). Such thinking about auditory impairment resonates with a later quote from Samuel Johnson, who said that it is "one of the most desperate of human calamities" because of how it curtails sociability.[66] To juxtapose the lady's letter with any of Justicia's own commentary about Campbell is to reveal the vastly refined perspective that Justicia possesses about her deaf friend: "Mr Campbell's House, by reason of the vast Variety of Company that frequented it, and the many whimsical Adventures that happen'd among them, was as proper a Scene of Mirth as any I knew, and Business or not Business, I was generally a Guest there once or twice a Week" (60). Justicia does not wonder or question, as the lady does, how it is possible that Campbell could be happy, or how he could bring together large gatherings of people. By contrasting Justicia's normalized understanding of deafness with the ignorance of tangential, insignificant characters, Haywood demonstrates that deafness might be viewed not as a severe impediment to happiness but as a natural course of life.

Such social vibrancy is spurred by Campbell's keen ability to perform different identities and to communicate in a variety of registers. This becomes especially pertinent for Campbell due to the many enemies that would question Campbell's authenticity as a deaf man and soothsayer. Early in the narrative, Justicia is one of these unbelievers. While at a social gathering, Justicia carries on a conversation with a gentleman who claims to have discovered the truth behind Campbell's lie in his physical mastery of him: "With this very Cane . . . I made him find both Tongue and Ears; nay, and beg Pardon like a School Boy" (4). Here, the gentleman positions himself as sexually ascendant, an aggressive top in a power play to subdue Campbell as a "School Boy" in need of a lesson.[67] Following the gentleman's pronouncement, Mrs. Bulweir, the hostess of the party (whose surname invokes John Bulwer), writes to Campbell, imploring him to come disguised as an aristocratic foreigner. Campbell soon arrives dressed as a "Ruffian Man of Quality, who could not speak a Word of English, and added a thousand plausible Circumstances, which sufficiently engaged the Belief of all that heard him" (4). Campbell's apt disguise proves successful: the cane-wielding gentleman does not recognize him and is thereby shown to have lied about meeting him previously. It is significant that Haywood's novel begins on this note, with Campbell posing as a foreigner who does not speak English, not far removed from his true identity as a deaf Scotsman who uses unconventional forms of communication. Despite this, Campbell's "Dress and Behaviour . . . were agreeable enough to be taken for what he was represented" and he successfully passes as a hearing foreigner (4–5). Haywood's portrayal of Campbell's passing performance indicates the ways in which one's national identity and embodiment are beholden to social mediation for meaning: a deaf individual performs these roles just as other members of polite society do. Moreover, this passage establishes Campbell as the text's master of disguise. His ability to overcome the cane-bearer's ploy for dominance indicates that he is a knave, not a fool. His shape-shifting performance of identity reveals that embodiment is the product of complex social and physical forces. Campbell's deafness is socially constituted, in other words, but his position within British society is no less real or material as a consequence.

Despite Campbell's marginal identity as a deaf, Scottish fortune-teller, Justicia asserts Campbell's heroism by positioning him as the center of rational thought and gallant deeds throughout the narrative. In this way, Haywood establishes Campbell as the occasion for the description and inset narratives of the clients that visit him. When Justicia first visits Campbell's house, for example, she describes Campbell's clientele, a "vast Number of Persons, who, by the Difference of their Garb, seem'd to be of all Conditions"—including an alderman's wife, a frightened young girl, and a four-time widow seeking advice on marrying a fifth time. Justicia's descriptions of these take up more narrative space than the details of Campbell's deafness or his remarkable methods of communication. Campbell's use of signed language is merely mentioned in passing, as Justicia writes: "[Mrs. Bulweir] made Signs to him, that I was her Acquaintance. . . . He made a Sign to his Servant; and immediately came up Wine and a Salver of Sweatmeats." Besides signing, Campbell uses writing to convey his thoughts, and this serves as his primary mode of communication: "After this little Regale he writ to Mrs. Bulwer, designing to know her Commands" (8). Unlike in *The History of the Life and Adventures of Mr. Duncan Campbell,* Haywood's narrative neglects to remark upon the extraordinary orientation of these communication modes, emphasizing *what* is communicated, and only briefly, *how* it is communicated. In this way, the narrative reveals that its focus is not the workings of the conjurer, necessarily, but the peccadilloes of the conjurer's clients. A wildly successful writer, Haywood would have been in tune with what would sell her writing to the public. As it turns out, what sells in a 1724 context is not the exoticism of a deaf Scotsman who possesses the second sight as much as the surreptitious sex lives of characters ranging in social status from button-makers, to servants, to high-ranking ladies.

The details of these women's scandals, and the lengths to which Justicia is willing to go to uncover these details, make up the bulk of the narrative; in contrast, Justicia positions Campbell as the means by which women's fallibilities become apparent. Through Campbell, Justicia comes to recognize her "Extravagancies" (80). After angrily rebuking Campbell over a letter whose contents reveal compromising information about the man she loves, Justicia learns that she needs Campbell in her life, if only to provide her with more opportunities to play voyeur. She apologizes to Campbell for "the heat of [her] Resentment" once she reflects "on the Injustice" of her actions (80). Campbell responds to her apology, confirming his role as father figure, "but his perfect good Sense taught him to be above taking Notice of those little Extravagancies which the weakness of my Sex (made weaker yet by my resistless Passions) had render'd me guilty of; he only smil'd when I made my Apology" (80–81). Campbell's gentle reprimand to Justicia for her insatiable curiosity indicates that he is a character with power, prestige, and responsibility. Much like in *Love in Excess*, in which female characters must learn to control and channel their sensibility into requited relationships with men, Justicia is prone to a range of excessive emotions prompted by the potential to discover stories of erotic scandal.[68] Haywood thus converts Campbell into a masculine authority figure who guides women, and in this way, Campbell sheds the cosmic queerness that excited spectacle among his attendants in *The History of the Life and Adventures of Mr. Duncan Campbell*.

Haywood's readership, who would have been accustomed to such sexually laden amatory fiction as *Love in Excess* or *The British Recluse*, perhaps would have approached *A Spy on the Conjurer* for more of the same. Ballaster notes that Haywood deviates from *The History of the Life and Adventures of Mr. Duncan Campbell* in her "swelling" and "distorting" of "the Duncan Campbell myth into a series of amatory tales around the same ladies the original novel had chivalrously protected."[69] According to Kathryn King, Justicia's drive to unearth the salacious specifics of Campbell's clients is indicative of the early novel form's "generic tendency to peer through chink holes."[70] Haywood's literary purpose, King argues, is to provide the reader with those "potentially scandalous bits" which Justicia's curiosity leads her to discover at every turn.[71] Curiosity, in this instance, "is depicted as a force strong enough to impel a well-bred woman to engage with zest and without shame in acts of theft, voyeurism, and unsurpassed indecorousness, to cross lines established by good taste and good manners."[72] A letter written to Campbell by a gentlewoman who has fallen in love with her father's servant, or a missive from a kept mistress who is not receiving enough financial support from her clandestine lover, provide far more shocking and scandalous material for Haywood's reading audience to consume than Campbell's deafness. In order for such scandal to come to light, however, the narrative must account for Campbell, who becomes a peephole for women readers to delight in, and arrive at, sexual knowledge. In this way, Haywood positions Campbell as the source of sexual intrigue, rather than the object of sexual desire.

Haywood also secures Campbell's moral authority through his second sight, which contrasts markedly with the demonic supernatural activity that ravages the bodies of a few of Campbell's clients. Bewitched characters whose bodies have been impaired by unnatural forms of witchcraft seek out Campbell's assistance. With Campbell's help, these characters regain control of their bodies, demonstrating the prophetic abilities of Campbell. One man loses control of his body to the point that he is unrecognizable: "He wou'd turn himself in a Moment, into as many different Posture-Masters, and fly upon those that endeavour'd to restrain him with a Strength, which visibly denoted he was agitated with Emotions, which might justly be call'd Supernatural. When he was out of these Fits, he look'd more like a Skeleton than any Thing that had Life, and was so weak that he could not go cross the Chamber without being supported by each Arm" (151). This passage reveals the disabling force of the unnatural forms of magic to which this man has been subjected, which can only be rectified by Campbell's honorable abilities. Campbell subsequently cures this man of his "agitated" state in a matter of weeks and performs similar feats throughout the novel. Campbell's ability to ameliorate bodily distress suggests that he is a prophetic means to regular spiritual living. Campbell has a vigorous body and sound mind, so that people can come to him for help with the regulation of their bodies. Part of what makes Campbell so potent is his ability to successfully straddle the threshold between what was called "natural magic" and polite, Christian society. Campbell's righteous, masculine, and decorous navigation of these two worlds allows him to thrive as a trustworthy soothsayer.

Campbell's reliability may also be attributed to the honesty he displays to his clients. Justicia claims that he is different from the average fortune teller because of his integrity: "[Other fortunetellers], to please the Fools, that put their Trust in them, always flatter them with Predictions of coming Happiness; but *He* . . . never deceives his Consulters with fictitious Hopes . . . he tells them, that he fears something of a Misfortune attends them, and endeavours, by a thousand Arguments, drawn from Morality and Christianity, to arm them for the coming Woe" (113). Campbell is not the stuff of typical, mercenary soothsayers because unlike them, he is incapable of deceit due to his "Morality and Christianity." By contrasting Campbell's Christianity with the tattered principles of his rivals, Justicia upholds Campbell as a bastion of morality and justifies his profession in an era in which reason and science-based rationality were coming to be increasingly important for public figures. By the turn of the eighteenth century, the second sight replaces witchcraft "as the predominant idiom through which 'non-rational' or 'popular' beliefs are understood by 'elites' because it was a kind of 'private' or 'secret' strand of thought within an ostensibly rational Enlightenment culture."[73] As the various print sources about Campbell attest, however, the divulging of such secrecy is a driving force of narrative. These public pronouncements of Campbell's supernatural practices help to foster his controversial celebrity.

Haywood asserts Campbell's heroism in the novel by emphasizing his masculinity, which he also demonstrates through his extraordinary fencing skills. When she first meets Campbell, Justicia inquires after Campbell's fencing lessons, which he has just undertaken. Campbell responds by conveying to Justicia that "he foresaw the Difficulties he should meet with in the World" and that such difficulties "would furnish him with frequent Occasions of using that Skill he was endeavouring to acquire" (143–144). Having the training of an Army enlistee turns out to be useful to Campbell as he is attacked with regularity. Justicia admires Campbell's physicality and ability to defend himself against his attackers. Nussbaum argues that unlike *The History of the Life and Adventures of Mr. Duncan Campbell*, in *A Spy on the Conjurer*, Campbell is "not emasculated."[74] Campbell's performance of manhood, though, ventures into the realm of the hypermasculine. As we have seen, he manages a household, plays father figure to Justicia, displays rakishness, and in the case of his swordsmanship, defends himself when ambushed by hostile forces in public spaces. For instance, he disarms a swordsman despite only having the use of one arm. Campbell is "as nimble as [the assailant], and presently disarm'd him, then shortening his Sword, put the Point to his Breast, and shew'd him what he could do, and obliging him to beg his Life, generously threw away his Sword" (145–146). Later on, the "twenty or thirty Gentlemen of Rank" who had been present for this scene "speak of this . . . very much to Mr. Campbell's Honour" (146). Campbell's weapon-wielding and courage in the duel are matched only by his gentility in sparing the other man's life. His "Honour" is that of a gentleman, and he is suitably admired by other gentlemen who have the privilege to observe him in action. Such fighting scenes in Haywood's novel draw from *The History of the Life and Adventures of Mr. Duncan Campbell*, in which Campbell is sometimes portrayed as larger-than-life. In Haywood's account, Campbell's strength is in his sword, a phallic symbol of his boundless strength.

Campbell's heroism in *A Spy on the Conjurer* reveals the excesses of his manly vigor. We could even think of Campbell as a precursor to the *supercrip* archetype, a modern-day portrayal of disabled people who, through extraordinary feats, seem to overcome their impairment and win over the respect and admiration of able-bodied people who would otherwise pity them.[75] Campbell's supercrip heroism is rooted in the marvels and miracles stereotypically associated with deaf subjects at that time. In Haywood's narrative, Campbell becomes the masculine ideal, and in this contrasting depiction from *The History of the Life and Adventures of Mr. Duncan Campbell*, in which Campbell is out of time, floating above the masses in saintly queer splendor, one observes wildly fluctuating popular portrayals of deafness. In this representational movement from queer angel to paternalistic, sword-wielding fighter, Campbell's body becomes a blank space upon which to project an array of gendered and sexed values for generic and narrative purposes. The contrasting portrayals of Campbell's character indicates the liminal character of deafness in the early eighteenth century, a period in which auditory impairment was used as metaphor to capture one's hardheadedness, and also a time in which actual deaf people existed on the margins of British society due to a false perception that they could not be educated. These works about Campbell call into question existing assumptions even as they enclose deafness within a larger audist system that maintains its primacy by accommodating variable forms of communicative exchange.

THE DEAF PROPHET'S GOLDEN YEARS: *THE SECRET MEMOIRS OF THE LATE MR. DUNCAN CAMPBELL*

From the depiction of Campbell's youthful angelic queerness in *The History of the Life and Adventures of Mr. Duncan Campbell*, to Haywood's amatory portrayal of the prophet as the apotheosis of mature manhood in *A Spy on the Conjurer*, early narratives from the Duncan Campbell Compendium trace Campbell's aging process in ways that are beholden to genre. *The History of the Life and Adventures of Mr. Duncan Campbell* focuses on the dual nature of the deaf seer's messages to Londoners: that, for one thing, he reveals personal futures in a spectacularly theatrical way, but that also, through his savvy intellect and communicative prowess, he demonstrates that deaf people could be integrated into hearing society. Haywood expatiates on the performative markers of Campbell's manly stoicism and physical vigor. The third and last extended narrative about Campbell, *The Secret Memoirs of the Late Mr. Duncan Campbell* (published after Campbell's death in 1732) is supposedly written from Campbell's point of view, constituting the form of a memoir.[76] *The Secret Memoirs* ruminates on the disabling fits to which Campbell is subjected in old age and, consequently, the ways in which he is often dependent upon the care of friends for comfort and recovery. In some ways, this makes perfect sense, for *The Memoirs* is a narrative about Campbell's last years of life. Campbell seems to have remained in the difficult position of earning his keep through soothsaying until his dying day. He is left to defend his practice, to convince his many detractors of an ever-elusive authenticity. As Campbell states at the end of the introduction, "This is my last Will and Testament to the Publick, and ought to be depended on as much as the last Words of a dying Man."[77] Campbell's "last Words" reveal that he is still plagued by naysayers and that he feels guilt about his previous actions. This culminating depiction of Campbell's life represents one last attempt to justify the veracity and righteousness of his miracles, one last print publication to convince a reading public that would have already been acutely aware of the seer's enormous reputation.

In *The Secret Memoirs*, Campbell is perhaps at his most conventional when recounting the fast-living of his youth. He recalls that he had once been motivated by carnal pursuit: "I confess I have been too much a Libertine, and have thought Drinking, Fighting, running away with Men's Wives and Daughters, Gentleman-like Qualifications, but these exploits were in my younger Years, and greatly owing to the Company I then kept" (15). Lamenting the unwise decisions of his young adulthood in such a confessional way aligns Campbell with other men of means. Here, the narrative draws directly on earlier depictions of the deaf seer as effortlessly attracting women due to his charisma and good looks. Campbell's recognition of the error of his sexually indulgent ways participates in the rising tide of the culture of sentimentality, in which pleasure-seeking libertines become respectable, mature gentlemen capable of empathy and elevated feeling.

Such a connection to the culture of sensibility helps to explain Campbell's loss of bodily control, which is emphasized at intervals through *The Secret Memoirs*. Campbell's reflection of his youthful libertine activity contrasts starkly with the lines that directly follow, in which the physical toil of his later years become apparent. He relates, "Of late, hard study, and a constant Application to my Business has brought Fits upon me" (15). The fits occur suddenly, consisting in "the most terrible Convulsions" that cause him "to distort [his] Face, and decay [his] Spirits with a forced Agony" (16). Though detractors insist that these fits are part of his huckster performance, Campbell insists that such disabling conditions have only caused him to lose out on business. Ultimately, he laments the way that his body betrays him in this state: "I have made use of my utmost Efforts to overcome this Humour; I cannot but look on it as Womanish, or at best a Pedantick one, but all I can do has hitherto been ineffectual" (16). This passage's documentation of Campbell's maturation into "womanish" sufferer of fits underscores anxieties surrounding emasculation. An early instance of this common misogynistic trope in eighteenth-century fiction, Campbell as man-of-feeling internalizes too much sensation and succumbs to a frenzied embodied response perceived to be typical of women. However, Campbell's convulsions do not always impede his abilities, for as he reveals later on, "the Infirmities of the Body have no Effect on it, but, on the contrary, it renders strong, for the Time, those Organs of the Senses thro' which it operates" (130). The narrative thus equivocates about the extent to which Campbell's fits impair him from his occupation or whether he is emasculated as a result. Such ambiguity falls in line with earlier narratives, since, as I have argued, Campbell's masculinity operates along a mobile continuum. Of course, gendered embodiment is never static or stable, and, in a patriarchal culture that values markers of male superiority, one's manhood is always at risk of emasculation. Nevertheless, the heightened degree to which Campbell's gender and sexuality oscillate between hypermasculinity, standard manhood, cosmic queerness, and womanish delicacy is suggestive of the mutability of fictional writing during the time. Campbell is available for any kind of representation that will please readers, and in the Duncan Campbell Compendium, so many forms of writing appear—poetry, novel, pamphlet, periodical, advertisement, and memoir. In this last narrative, the anxiety surrounding Campbell's masculinity reflects literary marketplace trends tied to the emerging culture of sensibility and the reformation of libertinism, the likes of which are epitomized in Samuel Richardson's *Pamela* (published eight years later in 1740).

Campbell's gender and sexual mobility likewise mirrors the doubts that surround the validity of his conjuring capabilities. In its representation of Campbell's maturation into old age, *The Secret Memoirs* attempts to manage the widespread skepticism that followed the prophet until his final days. As much as the narrator-as-Campbell attempts to present himself as an ordinary gentleman in *The Secret Memoirs*' opening pages, the extent to which he is trusted as a seer looms as a source of unease throughout the work. In even more pronounced ways than *A Spy on the Conjurer*, *The Secret Memoirs* dedicates ample ink to a defense of righteous conjuring. Several chapters explain how the second sight works, what the nature of apparitions is, how genii bring knowledge, and how Campbell is regularly victimized by the "ingratitude" and insensitivity of the masses (158). Regarding the latter of these narrative features, a closing inset narrative suggests that Campbell never really acquires the respect to which he feels entitled. Upon meeting an unknown gentleman at a tavern, Campbell agrees to assist the man in recovering a hefty fortune by traveling to Rotterdam. The gentleman, however, uses Campbell's foresight to arrange for the recovery of his fortune on his own, leaving Campbell stranded in Rotterdam without resources. Details of the transaction-gone-awry are somewhat hazy, but the resolution for Campbell is that he "never received one Farthing" (163). Campbell resolves to wash his hands of the affair entirely, offhandedly wishing retribution on the man's head: "But let his own rod lash him; the Ungrateful, sooner or later, may find one more ungrateful than themselves, and are punished by the very Crime they have been guilty of" (164). Like many prophets, Campbell is misunderstood and maltreated by the very people he would serve. In the end, the cosmically queer angel is tarnished by the unfeeling selfishness of fortune-seekers and left to die as a misunderstood visionary.

After recounting this strange turn of events in Rotterdam, Campbell swiftly concludes his narrative. He is, at last, unable to resolve the controversies that perpetually haunt him. In the closing lines of the account, Campbell reassures his readers that his central concern has always been his clients and not material gain, as critics would claim. He writes, "I assure them [i.e., his clients and followers], none has had, and will to the last Moment of my Life continue to have, their Interest more at Heart" (165). Campbell's use of "interest" here reveals the nature of the financial transactions that mark the relationship between his clients and him. The clients pay him for services rendered, but it is precisely these financial transactions that cause detractors to cry out against his fortune-telling as a mercenary act. Elsewhere in the memoir, Campbell justifies his payable prophecy by differentiating his own righteous supernatural practices with the witchcraft of the wicked. And yet the arguments against Campbell are significant enough: he is, after all, a soothsayer attempting to justify his strange practices to a skeptical reading public. The last of the major Campbell accounts reveals the exoticism that would accompany Campbell to his grave. Campbell's "last will and testament" magnifies the excesses that always accompanied depictions of his magnificent persona.

CONCLUSION

The Duncan Campbell Compendium both contests and reinforces audism by alternating between Campbell's genteel education and the awe-inspiring wonder of his marvelous deeds. At times in these works, Campbell effortlessly communicates with hearing interlocutors through his versatile communicative registers, and at others he performs his mysterious trade to the astonishment of clients and bystanders. The tension between these seeming retrograde and forward-looking passages could be said to reveal the transitional character of this period for the emergence of deaf subjectivity in Britain. After all, the narratives' fluctuation between Campbell's prophetic and polite attributes confirms some long-standing prejudices against deaf people while imagining their social inclusion through education. And to be sure, the early eighteenth century *is* a time in which the social position of deaf people is beholden to widespread misunderstandings that had been passed down from earlier periods. However, such a reading of the eighteenth century does not account for the fact that convincing arguments for deaf education—and indeed, the very pedagogical blueprint for educating young Campbell—came from the previous century, in which unprecedented proposals for establishing educational academies for deaf students in Britain, as well as the education of individual deaf pupils, proliferated among natural philosophers.

Moreover, Campbell's gender mobility destabilizes normative formulations of temporality, especially when he appears as cosmically queer prophet, navigating the heavens and earth to dispense divine wisdom to hearing clients. Campbell's queerness is elusive, however: he moves in and out of gender and sexual normativity throughout the compendium. These shifts are in some ways tied to Campbell's age, with the stage of his life determining his gender performativity. But Campbell's gender is also beholden to the genre of the narrative in which he is represented: he is queer and exotic in the travel narrative that is *The History of the Life and Adventures of Mr. Duncan Campbell*, paternally masculine in Haywood's amatory novel, and emasculated by old age and irregular health in *The Secret Memoirs of the Late Mr. Duncan Campbell*. Thus, the authors of these works exhibit diverse approaches to imagining deafness, revealing that deafness itself is a flexible form of embodiment in this period that could be bent to the will of the author and the demands of the genre. In time, such elasticity would harden to some degree with the establishment of formalized deaf education, the medicalization of deaf bodies, and asylum enclosure in the following century. However, Campbell's queer phenomenological experience of sensory perception, in which the intermingling of his senses grants him unique insights, is suggestive of the richness of deaf sensation that can be found in the writings of John Bulwer. Bulwer's philosophical impact on the Campbell Compendium enriches and complicates what we know about the discursive shifts regarding physical difference from the early modern period to the nineteenth century. In Bulwer's writings, deafness is not a sign of the miraculous or a curse, but an inevitable permutation of nature that contributes to the richness of language and sociability.

Beyond the unique insights that the compendium offers regarding the gradual emergence of deaf subjectivity, it also opens up the possibility for homoerotic bonds to figure centrally in narrative, especially in the passage from *The History of the Life and Adventures of Mr. Duncan Campbell* in which the male narrator and an array of young women gather around an otherworldly Campbell in communal adoration, or when Campbell experiences sound through queerly haptic means. The former of these scenes in particular imagines same-sex desire between men through the narrator's physical attraction to Campbell, as well as pleasurable, non-procreative forms of sexuality for women in their shared affection toward Campbell. In the following chapter, I will examine a widening chasm between same-sex and cross-sex intimacies in novels of sensibility from the mid-eighteenth century. Despite their massive differences, Samuel Richardson's *Pamela* and Sarah Scott's *Millenium Hall* each depict social reform through queer and disabled affiliations. For Scott in particular, a wide spectrum of embodiment and sapphic desire serve as vital components for the restructuring of British society.

NOTES

1. Nussbaum, *Limits of the Human*, 39.
2. Steele, *Selections from the Tatler, Spectator and Guardian*, 148.
3. Lamentably, there are no critical editions of these works. I have relied extensively on early editions at the Huntington Library, the Newberry Library, the British Library, Chawton House Library, and *Eighteenth Century Collections Online*.
4. I refer to the overall collection of writings about Duncan Campbell as a *compendium* due to their intertextual quality.
5. Krentz, "Duncan Campbell and the Discourses of Deafness," 45.
6. Lennard Davis calls Campbell a "fraud" and Harlan Lane sees him as a deaf impostor, for instance. See *Enforcing Normalcy*, 57; and Lane, *When the Mind Hears*, 106. However, according to Jan Branson and Don Miller's historical study, Campbell is a literary representation of "the educational potential of those who were deaf, mute, or both." Branson and Miller, *Damned for Their Difference*, 93.
7. Hall, "The Work of Representation," 18.
8. Krentz, "Duncan Campbell," 40.
9. Davis, *Enforcing Normalcy*, 59–63.
10. Ibid., 52. As Davis notes, by 1789, there were twelve schools for the deaf in Europe. By 1822, there were more than sixty spread across several countries.
11. The authorship of *The History of the Life and Adventures of Mr. Duncan Campbell* is a source of uncertainty. Daniel Defoe was once assumed to be the author, but this is a position that has been challenged by scholars who argue that Defoe likely would not have worked with the publisher of the narrative, Edward Curll. Some have asserted that William Bond is the likely author, while others have speculated that Bond and Defoe each had a hand in its creation. Moreover, in a recent essay, Essaka Joshua wonders if John Beaumont is another possibility. To avoid this debate, which is ultimately inconsequential for my argument, I omit the author's name when discussing *The History of the Life and Adventures of Mr. Duncan Campbell*. However, I also recognize that authorship of this novel is subject to new insights, and I hope that there will be certainty at some point in the future. See Turner, "Campbell, Duncan"; and Joshua, "Disability and Deformity," 60.
12. *The History of the Life and Adventures of Mr. Duncan Campbell*, 125, 128. All future references to the novel will appear in parenthetical citations.
13. Milton, *Paradise Lost and Paradise Regained*, 115.
14. Ibid., 116.
15. Ibid., 119.

16. Guy-Bray, "Fellowships of Joy," 1–20.
17. Ibid., 5.
18. Ibid., 2.
19. Nussbaum, *Limits of the Human*, 47.
20. Ibid., 48.
21. As Melissa Sanchez points out, in accounting for women's sexual pleasure in uneven power dynamics during the early modern period, we may challenge our own preconceptions about what constitutes "proper" or healthy sexuality for women. Melissa Sanchez, "Use Me But as Your Spaniel," 493–511.
22. Even though the engraving appears next to the very passage in which Campbell appears as a youthful, angelic messenger, the illustration of Campbell's face shows him to be conventionally masculine by the day's standards, as his periwig and cravat suggest.
23. Davis, *Enforcing Normalcy*, 63.
24. Miles, "Signing in the Seraglio," 115–134.
25. Bulwer, *Philocophus, or, The deafe and dumbe mans friend*, 1–2.
26. Ibid., 76.
27. Quoted in Stone and Woll, "Dumb O Jemmy and Others," 229.
28. Quoted in Reiss, *Theaters of Madness*, 72–73.
29. Sutherland, *The Brahan Seer*, 92.
30. Frazer, *Deuteroskopia*, 12–13, 24.
31. Ibid., 14.
32. Davis, *Enforcing Normalcy*, 55.
33. As noted in the introduction, Locke writes in *An Essay Concerning Human Understanding* (1690) that "men who through some physical defect can't utter words still manage to express their universal ideas by signs that they use instead of general words: and we see that non-human organisms can't do that." Despite registering a facet of his humanity, signers such as Campbell would face an uphill battle in establishing themselves as fully functioning members of polite society. For Locke, people with sensory impairments, though capable of embodying *some* intelligence and humanity, are still "remote" from possessing the knowledge that might be found in educated, hearing men. Locke, *An Essay Concerning Human Understanding*, 93.
34. Bulwer, *Philocophus*, A4; and Bulwer, *Chirologia*.
35. Wright, *Deafness*, 147.
36. Bulwer, *Chirologia*, 5–6
37. Wollock. "John Bulwer and the Significance of Gesture," 229.
38. Bulwer writes that if one of the senses is lacking in any respect, the other senses compensate. In the case of deaf people, sight compensates for hearing loss. For this reason, they have extraordinary vision, which enables them to read lips and intuitively discern the characters and personalities from peoples' visages. Bulwer reasons, "Insomuch as deafe and dumbe men, having a double defect, to wit of speaking and hearing, they usually have double recompense: this makes them good naturall Phisiognomers." Representations of Campbell from throughout the Compendium adhere to Bulwer's theorization of sensory perception, in which Campbell is depicted as able to converse with his clients through lip reading, writing, and signed language. Bulwer, *Philocophus*, 171.
39. Ibid., 171.
40. Ibid., 64.
41. Bearden, "Before Normal, There Was Natural," 38.
42. Ibid., 36.
43. Ibid., 35–36.

44. It was customary for the scrolls of stringed instruments of this period to represent the heads of humans or beasts.
45. Bone conduction is a naturally occurring phenomenon that enables profoundly deaf people in our day to hear sound via cochlear implants.
46. Ahmed, *Queer Phenomenology*, 3.
47. Ibid., 3.
48. Ibid., 7.
49. Bearden and Wollock argue that Bulwer deviates from Bacon's understanding of physical difference as an area in need of demystification and codification for the development of scientific knowledge. Rather, Bulwer has "a deep respect for bodies that vary from common forms and an empathic rather than an instrumental comprehension of the cultural situation of people with disabilities." Bearden, "Before Normal, There Was Natural," 35; and Wollock, "John Bulwer and the Significance of Gesture," 250.
50. Ahmed, 19–20.
51. Ibid., 20.
52. Ibid., 19.
53. *The Friendly Dæmon*, 233–234.
54. Wallis was later involved in a major controversy with William Holder, himself a Royal Society member, over the education of Popham. Holder claimed that Wallis did not give him credit for the work he had done with Popham and that Wallis had falsely taken all of the credit for himself. This led to a controversial exchange between the two, though Wallis is credited with having the more lasting effect on deaf education. The fallout from this controversy underscores the philosophical significance of educating deaf people in the time period preceding the early eighteenth century. See Branson and Miller, *Damned for Their Difference*, 83–84; Lane, *When the Mind Hears*, 103–106.
55. Shea, *The Language of Light*, 12.
56. Branson and Miller, *Damned for Their Difference*, 79–84.
57. Ibid., 105. In the later eighteenth century, Francis Green dedicated excerpts from both Bulwer and Wallis in *Vox Oculis Subjecta*, which demystifies the educational processes of the Braidwood family, who opened the first British school for the deaf in Edinburgh in 1760. Green, *Vox Oculis Subjecta*.
58. Branson and Miller, *Damned for Their Difference*, 79–81.
59. *The History of the Life and Adventures of Mr. Duncan Campbell*, third ed., 256.
60. Ballaster, *Seductive Forms*, 158.
61. Ibid., 153–195.
62. Haywood, *A Spy on the Conjurer*, 154. All future references to the novel will appear in parenthetical citations.
63. Lubey, *Excitable Imaginations*.
64. Ibid., 71.
65. As Lubey argues, eroticism is "a continuous unfolding of epistemology from the details of amorous scenes" through which "readers are thought to emerge from erotic episodes newly attuned to their own capacities for self-determination in moral and social matters." Lubey, *Excitable Imaginations*, 3.
66. Johnson and Boswell, *A Journey to the Western Islands of Scotland*, 144.
67. For more on the "school boy," see Straub's essay, "Men from Boys," 219–239.
68. Kelleher, *Making Love*, 97–130.
69. Ballaster, *Seductive Forms*, 167.
70. King, "Spying upon the Conjurer," 187.
71. Ibid., 187.

72. Ibid., 187.
73. Sutherland, *The Brahan Seer*, 91.
74. Nussbaum, *The Limits of the Human*, 49.
75. Shapiro, *No Pity*, 16.
76. While the writer of this particular narrative claims to have been Campbell himself, scholars have speculated that the author is either Haywood or Bond. Given the many similarities between *A Spy on the Conjurer* and *The Secret Memoirs*, I am inclined to believe that Haywood was the author, but this is speculative.
77. *Secret Memoirs of the Late Mr. Duncan Campbell*, 4. All future references to the novel will appear in parenthetical citations.

2

THE REFORMING BODIES OF SAMUEL RICHARDSON'S *PAMELA* (1740) AND SARAH SCOTT'S FICTION (1754-1766)

THIS CHAPTER WILL DISCUSS THREE of Sarah Scott's novels as well as Samuel Richardson's *Pamela* to examine how queer and disabled embodiment informs British novels that were published around the mid-eighteenth century. In *Millenium Hall* (1762), Scott imagines queerness and disability as pillars of a productive, self-contained sanctuary. Millenium Hall is an estate in which marginal figures in British society practice the Anglican principles of industriousness and charity. The queer and disabled inhabitants of the estate accommodate each other and achieve economic success. Not coincidentally, the organization of the household at Millenium Hall is a far cry from normative constructions of the gentry family. As is the case with other utopian accounts, Scott conceives of an ideal community that remedies the problems of the actual society in which she lives. Scott's critique is aimed in particular at patriarchal and corporeal standards that have violent consequences for women and variably-embodied people. A way to circumvent that violence, Scott suggests, is for these individuals to retreat from the hustle and bustle of town life, where they are subjugated by unsentimental men, to the countryside, in which matriarchal rule facilitates an inclusive community. Reform, for Scott, is built upon a queer pastoral foundation. In chapter 1, I argued that Duncan Campbell's adoring throng of young female attendants raises the prospect of women's homosocial companionship and willful subservience as viable alternatives to compulsory heterosexuality. The gathering of the angelic women around the deaf soothsayer's immobilized, cosmic body is suggestive of the ways in which disability is gendered and queered in the early eighteenth century. In that passage, young women express uninhibited, collective desire toward a male object. Such an eroticized imagining of female communality around disability reconfigures heterosexual relations, from the Restoration libertine model in which powerful men dominate women, to an alternative dynamic in which women experience eroticism

[71]

together in a noncompetitive, harmonious, and assertive manner. This scene in particular portrays subversive forms of female sexuality that challenge standard procreative practices. In an even more sustained manner than *The History of the Life and Adventures of Mr. Duncan Campbell*, Scott's *Millenium Hall* aligns disability with queerness and naturalizes the affective relations between them.

Scott offers a significant departure from Samuel Richardson's representation of embodiment in *Pamela*, the massively influential 1740 work that marks a critical moment for the development of the British novel. Richardson's narrative reflects a shift in literary tastes and cultural values as inscribed by the culture of sensibility. In his depiction of Pamela's unfaltering evasion of the repeated sexual assaults from her captor, Mr. B., Richardson's tale of attempted rape and conquest finally becomes one of marriage, serene domesticity, and class reconfiguration. To frame this drastic change in the narrative, Richardson advocates the cultivation of sentimental masculinity in men, which he depicts as a consequence of women's resistance to male sexual violence. He also imagines a dramatic shift in the negotiation of the contractual agreement between women and men in marriage, as Nancy Armstrong has convincingly shown.[1] What has been overlooked by scholars, however, is that Richardson shores up the relationship between Mr. B. and Pamela through his characterization of Mrs. Jewkes, the housekeeper and prison warden to Pamela. Mrs. Jewkes possesses a similar embodiment to that of several of Scott's fictional characters, but unlike them, she is imbued with a villainy that is apparent in her physiognomy. Mrs. Jewkes's physical disability and queerness, I argue, establish her as "opportunistic metaphorical device," a model of "narrative prosthesis" meant to strengthen the heterosexual union in Richardson's narrative.[2]

In contrast, through her critique of an arbitrary "common standard" that alienates so many individuals, Scott refuses to some extent such a two-dimensional representation of physical difference, opting instead to consider impairment as an inevitable facet of life that ought to be accounted for and accommodated. Throughout *Millenium Hall*, and to lesser degrees in *A Journey through Every Stage of Life* (1754) and *The History of Sir George Ellison* (1766), Scott critiques the imperatives of cross-sex, sentimental romance and reveals a capacious set of possibilities for those that do not fit the bodily or conjugal mold that Richardson imagines in *Pamela*. In her portrayal of queer, disabled bonds as viable alternatives to heterosexual union, Scott offers in *Millenium Hall* a vastly different account of corporeality from that of *Pamela*. *Millenium Hall* registers disability as "complexly embodied"—that is, Scott (who was herself disabled) represents impaired bodies as "possessing both social and physical form."[3] Impairment, in other words, is not merely a metaphor for Scott, as it is for Richardson: it is, instead, a source of both social *and* physical pain, and it serves as the basis for her restructuring of British society. Other novels from Scott, including *A Journey through Every Stage of Life* and *The History of Sir George Ellison,* reveal varying sketches of an eighteenth-century "ideology of ability" through their respective portrayals of a white, cross-dressing, working heroine on the lam in England and enslaved black characters in Jamaica.[4] I will examine Scott's development as a writer based on her shifting theorization of embodiment, as her fiction consistently fixates on variable bodies. Her novels expose heterosexuality's reliance upon gendered, racialized, and classed versions of ability and imagine a novel order in which same-sex bonds and impairment are the foundations for educational and social reform. Scott's novels allow us to consider the social limitations of communality in a class-stratified society and to understand why some variable bodies matter more than others during the mid-eighteenth century.

DISABILITY AND QUEERNESS AS NARRATIVE PROSTHESIS IN *PAMELA*

Mrs. Jewkes, the formidable housekeeper in *Pamela,* has not been regarded by scholars as a key element in Richardson's framing of a new kind of British domesticity. I would argue, however, that she plays a pivotal role in constituting Richardson's brand of heterosexual romance. Mrs. Jewkes's disabled and queer body becomes the prosthetic means by which Richardson imagines heterosexual domesticity as the product of sentiment, female virtue, class permeability, and the bifurcation of the public and private spheres. *Pamela* calls for the moral reform of sexually predatory men through a series of letters and diary entries written by the novel's upright, eponymous heroine. The significance and influence of Richardson's novel has been explored in rich detail by scholars. Nancy Armstrong, for example, argues that, through her speech and writing, Pamela writes herself into subjectivity despite the overbearing patriarchal system that would reduce her status to inert object. According to the narrative's logic, Armstrong argues, women can "negotiate" the terms of the marital contract, rather than merely function as passive objects of exchange between men.[5] Ian Watt argues that, in *Pamela,* Richardson creates a new ruling class, based on the unlikely union between a landed gentleman and a young, virtuous upper-servant. In Watt's reading, Richardson shows that the depravity of unrestrained libertine desire must be checked for a new order of bourgeois values to be established.[6] Pamela's narration also grants insights into a "secret history of domesticity," according to Michael McKeon, who argues that *Pamela* captures the delicate tension between eighteenth-century marriage as public institution and sexual pleasure as a private endeavor.[7] And, as Paul Kelleher has recently shown, sentiment is the key affective formation that must occur in the narrative for Pamela and Mr. B. to become a morally exceptional couple.[8] What has yet to be parsed, however, is the way in which the novel's consolidation of heterosexual romance is facilitated by Mrs. Jewkes, who triangulates and often absorbs the moral and physical conflict between Pamela and Mr B. Richardson uses Mrs. Jewkes as embodied metaphor to heighten the overall feeling of terror that young Pamela faces at the hands of Mr. B.; she comes to stand in metonymically for the unrestrained impulses of libertinism that must be curbed and channeled into virtuous sentiment.

In *Pamela*, Richardson rarely describes the shapes or motor functions of bodies, with one glaring exception. Mrs. Jewkes possesses a physically variable body, which is reduced to the realm of the physiognomic. Mrs. Jewkes first appears in the narrative as Pamela is transported to Mr. B.'s Lincolnshire estate, where Pamela is imprisoned and lives under the constant threat of rape. A monstrous double to Mrs. Jervis, the housekeeper that protects Pamela from Mr B.'s brutal sexual stratagems at the beginning of the novel, Mrs. Jewkes becomes Pamela's vigilant, terror-inducing warden. Shortly after her first encounter with Mrs. Jewkes, Pamela offers an unflattering portrait of the housekeeper's visage and overall appearance: "She is a broad, squat, pursy, fat Thing, quite ugly. . . . She has a huge Hand, and an Arm as thick as my waist. . . . Her nose is flat and crooked, and her Brows grow over her Eyes; a dead, spiteful, grey, goggling Eye, to be sure, she has. And her Face is flat and broad; and as to Colour, looks like as if it had been pickled a Month in Salt-petre."[9] Pamela's portrayal of Mrs. Jewkes indicates standard physiognomic thought, in which one's extraordinary outward appearance ostensibly mirrors one's inward moral destitution. Pamela's sustained attention to Mrs. Jewkes's facial features—the particulars of her "flat and crooked" nose and unkempt eyebrows—are supposed indications of deplorable sins that taint her soul.[10] Pamela consolidates her investment in physiognomy when she adds, "So that with a Heart more ugly than her Face, she frightens me sadly" (114). In establishing a correlation between foul heart and face, Pamela writes Mrs. Jewkes's deformity into the narrative as a corporeal repository of that which is uncouth and compromising to young women's virtue. At the same time, Richardson's narrative insinuates that Mrs. Jewkes's deformity is a visible indicator of the threat of uninhibited desire, which must be converted into chastity through resistance and restraint.

Besides her irregular facial features, Mrs. Jewkes assumes a vigorous masculinity that provokes anxiety in Pamela. Pamela follows her depiction of Mrs. Jewkes's facial characteristics with commentary on her indecorous gender: "She has a hoarse man-like Voice, and is as thick as she's long; and yet looks so deadly strong, that I am afraid she would dash me at her Foot in an Instant" (114).

Mrs. Jewkes's voice and "deadly" strength epitomize the physical terror for which Pamela accounts in her letters and diary entries. Pamela's alarm at the prospect that she could be harmed by Mrs. Jewkes's excessive strength resonates with the anxiety that Mr. B., authoritative lord that he is, represents to Pamela. Even Mrs. Jewkes's manner of walking is worthy of notice, which Pamela remarks upon when the two amble in the garden together, and Mrs. Jewkes is said "to waddle" (114). Richardson's prolonged attention to Mrs. Jewkes's peculiar physical appearance and unconventional mobility is a departure from his characterizations of other servant characters, such as Mrs. Jervis, whose righteousness and integrity elevate them above the degrading physical characterization bestowed upon Mrs. Jewkes. In widely disparate characterizations, the two housekeepers become foils to one another. The "editor" of the letters and diary specifies in the novel's didactic ending "that upper servants of great families may, from the odious character of Mrs. Jewkes, and the amiable one of Mrs. Jervis . . . learn what to avoid, and what to chuse, to make themselves valued and esteem'd by all who know them" (501). Amiable and odious, laudable and deplorable, Mrs. Jervis and Mrs. Jewkes carry their morality in their countenances and bodies. The odiousness of Mrs. Jewkes takes on the physical contours of facial irregularity and physical disability, while Mrs. Jervis is virtuously *dis*embodied. In *Pamela*, Richardson establishes physical difference as a visible marker of the depravity that he observes in British society.

Richardson's two-dimensional characterization of Mrs. Jewkes follows a representational pattern of disability in narrative that David T. Mitchell and Sharon L. Snyder identify as "narrative prosthesis," or the dependence of narrative upon disability for its very narratability. This is a four-part process that Mitchell and Snyder characterize in the following manner: "First, a deviance or marked difference is exposed . . . ; second, a narrative consolidates the need for its own existence by calling for an explanation of the deviation's origins and formative consequences; third, the deviance is brought from the periphery of concerns to the center of the story to come; and fourth, the remainder of the story rehabilitates or fixes the deviance in some manner."[11] Mrs. Jewkes's function in *Pamela* more or less adheres to this descriptive process. Matching step one of narrative prosthesis, Pamela's decidedly physical account marks Mrs. Jewkes's initial entrance into the narrative, setting her apart from other characters in manifestly bodily ways. Next, Pamela insinuates that Mrs. Jewkes looks the way she does due to her dearth of a moral compass (she refers to her as "wicked," "Jezebel," and "evil") (185). Mrs. Jewkes then becomes the central source of anxiety for Pamela over the course of several letters and diary entries. Pamela's struggle with Mrs. Jewkes typifies her struggle with Mr. B., from whom she must preserve "that

Jewel [her] Virtue" (14). And finally, as Mr. B. reforms, Mrs. Jewkes begins to rectify her behavior toward Pamela. At that point in her letters and diary entries, Pamela ceases to remark upon Mrs. Jewkes's physical form. In this way, Richardson imbues Mrs. Jewkes with what Mitchell and Snyder would call the "materiality of metaphor": her body represents in physical form the narrative's theorization of libertine reform and class-bound domesticity in "an embodied account of physical, sensory life."[12] Whereas Pamela's account of Mr. B. is typically devoid of his physical appearance, and Pamela is regularly called "Pretty-face," Mrs. Jewkes's glaring deformity is meant to function as an unwieldy prosthetic device upon which the narrative can ground its abstractions about indecorous libertinism and make visible its call for reform and regularity (39). In this sense, Mrs. Jewkes represents that which must be reconciled in young men such as Mr. B., who have the potential to do great harm to those within their sphere of influence.

Mrs. Jewkes's function as anomalous, material metaphor is only part of her narrative purpose, however; she also calls attention to the degenerate sexuality that Richardson would eradicate from British society. She carries Mr. B.'s licentiousness in her "goggling Eye" and "flat and broad" face (114). Her deformity is his excess. In this sense, Richardson complicates Mitchell and Snyder's formulation of narrative prosthesis by representing Mrs. Jewkes's queerness as that which, like libertinism, must be regulated. For example, Mrs. Jewkes expresses an erotic longing for Pamela that aligns her with Mr. B. Before she gives her extended portraiture of Mrs. Jewkes, in fact, Pamela describes her initial meeting with the housekeeper at an inn on the road to Lincolnshire as a moment in which she is "terrify'ed out of [her] Wits" due to Mrs. Jewkes's forwardness: "The naughty Woman came up to me with an Air of Confidence, and kiss'd me, See Sister, said she, here's a charming Creature! would not she tempt the best Lord in the Land to run away with her!" (107). Here, Mrs. Jewkes vindicates Mr. B.'s dishonorable intentions toward Pamela, who is objectified as a universal source of temptation due to her attractive appearance. Mrs. Jewkes becomes a grotesque symbol of tyranny, conflated in this instance with the uneven power dynamics that exist between Mr. B. and Pamela. Richardson's progressive thinking about Pamela's autonomy depends in this way upon Mrs. Jewkes's physical form, which manifests detestable tyrannical control.

Mrs. Jewkes's surrogacy for Mr. B.'s despotic sexuality is evident in the parallels between their individual assaults on Pamela. The "Air of Confidence" which Mrs. Jewkes assumes in her address to Pamela mirrors Mr. B.'s behavior toward Pamela, whom he regularly attempts to seduce and rape (107). In a passage that is typical of Mr. B.'s sexual violence, Pamela relates that "He by Force kissed my Neck and Lips" (32). Pamela subsequently escapes from Mr. B., only to fall "into a Fit with [her] Fright and Terror" (32). The narrative's oscillation between Mr. B.'s frightful attacks and Pamela's improvised defenses are repeated in Mrs. Jewkes's sexual advances to Pamela. As she accompanies Pamela to the Lincolnshire estate in a chariot, Mrs. Jewkes makes an unwelcome move on Pamela: "Every now-and-then she would be staring in my Face, in the Chariot, and squeezing my Hand, and saying, Why you are very pretty, my silent Dear! and once she offer'd to kiss me. But I said, I don't like this Sort of Carriage, Mrs. Jewkes; it is not like two Persons of one Sex" (108). The "carriage" to which Pamela refers is, on one level, the cramped chariot that transports the two characters to the Lincolnshire estate, the novel's new setting. In this case, the chariot is that which bridges the two settings of the novel, an interstitial, transitional space in which same-sex desire is for the first time introduced. "Carriage" also refers to the conduct of Mrs. Jewkes, who transgresses heteronormative gender and sexual codes when she attempts to possess Pamela's body. Mrs. Jewkes's disability and queerness are thus a materialization of Mr. B.'s cruel carnality and power. In his representation of Mrs. Jewkes's appearance and behavior, Richardson shows that libertinism is a morally bankrupt system in need of spiritual and domestic transformation. Through Mrs. Jewkes's variable body and desire, Richardson asserts the affective primacy of sentiment.

Even though she is far from the heroism of Duncan Campbell from the previous chapter, and the overall feeling of asylum and community that Scott represents in *Millenium Hall*, Mrs. Jewkes shares with these characters a critical literary function: her character encompasses the novel's imagining of society otherwise. While Campbell's performance of deaf literacy serves in part as a register of proposed changes in the realms of education, audibility, and sociability, Mrs. Jewkes epitomizes the excess of libertinism, a noxious system that, for Richardson, must be weeded out of British consciousness so that orderly domesticity may be established. Perhaps this is nowhere more apparent than when Mrs. Jewkes assists Mr. B. in one of his various attempts to rape Pamela. In this particular passage, Mr. B. assumes the appearance of another of the female servants, Nan, in his donning of "a Gown and Petticoat of hers, and her Apron over his Face and Shoulders" (202). Upon entering her room, Pamela does not at first recognize Mr. B. due to his successful camouflage. Finally, when the unspeaking "Nan" comes to bed, Pamela realizes that "Nan" is in fact Mr. B., who is at another of his duplicitous schemes. Mrs. Jewkes holds down one of Pamela's wrists to assist Mr. B. in his sexual assault of her. When Pamela faints under the pressure of these restraints, Mr. B. refrains from pursuing his nefarious design, but when Pamela regains consciousness, Mrs. Jewkes encourages him to continue: "And will you, Sir, said the wicked Wretch, for a Fit or two, give up such an Opportunity as this?—I thought you had known the Sex better.—She is, you see, quite well again!" (204). In light of this proposal for a renewed attack, Pamela faints a second time, and Mr. B. sends Mrs. Jewkes away from Pamela's bedroom. Mrs. Jewkes's presence in this scene allows Richardson to make her a scapegoat for Mr. B.'s actions. By dismissing her from the room, Mr. B. justifies his viciousness and atones for his attack on Pamela's person. However, in her promotion of Mr. B.'s reprehensible deeds, Mrs. Jewkes merely fulfills her obligations as one of Mr. B.'s upper servants—to facilitate the realization of her master's desires—and symbolizes the monstrosity of his base designs to execute his power over Pamela's body. Mrs. Jewkes, as a disabled, queer version of narrative prosthesis, represents that which must be eradicated: the base designs of the libertine, who Richardson unmans in the linens of a lower female servant to reimagine dominant sexuality as tyrannical perversity.

As Mr. B. changes his behavior due to his hearkening to the religious values and virtue embedded in Pamela's diary and letters, which he finally comes to acquire (in lieu of Pamela's body), Mrs. Jewkes also mends her ways. In this manner, Richardson converts deformity into virtue and queer vice into heterosexual righteousness. In a letter to her parents after her private wedding with Mr. B., Pamela writes of Mrs. Jewkes: "Her Talk and Actions are intirely different from what they us'd to be, quite circumspect and decent; and I should have thought her virtuous, and even pious, had I never known her in another Light" (378). Given Mrs. Jewkes's astonishing transformation, Pamela now refrains from disparaging caricatures of her. Mrs. Jewkes's physical difference is rehabilitated, in Mitchell and Snyder's terms.[13] It is no accident, I would add, that directly following her remarks about Mrs. Jewkes's piety and general improvements, Pamela shifts her attention to Mr. B.'s sphere of influence: "And this shews, that evil Examples, in Superiors, are doubly pernicious, and doubly culpable, because such persons are bad themselves, and not only to do no Good, but much Harm, to others" (378). Mr. B. has directly influenced Mrs. Jewkes, who has only acted under his orders to subdue Pamela. Once her surrogacy of Mr. B.'s base designs is no longer required, Mrs. Jewkes becomes Pamela's faithful servant. Mrs. Jewkes is a visible disruption to the order of virtue and seemly gentility that finally gets disciplined, transformed, and disembodied. She is a crucial means by which Richardson conveys his reformist message about heterosexual relations, in which sentiment must govern men's treatment of women and in which women are expected to somehow facilitate that change in men, as Pamela does for Mr. B. Heterosexual domesticity, in Richardson's terms, is marked by expelling the violence of men's sexual aggression toward women and by transforming the physiognomic registers of that violence through narrative. As a villainous same-sex desiring subject, Mrs. Jewkes allows Mr. B. to become a redeemable character. Mrs. Jewkes's body, so hideous and wretched to Pamela during her imprisonment at the Lincolnshire estate, is at last phased out as Pamela and Mr. B. establish their domestic happiness. When Mrs. Jewkes becomes pious, the shape of her body and peculiar facial features fall out of view, even as the details of a novel heteronormative order get established around Pamela's virtue and Mr. B.'s newly acquired sentiment.

CROSS-DRESSING AND DISABILITY IN SARAH SCOTT'S *A JOURNEY THROUGH EVERY STAGE OF LIFE*

In *Pamela*, deformity and queerness are concentrated in one character, Mrs. Jewkes, whose presence in the plot allows Richardson to resolve narrative tension by rehabilitating her in the novel's final pages. As Mrs. Jewkes's physical presence becomes invisible, the triangulation of sex and power that had hitherto animated the novel disappears, leaving Pamela and Mr. B. in a good place—narratively speaking—to marry. Richardson thus uses disability and queerness to shore up the harmonious heterosexual romance between his two main characters. In Sarah Scott's fiction, the relationship between disability and queerness is more complex and varied than what Richardson conveys in *Pamela*. Scott's novels, written in the decades following *Pamela*, reveal Scott's evolution of thought regarding the role that the body plays in her reformist vision. In what remains of this chapter, I chart Scott's development as a writer through her theorization of the body. Scott writes about an array of constructed embodied forms, focusing on disability, sexuality, gender, and race. One of Scott's earliest novels, *A Journey through Every Stage of Life*, for instance, cleaves queerness from disability, celebrating the former of these at the expense of the latter. Like *Millenium Hall*, *A Journey through Every Stage of Life* depicts female characters as vital contributors to the public good and as savvy breadwinners. However, it also defines these young women's capital-accruing vitality by satirizing aging, disabled characters that also populate the narrative, making this a rather different account about embodiment from what Scott would later imagine in *Millenium Hall*. In *A Journey through Every Stage of Life*, Scott shows that women's work requires a public performance of maleness and youthful vitality that is realized in juxtaposition with aging, delicate, and disabled women.

In its very first lines, *A Journey through Every Stage of Life* establishes its feminist outlook. The novel's form is composed of a series of frame tales related by a maid, Sabrina, to a young princess, Carinthia, who, like Pamela, is imprisoned by a powerful man. In this case, the jailor is a megalomaniacal cousin who is the recently appointed regent of a fictional kingdom, Aramant. Because she "feels a Mother's fondness for her Royal Charge," Sabrina sets out to entertain and educate

Carinthia by relating to her a series of stories that identify the destructive effects of patriarchy on young women.[14] The first of these inset narratives, "The History of Leonora and Louisa," pits a wicked stepmother named Arabella against a young, strong-willed heroine named Leonora. Arabella is abusive toward Leonora and her dear cousin, Louisa. In time, Leonora and Louisa feel compelled to run away from home. In the picaresque tale that follows, the cousins travel to Buxton so that Louisa can take the waters for her health, and then, they move on to London. Along the way, the narrative alludes to the heterosexual bonds that await Leonora and Louisa back at home. And yet despite the heteronormative undercurrents to "The History of Leonora and Louisa," the narrative also interrogates the very patriarchal structure that is perpetuated through marriage. Gary Kelly argues that the inset narratives that Sabrina relates to Carinthia act as "a relief and as illustration of the vicissitudes of women's lives under patriarchy" and that they contain "elements of explicit feminist protest."[15] Eve Tavor Bannet concurs, claiming that *A Journey through Every Stage of Life* is every bit as "feminist" and "formally experimental" as *Millenium Hall*.[16] I would add that what is unique about Scott's particular brand of feminism is the way in which gender mobility, physical ability, and sapphic desire intertwine to raise the possibility of women's successful occupation of the male-dominated public sphere.

A Journey through Every Stage of Life captures Scott's budding exploration of how sapphic desire is tied to labor. Leonora, who cross-dresses in order to garner wages in various male-oriented professions to support herself and Louisa, regularly excites desire in the women that she meets while donning professional habits. Leonora becomes an object of admiration, for example, when she addresses a series of sermons to the local parishioners in Buxton as a clergyman. Her execution of this bold enterprise turns out to delight a group of young women, who immediately fall in love with her. At the same time, Leonora's sermons remedy the shortcomings of callous male clergymen. When she mounts the pulpit, she does so "with an Air so bashful and disconcerted" and announces her talk "with so faltering an Accent, and so many Blushes, that gentle Compassion sat on every Countenance" while "the Warmth of her Heart soon took off her Attention to her Audience, and left her only just Modesty enough to grace her Words, and give her the Air of Advice and Entreaty, rather than of commanding Injunctions" (26). Here, Scott illustrates gender norms that are typical of the woman of sensibility— "Blushes," "faltering" speech patterns, softness—as desirable foils to the assertiveness of "the bolder Sex" (26). Consequently, Leonora's sermon proves palatable to the women in the audience. As Ula Klein has argued, Leonora's femininity, which is in part symbolized by her lack of a "beard," among other conventionally masculine markers, attracts the attention of other female characters.[17] After the sermon, a fawning throng of young ladies announce in unison that "Truths divine came mended from her Tongue" (26). The sweetness and delicacy of Leonora's speech and person gently persuade her audience to comply with her message, underscoring the tale's recurring concern with rectifying the public, professional errors typical of men. Moreover, the erotic connotations invoked by Scott's portrayal of Leonora's sweet tongue, perhaps a coded reference to cunnilingus, suggests that, like *Millenium Hall,* "The History of Leonora and Louisa" explores the potential for sapphic bonds to amend the errors of patriarchal rule.

In all of the professions that she takes on, which besides clergyman include painter and headmaster, Leonora balances feminine delicacy with a physical vitality that is typically associated with men in this period. Her bodily ability marks her as heroically distinctive from the other female characters that are drawn to her. These peripheral, delicate characters desire Leonora for her public displays of strength. Crucially, Scott depicts Leonora as *able* to perform each of her occupations due to her physical constitution and education. Leonora is "tall, her Limbs formed in the exactest Proportion" (10). Besides this physical advantage, Leonora has the sensibility requisite of a young woman but also understands how to comport herself while cross-dressing due to the male education she has received. Precocious as a youngster, Leonora surpassed her brothers in their lessons, giving her a well-rounded upbringing in which she freely partakes of both conventional femininity and masculinity: "The very quick Progress Leonora made in everything she chose to undertake, afforded her the Means of acquiring female, as well as male, Accomplishments" (10). Through Leonora, Scott advocates for the benefits of an androgyny that balances a beautiful and well-proportioned body with active forms of learning. As in her later fiction, Scott endorses education for young women that would put them on equal footing with young men, and she launches an implicit critique against a system in which educated women have few opportunities to demonstrate their intellectual aptitude. Through Leonora's cross-dressing, Scott shows that the social regulation of gender should be critiqued and reconfigured.

Through its portrayals of young characters challenging existing frameworks, "The History of Leonora and Louisa" insinuates that youthful vivacity reworks limiting gender norms that are attributed to the older generation. Scott asserts Leonora's corporeal strength by juxtaposing her vital body and active mind with disabled and aged characters that she encounters on her journey. There is Louisa, for instance, Leonora's chronically ill cousin whose impairments make Leonora the logical candidate to be the wage-earner during their travels. Moreover, an aged widow, Lady Haines, falls in love with Leonora when she is working as a clergyman. Lady Haines's lameness makes visible her heightened delicacy, distinguishing her from Leonora, who typically walks several miles a day in the countryside surrounding Buxton. When the two walk together, the difference between them is clear: "If the weather tempted them abroad, Lady Haines never let slip the Opportunity of leaning on Leonora's Arm to support her feeble Steps, for she was too delicate to be a good Walker." (52). Here, Scott playfully satirizes Lady Haines's excessive sensibility to emphasize Leonora's vigorousness in her daily routines. Leonora's youth poses the possibility for women to be dynamic in mind and body; Lady Haines, with her age and mobility impairment, represents an old-guard, anti-feminist delicacy that fades to the margins of the narrative. She is not to be imitated by young women.

At intervals in "The History of Leonora and Louisa," Scott uses the prospect of women's intimate, physical bonds to create irony, but she also considers the possibility of sapphic households. For instance, while suffering from a headache, Lady Haines implores Leonora (who is cross-dressed as a clergyman at this point) to attend to her in her sick bed. Pressed by Lady Haines, the two proceed to "represent an Interview between" Pope's Abelard and Eloisa, "when Love approached Eloisa under Friendship's Name" (57). Their role-play permits Lady Haines occasion "to caress Leonora so fondly" that Leonora feels that she must put a stop to it: "After having unsuccessfully thrown out some Reproofs for Eloisa's Forwardness, [Leonora] found it necessary to resume her own Character, and to tell her Ladyship, that these Sort of Amusements were not prudent" (57–58). The comedy of the scene is rooted in Lady Haines's passionate expression of sexual desire—supposedly at odds with her age and bodily state—for what she thinks is a young man, but who is actually a young woman. However, despite her reproof of Lady Haines, Leonora is genuinely curious about marrying another woman and becoming the head of a household. Leonora sees herself "settled in a small House, with more Sash window than Wall; a little Garden of Ever-greens before it, a Church shadowed with solemn Yews behind . . . and a cleanly mincing wife, with a multitude of Cherry-cheek'd Children with the House thus properly situated" (31). The conventional arrangement of this quotidian domestic scene, in which the particulars of the household and garden are imagined in vivid detail, offer a brief glimpse into a healthy sapphic domestic arrangement. The "cleanly mincing wife" and "Cherry-cheek'd Children," whose health is suggested by their facial complexion, imply that this is as normal and healthy a family as any could be. This brief but affirmative vision of queer family life indicates Scott's upholding of same-sex domestic arrangements as socially viable.

In Leonora's queer fantasy, she is cross-dressed as a clergyman, successfully occupying a male profession. Her cross-dressed domestic dream resonates with the phenomenon of the "female husband," a contemporary source of public and writerly fascination. Henry Fielding's account, *The Female Husband: or, the Surprising*

History of Mrs. Mary, alias Mr. George Hamilton (1746), published just eight years before Scott's novel, purports to give a true account of an individual, Hamilton, who marries three different women while traveling about Britain as a quack doctor.[18] Female husbands such as Hamilton were accused of ensnaring unsuspecting women into marriage and continuing the charade through their use of dildos with their wives. Given its content, Fielding's pamphlet is a possible touchstone for Scott's portrayal of Leonora's public performance of maleness and of the sapphic domestic fantasy embedded therein. Both Fielding's Hamilton and Scott's Leonora are seasoned travelers who have mastered the ability to pass as male. Both work in male professions and desire the company of women. Both are queer in their rejection of heteronormative domesticity and gender norms. One significant distinction between Scott's portrayal of Leonora and Fielding's depiction of Hamilton is form. Fielding's pamphlet is, after all, a criminal biography, while Scott writes of a heroic character in a novel. While Fielding represents in a picaresque manner Hamilton's unsuccessful masquerades as a male quack doctor, Leonora possesses a sound education and moral formation, which allow her to excel in a variety of professions, even if she would be, like Hamilton, a vagrant.[19] Unlike Hamilton, Leonora is a laudable representation of what young women can achieve through creativity and resilience. Leonora's mobile performance of gender is the occasion for Scott's celebration of women's empowerment. Moreover, her domestic fantasy substantiates the loving and productive contours of same-sex households.

After a series of misadventures, including wrongful imprisonment for murder, Leonora sees that her vagrant mobility is ultimately unsustainable and even dangerous. She realizes that she must return home to the standard domestic life that awaits her. The narrative concludes with Leonora, now dressed in regular female attire, marrying a reformed libertine named Calidore. Scott's heteronormative conclusion does little to resolve the various forms of queer desire that permeate the narrative, though the tale dispenses with disability and aged bodies rather handily. In concluding the frame tale, Sabrina makes the following concluding remarks about Leonora: "And here . . . I shall drop her; a Novel would make but a bad Figure carried on beyond Marriage, and as I began Leonora's History in order to shew . . . how capable our Sex might be of preserving Independence . . . she might rather serve as an Argument, that, let our Talents be equal or superior to them, our Spirits above Controul, still sooner or later we become their Dependents, perhaps their Slaves" (159–160). Sabrina reveals that novels end at marriage because of how circumscribed women's independence becomes at that point. Sabrina teaches Carinthia that women should preserve their autonomy as long as they can because the domestic sphere is an inescapable form of enslavement.

This "common . . . thing" of marriage, which as Scott learned through her own short, disastrous marriage, may not be a desirable state of affairs for young women after all.[20] Scott establishes Leonora's working abilities by juxtaposing her well-shaped form to the several *un*productive, disabled characters that populate the tale. The prospect of a life on the lam or in prison returns Leonora to heterosexual respectability, but marital life is undoubtedly an institution about which Scott is highly critical and would later challenge in an even more overt manner in *Millenium Hall*.

SCOTT'S CRITIQUE OF THE "COMMON STANDARD" IN *MILLENIUM HALL*

Scott's fictional portrayal of disability and aging undergo significant developments from *A Journey through Every Stage of Life* to *Millenium Hall*, the latter of which scrutinizes the arbitrariness of socially driven bodily standards that reduce variably-embodied people to the realm of the physiognomic (as we have seen in Mrs. Jewkes and in Scott's own depiction of Lady Haines). The characters in *Millenium Hall* betray Scott's deep discomfort with a system that denies dignity to the physically disabled and aged, a system in which variable bodies are viewed as monstrous vessels of immorality, as emblems of weakness, or as manifestations of wonder. In *Millenium Hall*, Scott offers a vivid model of what Tobin Siebers would call "complex embodiment," in which she elucidates a keen "awareness of the effects of disabling environments on people's lived experience on the body."[21] Moreover, she explores the factors that impact disability, such as "chronic pain, secondary health effects, and aging," which stem from the body and not the environment.[22] Scott understands, in other words, that the body is a product of the social arrangement of impairment as well as one's particular physical constitution. Scott imagines a woman-led utopia that undoes the injustices which confront variable people and those who do not adhere to genteel heterosexuality. She views disabled and queer affiliation as the center of an ethical framework that makes possible social reform, and she does so in part through her critique of the corporeal and sexual standards that relegate so many to the peripheries of British society.

Scholars have examined *Millenium Hall* for its extraordinary envisioning of utopia, for its depiction of queerness, and for its unusual (for the time) take on embodiment. Alessa Johns, for example, argues that Scott "embraced liberal ideas of individual rights and property" in her planning of "utopian communities in which these rights furthered the capacity, most often of women, to carry out Christian responsibilities."[23] For Johns, Scott's utopian vision adapts existing contractual language to reconfigure society in a gynocentric fashion that relies upon Christian principles for moral coherence. Queer readings of Scott's novel often focus on its portrayals of non-normative sociability and desire. George Haggerty claims that the "unnatural affections" among the heads of the estate are suggestive of a maternal homoeroticism that contributes to the novel's general inversion of Oedipal structures and subversion of patriarchal standards.[24] In her reading of the novel's representation of "anomaly," Felicity Nussbaum argues that physical difference "is a recommendation for a position at Millenium Hall" and that, throughout the narrative, "the culture's devaluation of deformity is reversed."[25] Whether exploring female friendship or the possibility of sapphic conjugality, these scholars tend to agree that *Millenium Hall* contains both progressive and conservative elements for the way that it simultaneously posits moral reform and reinforces class hierarchies. Scott and the Bluestocking Circle with whom she is generally affiliated are now known for their proto-feminist thinking, but also for lacking the radical politics that would inform later generations of women writers, especially Mary Wollstonecraft. While it is the case that, in her uncritical upholding of the British class system, Scott exercises a "compensatory conservatism" that Susan Lanser identifies as a "screen" for Bluestocking sapphism, she can be more radical than she is generally allowed, for she also advocates for better living conditions for gentlewomen and disabled people.[26] Scott's fiction indicates a capacious set of possibilities for disabled and queer people, depending upon their class status.

Millenium Hall designates the close-knit, loving bonds among the aging mistresses of the estate as the foundations for social reform. In considering Scott's own biography, as well as that of her long-term partner Lady Barbara, Scott's emphasis on disability and same-sex conjugality is not terribly surprising. Her assorted bouts with illness, including the smallpox she contracted in her teens which permanently scarred her face—not to mention Lady Barbara's heart failure, recurring headaches, and stomach pains—were difficulties which were at least partially responsible for the couple's removal from society to the slow-paced village of Batheaston, outside of Bath, in 1760.[27] Given that Bath was a wellness center for people with a variety of health conditions in the eighteenth century, it made sense for the couple to settle where they did, still near Bath, but in a place where they could live comfortably on their somewhat meager collective income.[28] While in Batheaston, Scott and Lady Barbara employed intellectually and physically impaired domestic servants and even started a school for indigent young women, a version of what Scott writes into *Millenium Hall*, though on a smaller scale.[29] Even before they settled in Batheaston, the idea of employing disabled servants appealed to Scott. In a 1752 letter to her sister, Elizabeth Montagu, Scott writes about a maid she and Lady Barbara have employed who is "a well meaning simpleton, who, was not her understanding still in its minority, I might call a Woman; & a more useful Domestic . . . to whom nature instead of the sense of hearing has given numberless virtues, & indeed made almost a miracle for her station."[30] Scott's letter reveals her belief in a compensatory model of disability, in which people with impairments are recompensed for their supposed deficiencies with "virtues." In this case, the maid's deafness and intellectual impairment are no stumbling blocks to "her station," and she is miraculously efficient in the way that she goes about her work, even if Scott also infantilizes her. Scott's desire to surround herself with physically and intellectually impaired servants indicates reform-minded principles in which variable embodiment is the rule, not the exception—where disability is the gateway to community building.[31] Scott finds in the utopian genre an exemplary literary venue for the fictionalization of her ideals. In *Millenium Hall*, the bucolic estate is a respite from the unforgiving outside world. This rendering of utopia, as Hilary Brown affirms, is one that "stands in complete opposition to contemporary gentry capitalism," but is also a renouncement of cruelty to women, a treatise against the maltreatment of the disabled, and a proclamation of what constitutes a family—not blood, but choice and love.[32] Though it is a family in which the members know their place, it is also one that relies on choice, circumstance, and love for its very formation, or what we might think of as queer network affiliations based on divine intervention.

Scott manages these literary objectives by offering a direct challenge to normative thinking about the body, and she frames the narrative to introduce uninformed men to this ambitious project. Upon their accidental discovery of Millenium Hall, Sir George Ellison, the author of the epistle that frames the narrative, and his traveling companion, Lamont, are soon asked to reflect upon their ignorant assumptions about variable bodies. As she shows Ellison and Lamont around the estate, Mrs. Mancel, one of the estate owners, remarks upon the violent consequences that corporeal standards have on short-statured inhabitants that they purchased from freak show entertainers: "Here they find refuge from the tyranny of those wretches, who seem to think that being two or three feet taller gives them a right to make them a property, and expose their unhappy forms to the contemptuous curiosity of the unthinking multitude."[33] Mrs. Mancel criticizes the propensity of insensible people to derive pleasure from the exhibiting of bodies in public spaces. In such a milieu, she implies, there is an unjustifiable distinction between what gets construed as natural and unnatural. Mrs. Mancel identifies the continuity of a discursive framework in which physical difference functions either as a token of the miraculous, or as a manifestation of evil, by invoking Procrustes. In Greek mythology, Procrustes used what Mrs. Mancel calls a "necessary standard" to determine whether his victims should either be stretched or have their limbs cut to fit his metal bed (72). This imposing of bodily norms is a considerable problem in contemporary British society, according to Mrs. Mancel: "But is not almost every man a Procrustes? We have not the power of shewing our cruelty exactly in the same method, but actuated by the like spirit, we abridge of their liberty, and torment by scorn, all who either fall short, or exceed the usual standard, if they happen to have the additional misfortune of poverty" (72). From her employment of the phrase "necessary standard," to that of "usual standard," and finally, on the following page, "common standard," Scott repeatedly qualifies the violence of Procrustean norms as beholden to arbitrary social forces, for what is "necessary" or "usual" or "common" in the outside world has no place in the self-contained sanctuary (72–73). The inclusion of "poverty" in this discussion speaks to the class-based formulation of society that the estate represents, with destitution a "misfortune" that requires the charitable deeds of the estate owners to be overcome. Mrs. Mancel thus sees it as a responsibility of her station to expose corporeal vulnerability as especially detrimental to impecunious members of society. This significant caveat notwithstanding, in her exposing of bodily norms as inherently illogical, Mrs. Mancel posits impairment as a naturally occurring variation that cuts across the British class system. Through Mrs. Mancel's voice, Scott establishes embodiment as existing along a diverse spectrum, which becomes, for her, the only dependable way to conceive of bodies. By invoking Procrustes, Scott ties her queries about the body to a critical tradition that extends as far back as the Classical Age.

Scott's critique of corporeal regularity complicates the emergence of the idea of "normalcy" that Lennard Davis identifies as occurring well after the publication of *Millenium Hall*. For Davis, the nineteenth century witnessed a variety of intellectual developments, such as the rise of statistics, the bell curve, the novel, eugenics, and psychoanalysis, all of which defined themselves in relation to the emergence of an average or "norm." For Davis, prior to the nineteenth century, all bodies, regardless of shape or ability, were viewed as falling short of a godly ideal.[34] This framework for understanding the body, however, does not adequately explain the hierarchical range of bodies in *Millenium Hall*, in which there is a clearly defined notion of those that adhere to, or fail to adhere to, acceptable bodily forms. Scott's use of "standard" allows for some nuanced insight into how bodies were conceived before "normal" was imbued with a notion of a statistical average.[35] The *Oxford English Dictionary* defines *standard* as "an authoritative or recognized exemplar of correctness, perfection, or some definite degree of any quality" and "a rule, principle, or means of judgment or estimation."[36] As Scott proclaims through the character of Mrs. Mancel, there is a socially constructed notion of what bodies should look like, how they should move and function, and so on.[37] By qualifying "standard" with modifiers such as "usual" and "common," Scott identifies the very subjective nature of such an "authoritative" rendering of the body. The hermetically sealed estate as a whole becomes the imagined means by which Scott pushes back against these subjective conditions, for it is the goal of the estate owners to reconfigure British society by emphasizing the meaningful contribution of impaired bodies to the greater good. In fact, in both the narrative and description that compose the novel, Scott identifies a variety of standards that cause harm, including those that underpin compulsory heterosexuality and ableism. Scott asserts same-sex intimacy and disabled embodiment as interrelated sources of happiness and productivity to counter these arbitrary norms.

Scott's utopia challenges the various standards that shape British society, ranging from corporeal norms to norms that govern how intimacy works. Though she stops short of portraying same-sex eroticism among the variably-embodied women that run the estate, Scott imagines the relationships between the women of the estate as sapphic—a classed term used with regularity in the mid-to-late eighteenth century, typically in reference to women whose primary inclination is to be with other women.[38] Susan Lanser regards sapphism as both encompassing and exceeding the scope of "sexual acts" to encapsulate "desires and penchants that give primacy—even momentary primacy—to same-sex bonds through words and practices amenable to an erotic rendering."[39] The "words and practices" of Scott's novel indicate an "erotic rendering" of the estate-managing women's desire for one another. Moreover, the manner in which Scott affirms affective community is clearly stratified along British class lines. Lanser would deem this a form of "compensatory conservatism," in which unmarried genteel women who pursued relationships or cohabitated with other women safeguarded themselves from accusations of "oddness" behind their accrual of cultural capital, imbuing their status with a respectable "public relations" visibility.[40] One well-known couple, Eleanor Butler and Sarah Ponsonby (widely known in their day as the Ladies of Llangollen), are models of compensatory conservatism. They hosted well-known visitors in their impeccably decorated home and beautiful garden and were widely regarded as lovers, though they were rarely derided or censured for it.[41] Compensatory conservatism is likewise a means for Scott to distance herself from potential accusations of social deviancy. From its reform principles to its narrative structure, *Millenium Hall* offers sapphism as a disruptive force to the interrelated social constructs of patriarchy and ability. Scott imbues the disabled and queer inhabitants of the estate with the potential to reform British society.

The estate owners' sapphic relationships are characterized by a combination of conjugal and group intimacies. Scott registers this harmonizing of the conjugal with the communal in a series of inset narratives, which interrupt the description of the male letter writer, Sir George Ellison. In using Ellison's male perspective to describe the estate, Scott increases the rhetorical efficacy of her novel to a reading public accustomed to male authority. Further, as Caroline Gonda argues, Scott's use of a male point of view in Ellison protects Scott from "any possible accusations of separatism or man-hating."[42] Mrs. Maynard, however, regularly interjects herself in Ellison's letter with a series of detailed narratives about the ladies that run the estate. In this way, she becomes "the master of the discourses in utopia."[43] These frame tales relate the ladies' biographical circumstances, particularly how they discover in one another the affection and fortitude necessary to shoulder the harsh realities of their respective comings-of-age and courtship adversities. In the characters' stories, each individual woman encounters danger and distress, and at last finds refuge and purpose in a community of like-minded peers. Even if there is an absence of eroticism throughout the narrative, *Millenium Hall* extends a comprehensive social framework that privileges queer kinship over anything approximating standard gentry household configurations. Miss Mancel and Miss Melvyn's relationship bears this out: theirs is a commitment in economic and emotional terms: "The boundaries and barriers raised by those two watchful and suspicious enemies, Meum and Tuum ["mine" and "thine"], were . . . broke down by true friendship; and all property laid in one undistinguished common" (93). Thus, "true friendship" is the sum of each member, and in the social system of the estate, each individual's importance is supplanted by the collective as a whole. On the estate, the value of an individual is based on the extent to which she facilitates the advancement of the community.

Miss Mancel and Mrs. Morgan's collective mentality acts as the founding democratic principle of Millenium Hall. The remaining inset narratives likewise detail the biographies of the other estate managers. Each individual woman comes of age despite a variety of difficulties to inherit sizeable incomes from deceased parents or husbands. In time, they find one another, and their money goes into the "common stock" of the estate (218). Each contribution facilitates new projects. Mrs. Selvyn's influx of money, for example, provides the means for the establishment of a house for indigent gentlewomen. Mrs. Selvyn's narratives about each of the ladies of Millenium Hall are individual histories, not communal ones, and this serves as a limitation to the novel's endorsement of community. However, even though these histories begin as individual accounts (with the exception of Miss Mancel and Mrs. Morgan, who are narrated jointly), they are finally woven together to form a complete picture that is, in the novel's present tense of utopian description, the bastion of the communal Christian ideal. The characters' names are suggestive of this collectivity. Scott's repetitive use of M in the names, Miss Melvyn (Mrs. Morgan), Miss Mancel, Mrs. Maynard, and Lady

[89]

Mary Jones invokes a shared identity. There is exact rhyme between the surnames Selvyn and Melvyn and near rhyme between these and "Trentham." The interchangeability among the ladies' surnames reduces the importance of the individual in the interests of promoting a coalition of like minds and purposes. Even the characters' dress is uniform. Upon first meeting the estate owners, Ellison remarks that they appear in "the same neatness" and in "the same simplicity and cleanliness." They all wear a "lutestring night-gown, though of different colors," and there is nothing "unfashionable in their appearance, except that they were free from any trumpery ornaments" (61). Their dress, names, and united purposes diminish individualism. As singlewomen, they are subjected to the interests of men, but as a group, they harness their status and resources to build an estate that counters woes related to heterosexual courtship and familial failure. The structure of the narrative and of Millenium Hall itself are in these ways contingent on sapphic bonds. Through these same-sex intimacies, Scott imagines a society that is productive, bucolic, and communal.

ACCOMMODATION AND COMMUNITY IN *MILLENIUM HALL*

Beyond its endorsement of collectivity, *Millenium Hall* registers women's variable embodiment as a prerequisite for inhabiting the estate. The spectrum of bodies that Scott represents indicates one of the notable characteristics of her utopian project: to re-envision gendered bodies of various kinds as capable of generating income through productive labor. In this way, Scott suggests that men's able bodies are not the only ones capable of advancing economic interests. *Millenium Hall* asserts such a philosophy from the beginning of the narrative through Ellison's manifestly physical description of the estate owners. For example, Mrs. Selvyn's "features are too irregular to be handsome" and Mrs. Trentham has "features and complexion [that] have been so injured by the smallpox, that one can but guess they were once uncommonly fine." Besides these women, stand Lady Mary Jones, who is "thin and pale" with a "countenance, which sickness has done its utmost to render languid," and Mrs. Morgan who is "upwards of fifty, tall, rather plump" (60). Clearly, these women share effects of lived experience (pockmarked face, thinness, chronic illness, paleness) that were typical for the time. Of all of the estate owners, only Mrs. Mancel adheres to more regular forms of female beauty, with her "elegance of figure" and grace "in every motion." And yet, like Mrs. Morgan, she has passed marriageable age, excelling "in every beauty but the bloom, which is so soon faded, and so impossible to be imitated by the utmost efforts of art" (60). In their advanced age and scarred bodies, the women stand together as emblems of a communal matriarchal power that runs through the estate. Scott thus conveys a vision of variable embodiment that accounts for the malleability of the body, which is shaped by the inevitable pressures of disease, of injury, and of aging. Ellison initially characterizes the estate owners' bodies in terms of the worth that they would be assigned outside of the estate in polite society: irregular, plain, and past marriageable age, these characters would seem to have little to contribute according to the standards imposed by genteel patriarchy. This characterization of the intrinsic worth of physical variability and age stands in direct opposition to what Richardson represents in Mrs. Jewkes and also shows Scott's growth as a writer. Perhaps because nearly a decade passes between the publication of *A Journey through Every Stage of Life* and that of *Millenium Hall*, Scott has herself grown older and has reflected on the aging process. In any case, *Millenium Hall* establishes aging as that which has inevitable consequences on the body but also as a facet of lived experience that is especially challenging for women of various classes.[44]

Throughout *Millenium Hall*, Scott reinforces class hierarchies. Like the estate owners, the servants and laborers of the estate likewise represent physical variability, though in even more pronounced ways. From the lame and blind musicians and deaf laborers, to the short- and tall-statured people that live in the estate's enclosure, Millenium Hall houses a wide range of bodily forms (63, 73, 168). These characters appear at intervals throughout the narrative and are typically accompanied by some kind of justification or explanation. A housekeeper who is impaired, for instance, finds in Millenium Hall her one and only refuge. She relates to Ellison that, upon losing the use of a hand after suffering a fever, she "was advised to apply to these ladies, and found what had hitherto been an impediment, was a stronger recommendation than the good character I had from my last place" (168). She continues, "I am sure I have reason to value these distorted fingers, more than ever any one did the handsomest hands that ever nature made" (168). By imbuing her disfigured hand with intrinsic worth, the housekeeper counters Ellison and Lamont's ableist presuppositions about labor and bodily function. The housekeeper finds in Millenium Hall the best of all possible scenarios for, along with the other servants with whom she works, "there is no family where the business is better done; for gratitude, and a conviction that this is the only house into which we can be received, makes us exert ourselves to the utmost; and most people fail not from a deficiency of power, but of inclination" (169). Because the estate owners offer a last resort for labor or servitude to those that are often deemed undesirable, the estate's inhabitants do their utmost to accomplish the various tasks assigned to them. *Millenium Hall* recasts disability, from the contemporaneous view that impairment embitters the individual, to a physical state that motivates that individual to promote the advancement of society as a whole.[45] Scott's model of labor not only accounts for an array of bodily abilities: it suggests that disability is an ideal state because it serves as the catalyst for the realization of a smoothly run estate.

Scott's model of labor is also based on a model of exchange that is contingent on bodily ability. When the narrator and Lamont meet one of the estate's elderly, impoverished inhabitants, they learn about this system from her:

> There are twelve of us that live here. We have every one a house of two rooms, as you may see, beside other conveniences, and each a little garden, but though we are separate, we agree as well, perhaps better, than if we lived together, and all help one another. Now, there is neighbour Susan, and neighbour Rachel; Susan is lame, so she spins cloaths for Rachel; and Rachel cleans Susan's house, and does such things for her as she cannot do for herself. The ladies settled all these matters at first, and told us, that as they, to please God, assisted us, we must in order to please him serve others; and that to make us happy they would put us in a way, poor as we are, to do good to many. (66)

As the elderly woman indicates, individual home ownership is a given on the estate, and yet, much like the ladies that run the estate, whose individualism merges into the collective whole, the women from these homes depend upon one another for subsistence. Their labor is based on communal and interchangeable accessibility. Susan and Rachel, though each impaired in their distinctive ways, assist each other by completing tasks that the other would not be able to accomplish on their own. This enables each estate inhabitant to actively participate in the estate's core principle of industriousness. Each of the estate members works toward the common good of caring for one another, which in turn keeps the estate prosperous. Through this organization, the estate becomes accessible to figures of varying bodily types. So, while Scott's utopia does little to upset class hierarchies, it does reconfigure the way that labor and exchange function by assuming that *all* bodies vary in form and function and that therefore the best way to run a society is by thoughtfully accounting for one's unique physical abilities.

However, Mrs. Mancel's thoughtful interrogation of bodily standards does nothing to untangle class-based hierarchies. After all, the laborers and servants that occupy Millenium Hall are relegated to separate parts of the estate, and their presence in the narrative often elucidates the estate owners' genteel beneficence and condescension. Ellison, for example, discovers that the laborers learn to follow the principles of the estate owners, as one inhabitant explains, "We used to quarrel . . . but the ladies condescended to make it up amongst us, and shewed us so kindly how much it was our duty to agree together, and to forgive everybody their faults . . . now we love each other like sisters" (67). The woman's description of her own moral enhancement and that of her neighbors underscores their subordination to the estate owners. And yet there are crucial alignments between these two sets of characters that endow Scott's novel with an overall feeling of community and asylum. All of the inhabitants on the estate are outcasts, regardless of their station, and the manner in which they work together indicates a familial bond of sorts, however hierarchical that might be. Kristina Straub has shown that the relationship between masters and servants may be characterized by such family-like ties, and that, in an ambivalence that stratifies both "love and class conflict," the two share an intense "need for one another" both in terms of the cynical—profit and exploitation—and in terms of the emotional—in their "desire for connection."[46] *Millenium Hall* represents this relationship without ever really questioning the ideological assumptions that undergird it, and therein we observe Scott's classist conservatism. But Scott also renounces and rectifies cruelty to women and maltreatment of the disabled and proclaims in their place a viable formation of queer family. In Scott's construction of the household we may observe the heavenly "asylum" that rectifies the wrongs of British society (58). To be certain, labor of various kinds is central to the society. The estate owners and residents toil and are thus productive contributors to the greater good of the estate, as I have shown, but the capacity to labor is a key component to the definition of *disability*. By portraying women of varying bodily abilities performing labor, Scott does not exactly undermine the contemporaneous conceptualization of ability, but she refutes the idea that only certain bodies are capable of being productive.

RACE AND ABILITY IN *THE HISTORY OF SIR GEORGE ELLISON*

In *Millenium Hall*, Sarah Scott creates a utopian society that positions variably-embodied and queer characters as the essences of a reconstituted British society. Scott's novel counters the physiognomic, metaphoric function of disability that is often evident in fiction, including in Richardson's *Pamela*. Moreover, Scott captures the complex manner in which impaired bodies are formed: in the way that society creates disability, in the way that aging and illness enhance impairment, and in the way that such social obstacles and physical realities regularly intertwine to shape the lives of people with impairments. Up to the publication of *Millenium Hall*, Scott had written extensively about gender mobility, disability, ugliness, and queerness as critical facets of embodiment with tangible social and corporeal consequences.[47] Scott's narrative solutions to the effects of these extraordinary forms of embodiment range from the creation of self-contained communities to the advancement of the individual through the accrual of education and virtue. These reform measures depend upon entrenched class hierarchies that extend to the question of slave ownership. *Millenium Hall*, for instance, makes passing reference to the ladies' purchase of short-statured people from freak show entertainers who had used them as spectacles for money. The ladies enclose these individuals on the estate, away from the prying eyes of society, where they learn to live a virtuous, hardworking, and dignified life after the manner of their new owners. Scott imagines such benevolent slave ownership, when informed by sentiment, to improve the deleterious living conditions of variable people. Scott addresses the topic of enslavement in a much more sustained and focused manner in a quasi-sequel to *Millenium Hall*, *The History of Sir George Ellison*, written four years later. In this novel, Scott asserts a more ambitious agenda for her reformist doctrine by setting the narrative outside of the confines of England, in Jamaica. *Sir George Ellison* also adds a critical dimension to Scott's depiction of complex embodiment and the ideology of ability; she depicts the lived experience of enslaved black people as analogous to the white disabled servants who live at Millenium Hall. Scott also portrays the system of chattel slavery as hideously inhumane. Through Ellison's sensibility, Scott advocates for improved plantation conditions in Jamaica, where slavers' ruthless physical abuses were utterly appalling.[48] A crucial part of Scott's argument is economically oriented, for, as she suggests throughout the narrative, if enslaved people live under optimal conditions, they may become more productive, more *able* to do the grueling labor required of them. Scott thus imagines blackness as a social disability but also suggests that black bodies are quintessentially able bodies. In *Sir George Ellison*, Scott creates a sentimental fantasy of plantation reformation based on a racist ideology of ability.

Given its detailed exploration of the conditions of slavery, *Sir George Ellison* enjoyed an eighteenth-century, transatlantic afterlife which eclipsed that of her other novels.[49] Due to the way that Scott portrays plantation life in Jamaica (which she envisioned through her own research and through conversations with Creole people that she knew intimately at Bath), the novel felt true-to-life to readers of Scott's day, on either side of the Atlantic.[50] Jamaica was a place of intense political instability, and abolitionists were beginning to speak out against the horrors of slavery.[51] The novel relates the life of George Ellison (the narrator of *Millenium Hall*), who at twenty-one years of age departs England for Jamaica, where he intends to boost his father's limited finances through capitalistic venture. In time, he marries into plantation ownership but finds his wife's exploitation of slaves to be repugnant. Ellison begins to instill change in the way that their plantation is run, eliminating harsh corporal punishment and slave sales, among other things. Scott's sentimental novel impacted readers of varying backgrounds, including Ignatius Sancho, one of the most visible and prolific of black British writers from the period. Sancho found in Scott's novel a laudable critique of chattel slavery. In a letter to Laurence Sterne, Sancho writes, "Of all my favourite authors, not one has drawn a tear in favour of my miserable black brethreren—excepting yourself, and the humane author of Sir George Ellison."[52] As Sancho indicates, Scott's "humane" depiction of plantation life is very much steeped in the tradition of sentimental literature, aligning her with the likes of Sterne. According to Eve Tavor Bannet and Betty Rizzo, *Sir George Ellison* is, for its time, progressive in its restructuring of plantation life, even if it stops short of calling for abolition all together. As Rizzo claims, Scott's reluctance or inability to imagine a society devoid of slavery is evidence of what "she could and could not propose" given the "intellectual" circumstances of her day.[53] This is a crucial point to keep in mind. Like all writers, Scott would have been able to work with the tools—intellectual and imaginative—at her disposal, and she may have had to make difficult decisions about how far to extend her critique in order to successfully sell her work.[54] Regardless, *Sir George Ellison* offers a one-dimensional representation of characters of color. They lack subjectivity in that they never speak, nor are they granted character development. Scott's novel also reflects the fluid understanding of race of her day, which is informed not by the sorts of rigid black and white binaries that structure our thinking today, but instead by "categories of difference" such as religion, climate, and class.[55]

Ellison is, if nothing else, prototypically Anglican in his rational and sentimental ethics. Rather than promoting the overturning of structures of oppression, Scott writes of how the likes of Ellison can work within existing systems to enact change. *Sir George Ellison* explores the influence of landed, genteel men, as Ellison touches the lives of servants, captive laborers, and peers alike through his sentimental words and deeds. While Ellison is not an abolitionist, his highly cultivated sensibility is at odds with his newfound position as slaver: "Slavery was so abhorrent to his nature, and in his opinion so unjustly inflicted, that he had hitherto avoided the keeping of any negroes; chusing rather to give such advantages to his servants."[56] Ellison initially prefers to employ the British servants that have accompanied him to Jamaica, but he soon realizes that it would be impossible to maintain his estate without free labor. In short order, Ellison decides to take concrete measures to ease the slaves' burdens. He proselytizes his approach to the surrounding community, and he becomes an emissary of sentiment and religious virtue to the morally compromised creole population that has been inured to the brutalities of chattel slavery.

Under Ellison's guidance, the captives on his plantation become much more productive than those of the surrounding plantations. Another benefit to improved slave management, according to *Sir George Ellison*, is an increase in business. In the structure of chattel slavery that Scott invokes, enslaved peoples are valued for their *ability* to labor. Often represented in print as monstrous, as marked by harmful climates, or as inferior manifestations of humanity through discourses of scientific racism that emerged in the eighteenth century, black people, especially black men, also epitomized for many white slavers the pinnacle of physical strength.[57] Given this popular perception, it is hardly surprising that a benefit of Ellison's reform measures is that the individuals on his plantation become "stronger" (17). By comparison, "the natural strength of those who belonged to other masters" are "consumed by hardship and hunger" (17). In time, Ellison's decision to ease the amount of labor heaped upon his captives' shoulders, and to better nourish and civilize them, has optimal results for capital in that they are "*able* with so much ease to do so much more work" (40, emphasis mine). Scott thus establishes slaves' increased ability to exert themselves on the plantation as an effect of Ellison's treatment of them with "as much ease and enjoyment as they could enjoy" (40). The physical ability of enslaved peoples correlates directly with the manner in which they are treated by masters, and, like the inhabitants of Millenium Hall, the "lowest" of society are rendered civilized, happy, and hardworking. In both *Millenium Hall* and *Sir George Ellison*, Scott betrays an assumption that variable and black bodies can be honed as instruments of labor. If the system is to persist (and persist it must, for Scott) then it is the slaver's responsibility to create better conditions for servants and enslaved people. For Scott, land ownership in the British Isles and plantation ownership in Jamaica are analogous positions of power, and the boundary between free servant and slave is not necessarily discrete.

Class and servitude-slavery distinctions aside, in terms of their embodiment, there are significant differences between the short-statured and disabled servants of Millenium Hall and the captives on Ellison's plantation. Crucially, the enslaved people in Jamaica are uniformly represented as being free of physical impairment and as having bodies that can be strengthened in ways that the inhabitants of Millenium Hall cannot. However, just like the short-statured characters that live in the enclosure in *Millenium Hall*, the enslaved characters of *Sir George Ellison* have been maltreated by tyrannical, sadistic masters in Jamaica: "By the barbarity and tyranny of their overseers they shall frequently be punished, even when they are not guilty; and looking upon these sufferings as a misery attending their condition, they do not endeavor to avoid what they cannot always prevent" (23–24). Ellison's critique echoes Mrs. Maynard's commentary about freak show entertainers, in which she claims that the "tyranny of those wretches" expose variably-embodied people to the malicious whims of the "unthinking multitude" (72). These parallel scenes indicate that plantation owners in Jamaica and freak show managers in

England lack the requisite sensibility to be good proprietors, thereby creating the harmful conditions that Scott critiques. For Scott, tyranny is at its most malignant when those that are socially alienated are subjected to barbarity by cruel, unfeeling rulers. Thus, the power differential between slave owner and enslaved person, or freak show entertainer and variably-embodied performer, is "not natural" but "merely adventitious" (27). As Ellison tells his wife, "When you and I are laid in the grave, our lowest black slave will be as great as we are; in the next world perhaps much greater" (27). Here, Scott recognizes that all are equal in the eyes of god, but that due to political circumstances, inequality is the accepted order. Ellison's faith in a just afterlife, in which all is rectified for the "lowest" of society, undercuts the urgency of the social upheaval that would be necessary to permanently remedy the deplorable conditions which so many people face. Even as Scott identifies analogous systems of oppression for white servants and enslaved black people, both *Millenium Hall* and *Sir George Ellison* reinforce the very capitalistic system that perpetuates such oppression in the first place. As in *Millenium Hall*, the social and political parameters in *Sir George Ellison* are firmly set, but in each narrative, the benevolent landowner finds ways to work within that system, to reimagine it in order to improve the lives of those that are denigrated by that system.

In this beneficent, paternalistic spirit, Ellison employs tactics to alleviate the captives' distress. Just as in *Millenium Hall*, in which the inhabitants are given their own cottages and gardens to cultivate produce, Ellison improves housing conditions by building "a great number of cottages" which he "assigned to each family . . . with a little piece of ground adjoining, well stocked with vegetables, the future cultivation of which he left to themselves" (29). By creating pockets of autonomy within the confines of his land, Ellison inspires the slaves to improve their moral character and behavior so that they will not require the corporal punishment which he finds so abhorrent. Ellison functions as sentimental father figure to the individuals on his plantation, whom he chooses to look upon as "free servants" or "children" and for whose welfare he is "anxious and watchful" (31). His paternalistic care is manifested in the school that he establishes, a project also undertaken by the ladies of *Millenium Hall*. For Scott, variably-embodied, white laboring English servants and black slaves in Jamaica are both in need of education to become civilized. Still, both sets of oppressed people fall in line within the established hierarchy, productive in their labor due to their "gratitude" to the landowners and the judiciousness which they learn from their superiors: "Prudence will bind [them] to good behaviour" (31). In this way, both *Millenium Hall* and *Sir George Ellison* interrogate the socially driven contours of physical ability by asserting the capabilities of all bodies to be productive. However, according to Scott, black bodies are especially capable of labor, reinforcing a racist ideology of ability even as it critiques the chattel slavery system that it ultimately justifies.

Scott's novels, when considered together, allow insight into how bodies are culturally and physically constituted in the mid-eighteenth century. Throughout her fictional career, Scott redeems women, the queer, the disabled, and the deformed inasmuch as they enjoy the classed privilege which enables them to possess the requisite education. Those that live in servitude or in slavery, however, are dependent upon their masters for nourishment and the civilizing influences of religion and education. Servants' and slaves' lives are substantially improved in Scott's utopian reckoning, but to replicate such a model, the landowner must attain the proper sensibility, which, in this sense, aligns Scott with the sentimental ethos of Richardson. In such a model, so many lives are dependent on the genteel individual, and in this, Scott delineates the limits of her social critique. Scott, however, captures the essence of complex embodiment in her fiction, in which an array of factors inform (dis)ability. The ultimate indications of corporeal experience, for Scott, are to be found in the individual's class status as well as in their skin complexion and geographic location.

CONCLUSION

Samuel Richardson's use of narrative prosthesis in *Pamela* and Sarah Scott's sustained focus on complex embodiment throughout her writing career allow for a kaleidoscopic understanding of how physical ability was constituted in the contexts of labor and reform during the Age of Sensibility. Both authors use their novels to imagine society anew. Richardson, with his softening of the violent impulses of Mr. B.'s libertinism through Pamela's virtue and Mrs. Jewkes's queer deformity, and Scott, with her comprehensive reformist vision that addresses the vulnerability of so many people within British society, offer a diverse set of corporeal models in their novels. For Richardson, Mrs. Jewkes's body is merely symbolic and ultimately peripheral to the heterosexual romance that dominates the plot. Her place in the narrative is to make visible those mortal sins that are to be reined in if tranquil heterosexual domesticity is to be attained. Phased out by *Pamela*'s end, Mrs. Jewkes is not just a cautionary tale but the means by which Richardson establishes the harmonious tenor of Mr. B.'s household. For Scott, however, embodiment poses a dynamic set of representational possibilities. Her fiction reflects a deeper understanding of how the cultural and physical experiences of disability shift according to gender, sexuality, and race. Moreover, her interweaving of these facets of lived experience, along with the diseases and aging process that mark the body, underscore her body-oriented feminism, which shifts from novel to novel but which is always loyal to established class hierarchies. In light of these diverse authorial approaches that are, in their own necessarily limited ways, representative of the mid-eighteenth century, we observe a capacious set of possibilities for the body's role in reforming fictions. Queer, variable bodies such as Mrs. Jewkes's secure the primacy of heterosexuality, but also, as in *Millenium Hall*, configurations of disability and queerness exceed the metaphorical to become an embodied life course for those that do not adhere to the corporeal or classed standards of heterosexual domesticity. Disability thus plays a foundational role in granting legibility to heterosexuality and queerness at mid-century. Race functions as an analogue to disability for Scott, but this analogue is ultimately compromised by a racist ideology of ability based on the idea that black bodies represent the apotheosis of physical prowess, and by Scott's ultimate exoneration of chattel slavery. Such thinking resonates with contemporaneous views of black bodies as perfectible, as quintessentially able to perform the grotesque labor imposed upon them.

It might seem surprising that, given all of the attention to impairment and disease in her fiction, Scott offers no discussion of medicine or medical intervention. We might attribute this to Scott's propensity to imbue physical difference with moral, religious, and economic value. Scott shows little interest in the idea of medical treatment or health, perhaps because she is accustomed to the idea that, while physicians and medical experts often promised physical gains to those that suffered from disease or impairment, few *actual* gains occurred during the eighteenth century.[58] In any case, the idea of health was still an emerging concept at this time. Given Scott's representation of so much impairment and chronic illness, it is reasonable to surmise that any combination of these reasons may explain why doctors are all but absent in her fiction. Scott's silence on the matter, however, is not in standing with the wide proliferation of medical tracts that occurred throughout the later part of the eighteenth century. The authors of these pieces were professional writers like Scott and Richardson and were in need of money for sustenance. The line between certified doctor and quack, like successful writer and hack, was sometimes difficult to discern. In this utterly disordered environment, medical intervention, what we might think of today as a medical model of disability, hardly existed. The idea, for example, that a medical practitioner could "cure" a person with impairments was still in its embryonic stages.[59] Given this historical context, how might a novel about medicine, disease, and impairment add to our understanding of disabled and queer embodiment in the eighteenth century? Like Richardson and Scott, Tobias Smollett raises questions about the degree to which the body is a product of diverse factors, but he tackles other questions in his probing of the relationship—metaphoric and literal—between health and sexuality in his 1771 novel, *The Expedition of Humphry Clinker*, the subject matter of the following chapter.

NOTES

1. Armstrong argues that, through her speech and writing, Pamela becomes empowered against aristocratic modes of patriarchy. For Armstrong, the fact that Mr. B. is a member of the older landed gentry is crucial to Richardson's reformist rhetoric. In *Pamela*, the gentry is a "permeable" class that one could enter through marriage. Woman is thus shown to "negotiate" the terms of her sexual contract, rather than serve as mere object of exchange between men (120). With *Pamela*, Armstrong argues, Richardson creates a new ruling class, in which a servant girl converts the upper gentry and aristocracy to virtuous domestic values. Armstrong, *Desire and Domestic Fiction*, 125–141.
2. Mitchell and Snyder, *Narrative Prosthesis*, 47.
3. Siebers, *Disability Theory*, 30.
4. Ibid., 7–11. According to Siebers, the "ideology of ability" is "at it simplest a preference for able-bodiedness" and "as the baseline by which humanness is determined" (8).
5. Armstrong, *Desire and Domestic Fiction*, 120.
6. Watt, *The Rise of the Novel*, 135–173.
7. McKeon, *The Secret History of Domesticity*, 657–658.
8. Kelleher, *Making Love*, 131–168.
9. Richardson, *Pamela*, 114. All future references to the novel will appear in parenthetical citations.
10. Richardson's disparaging, colorful description invokes characterizations of male members of the ugly club in Liverpool, from around the same period, who were caricatured in a similar manner. *The Ugly Club Manuscript, 1743–1754* gives details about the physical appearance of ugly gentlemen that belong to this social club. In these descriptions, close, satirical attention is paid to an individual's facial features, such as what may be observed in Mrs. Jewkes. For instance, one John Kenyon is described in the following terms, "A very Oblong Visage. Sallow Complexion. Largeish Eyebrows. Cock Eye'd. A pretty long Nose. Lanthorn Jaws. On the whole very much like the Picture of King Charles 2nd in a huge full Bottom'd Wig." *The Ugly Club*, 38.
11. Mitchell and Snyder, *Narrative Prosthesis*, 53.
12. Ibid., 63.
13. Ibid., 53.
14. Scott, *A Journey through Every Stage of Life*, 2. All future references to the novel will appear in parenthetical citations.
15. Kelly, "Introduction" to *Millenium Hall*, 22.
16. Bannet, "Life, Letters, and Tales in Sarah Scott's *A Journey through Every Stage of Life*," 233–259.
17. Ula Klein explores same-sex eroticism and cross-dressing in *A Journey through Every Stage of Life* in "Eighteenth-Century Female Cross-Dressers and Their Beards," 119–143.
18. For readings of Fielding's *The Female Husband*, see Castle, "Matters Not Fit to Be Mentioned," 602–622; and Nicolazzo, "Henry Fielding's *The Female Husband*," 335–353.
19. According to the Vagrant Act of 1744, earning money through fraudulent means, as Leonora does, would be considered an act of vagrancy. See Nicolazzo, "Henry Fielding's *The Female Husband*."
20. Sarah Robinson married Sir George Lewis Scott, a mathematician and tutor to the Prince of Wales. Merely one year after their marriage in 1751, Sarah's brothers and father removed her from her husband's home. As Caroline Gonda and Betty Rizzo both note, the exact

reason for the newlyweds' separation is unknown—though Gonda surmises that it is likely due to some illicit behavior on George's part, and Rizzo speculates that he may have had same-sex relations, that he possessed "libertine inclinations," or that he discovered a romantic relationship between Sarah and Lady Barbara. See Gonda, "Sarah Scott and 'The Sweet Excess of Paternal Love,'" 522–523; Rizzo, *Companions Without Vows*, 304.

21. Siebers, *Disability Theory*, 25.
22. Ibid., 25.
23. Johns, *Women's Utopias of the Eighteenth Century*, 109.
24. Haggerty, *Unnatural Affections*, 93–94.
25. Nussbaum, *The Limits of the Human*, 156.
26. Lanser, "Befriending the Body," 184, 189.
27. Rizzo, *Companions Without Vows*, 311.
28. Ibid., 307.
29. Ibid., 311.
30. Sarah Scott, *Sarah Scott to Elizabeth Montagu, 15 January 1752*. Letter. From the Huntington Library, *Montagu Collection*.
31. Siebers, *Disability Theory*, 25.
32. Brown, "Sarah Scott, Sophie von La Roche, and the Female Utopian Tradition," 472–473.
33. Scott, *Millenium Hall*, 72. All future references to the novel will appear in parenthetical citations.
34. Davis, "Introduction: Normality, Power, and Culture," 1–14.
35. See Travis Chi Wing Lau's thought-provoking essay, "Before the Norm."
36. "Standard, n" *OED Online*.
37. Elizabeth Bearden argues that early modern conceptualizations of disability have been "oversimplified" and that "concepts of nature" help to define early modern disability. See Bearden, "Before Normal There Was Natural," 34.
38. As Susan Lanser has argued, sapphism is distinguishable from earlier homoerotic configurations and later lesbian ones in its class specificity. Lanser, "Befriending the Body," 184.
39. Lanser, "Bluestocking Sapphism and the Economies of Desire," 259–260.
40. Lanser, "Befriending the Body," 185, 189.
41. See Brideoake, *The Ladies of Llangollen*.
42. Gonda, "The Odd Women," 113.
43. Kelly, "Introduction" to *Millenium Hall*, 29.
44. For more on the significance of aging for Scott's representation of deformity in *Millenium Hall*, see Reeves, "Untimely Old Age and Deformity," 229–256.
45. In this, Scott aligns herself with William Hay, who argued against Sir Francis Bacon in his 1754 *Deformity: An Essay*. Bacon had written in 1612 that people with disfigured, crippled, or otherwise disabled bodies have "unnatural affections" due to the visibly apparent ways that they have been wronged by nature: "Deformed persons are commonly even with nature, for as nature hath done ill by them, so do they by nature; being . . . void of natural affection; and so they have their revenge of nature" (500). In other words, for Bacon corporeal difference guarantees social transgression: to be deviant in body is to be deviant in comportment. Bacon goes on to argue that this social liminality causes "deformed persons" to "rescue and deliver themselves" from the "scorn" of society (500). Since they have been subjected to ridicule, these individuals "watch and observe the weakness of others, that they may have somewhat to repay" for their various tribulations (500). Deformed persons, according to Bacon, are thus embittered and are to be watched closely. Hay counters this by arguing that deformity imbues an individual with virtue, temperance, and intellect. See Bacon, *The Works of Francis Bacon*; and Hay, *Deformity*.
46. Straub, *Domestic Affairs*, 1.

47. One of Scott's novels that I do not account for in this chapter is *Agreeable Ugliness*, her 1754 loose translation of a French novel, *La laiduer aimable*. I have written about this novel elsewhere, in Farr, "Attractive Deformity," 181–201.
48. Wilson, "The Performance of Freedom," 45–86.
49. In Britain itself, Scott's novel went through eleven printings by 1800. Beyond England, as Eve Tavor Bannet points out, there was an American edition of Scott's novel that emerged in 1774, James Humphrey's *The Real Man of Sensibility: Or the History of Sir George Ellison*, and later on, Scottish versions of *Ellison* appeared in 1795 and 1797. These versions considerably altered Scott's depictions of the plantation reform. See Bannet, "Sarah Scott and America," 631–656.
50. Ibid., 635–637.
51. Wilson, "The Performance of Freedom," 52.
52. Quoted in Edwards and Dabydeen, *Black Writers in Britain, 1760–1890*, 27.
53. Rizzo, "Introduction" to *The History of Sir George Ellison*, xxxii.
54. Rizzo argues that Scott was writing to support herself, and therefore did not have the luxury to throw caution to the wind in her representation of slavery. Ibid., xxv.
55. Roxann Wheeler argues that in eighteenth-century Britain, race was constituted in a far more fluid manner than it is today. Britons understood complexion to be mutable and informed by climate. Class, religion, and commerce, among other factors, informed "categories of difference" that informed racialized thinking. Wheeler, *The Complexion of Race*, 5–6.
56. Scott, *The History of Sir George Ellison*, 18. All future references to the novel will appear in parenthetical citations.
57. James, "Gwendolyn Brooks, WW 2, and the Politics of Rehabilitation," 136–158.
58. Porter, *The Greatest Benefit to Mankind*, 248.
59. A recent essay from Jared S. Richman explores an early example of the medical model of disability: the invention of speech pathology in the later eighteenth century in Britain. See Richman, "The Other King's Speech," 279–304.

3

CHRONIC ILLNESS, MEDICINE, AND THE HEALTHY MARRIAGES OF TOBIAS SMOLLETT'S *THE EXPEDITION OF HUMPHRY CLINKER* (1771)

A LITERARY HISTORY OF DISABILITY covering the eighteenth century would be incomplete without attending to some of the medical concerns that proliferated during the period. Given the ways in which disability and medicine are often in uncomfortable relation to one another, however, such an endeavor poses unique challenges. Beth Linker has called attention to the ways in which this plays out in historical inquiry. For Linker, historians of medicine and historians of disability rarely engage in shared conversations despite the various ways "in which the actual histories of disease and disability overlap."[1] This is because studies of medicine tend to focus on typical conceptions of disease history, in which impairing conditions that result from disease are hardly a primary concern, while disability scholars' mistrust of medicine, stemming from the curative, medical model of disability, often pushes medical history to the margins of their own inquiries.[2] However, as Linker persuasively argues, we can enhance our understanding of past and present configurations of embodiment and medicine if we examine these jointly.[3] As Emily B. Stanback has demonstrated with the publication of her recent book, *The Wordsworth-Coleridge Circle and the Aesthetics of Disability*, such cross-fertilization facilitates rich insights into the "porousness" of later eighteenth and early nineteenth-century conceptions of disability, medicine, literature, and science.[4] Tobias Smollett's novel *The Expedition of Humphry Clinker* (1771) is an ideal literary text for a critical disability-medical reading, for in it, Smollett imagines the disabling effects of chronic disease alongside a wide range of medical interventions. Smollett's last novel is an epistolary tale that offers multiple perspectives from an extended family of letter writers as they travel around the South of Britain and eventually up to Scotland and Wales. Along the way, they experiment with an array of therapeutic treatments for their physical and psychological disorders. The most prolific of these letter writers, an irascible, elderly gentleman named Matthew Bramble, often writes of the persistent pain he experiences due to his gout and rheumatism. Despite Bramble's eventual cure, *Humphry Clinker* is suggestive of the ineptitude of medicinal intervention to treat chronic disease, highlighting in turn the limitations of eighteenth-century medicine in managing pain and impairment.

Scholars have mined *Humphry Clinker* for its profound insights into eighteenth-century medicine. Paul-Gabriel Boucé, Aileen Douglas, Paul Erickson, Allen Ingram, B. L. Reid, and William West have explored the novel's charting of Bramble's "journey to health" with productive and illuminating results. However, critics have neglected to consider the disabled bodies that appear at almost every turn of this fictional expedition.[5] Their presence disrupts what Douglas identifies as the novel's progression from the "disorder" of illness and impairment to the "order" of health and ability.[6] Characters populating *Humphry Clinker* experience blindness and lameness, physical disfigurement, and an assortment of impairments and chronic diseases. Some of these characters, such as Bramble's sister, Tabitha Bramble, and his often unwell niece, Lydia Melford, write letters of their own; Humphry Clinker, the novel's impoverished titular character whom the family meets on the road from Bath to London (and who turns out to be Bramble's illegitimate son) suffers from fever and is at the point of starvation when he first appears as an emaciated "tatterdemalion"; and still other variable bodies hover around the periphery of the narrative, unsettling the novel's gradual consolidation of corporeal regularity.[7] These characters' "unruly resistance" to corporeal health provides much of the narrative drama and body-oriented comedy.[8] Smollett ultimately does not excise these non-normative bodies from the social world he imagines. In fact, manifestations of physical difference unsettle the plot until the very last epistles bring the novel to a close. As the narrative progresses—as the letter writers weave together a tale from varying viewpoints—illness and disability are converted into some semblance of health and ability. But ultimately, through his portrayal of characters "that resist or refuse the cultural scripts assigned to them," Smollett reworks to some extent the comedy genre, in which a happy marital resolution typically restores order to the imagined social landscape.[9]

And yet chronic pain, disability, and medical treatment are only part of Smollett's story, as the various romantic attachments that finally come to fruition by the novel's last epistles suggest. *Humphry Clinker* represents Bramble's transformation from ill codger to healthy gentleman even as it narrates a series of heterosexual courtships that end favorably despite the trials that regularly beset them. Bramble's physical constitution and the impaired, diseased bodies that often appear throughout the narrative mirror the cross-sex courtship disarray of spouse seekers, including Tabitha, Win Jenkins (Tabitha's servant), Lydia, and

Humphry Clinker. In each of these characters' romantic ventures, Smollett tethers illness and disability to courtship irregularity. That the narrative at last establishes bodily wellness and matrimonial harmony simultaneously is no coincidence; rather, these mutual resolutions confirm that, in their ideal form, health and heterosexual bliss appear as a linked state. From this perspective, the term *healthy marriage* functions as a lexical indicator of how robust bodies grant heterosexual romance its legibility and primacy, and offers a medical dimension to this book's exploration of heteronormativity and able-bodiedness in the eighteenth century. However, Smollett imagines various kinds of romance, including a marriage between Tabitha Bramble and Obadiah Lismahago, aging partners who represent a queer displacement of the reproductive futurity that *Humphry Clinker* otherwise asserts. By staging romance in this way, Smollett shows that aging and variable bodies have their own part to play in the construction of intimacies, for though his narrative at last would appear to eradicate disability and illness, these inevitable states of being loom on the horizon of the novel's closure. Even as Smollett's portrayal of chronic illness and disability serves the purposes of metaphor—the body in pain, after all, is a significant catalyst for the plot—*Humphry Clinker* also registers the embodied agony of chronic pain that insistently undermines its avowal of healthy heterosexuality.

LIBERTINE EXCESS AND GOUT IN THE EIGHTEENTH CENTURY

Beyond simply functioning as metaphors for narrative disorder, Smollett's diverse depictions of physical variability and chronic illness underscore the vulnerability of the body in Enlightenment Britain, a setting in which the grandiose promises of science did little to advance the treatment of disease and disability in spite of the explosion of medical print materials which promised to either explain or cure such conditions. As Roy Porter has shown, the eighteenth century was a time of "great expectations" and "disappointing results" for medicine.[10] Smollett frames gout in a multivalent manner, giving his readers insight into the physical and social difficulties of pain management, something that he himself confronted as he wrote the novel.[11] Undergirding Smollett's portrayal of pain is his sustained engagement with classed and gendered medical concerns of the day. Due to Smollett's own medical training, *Humphry Clinker* is conversant with medical tracts about chronic disease, many of which charged that wealthy men bring gout and rheumatism on themselves and that, consequently, they can also heal themselves by taking the right measures.[12] In what Boucé calls *Humphry Clinker*'s "therapeutic function," Bramble's journey represents a hopeful vision of an aging man who manages chronic pain not through medical intervention, but through exercise, travel, and the acquisition of a sense of pastoral calm that can only be appreciated in juxtaposition with the disarray and disquiet of town life.[13] What scholars have yet to parse, however, is the extent to which *Humphry Clinker* reinforces one of the lasting stereotypes of disabled embodiment: that impairment is an obstacle for the individual to overcome and that one may do so through perseverance. As disability studies scholars have argued time and again, however, the struggle for perfect health, or for wholeness, is an elusive fantasy.[14] *Humphry Clinker* participates in this fantasy by imagining health as an achievable state of being for resilient heterosexual characters.

In his depiction of the relationship between Bramble and his doctor, Smollett reveals the contours of contemporaneous doctor-patient dynamics. In the opening lines of the novel, for instance, Bramble writes in an epistle to his dear friend, Dr. Lewis, about what ails him, setting the stage for the forthcoming narrative that charts his family's voyage from the inaccessible cityscapes of South Britain, with its densely populated and irrationally organized cities and spa towns, to the pristine country vistas and purifying airs of Scotland and Wales: "The pills are good for nothing—I might as well swallow snowballs to cool my reins" (5). Bramble identifies the ineffectiveness of the medicine at his disposal and then proceeds to chide his doctor, "I have told you over and over, how hard I am to move; and at this time of day, I ought to know something about my constitution" (5). In his questioning of Dr. Lewis's diagnosis and prescription, Bramble takes ownership of his aging body, asserting an agency associated with his gender, class, and extensive experience with chronic disease and infirmity.[15] The invalid in this doctor-patient exchange diagnoses himself, which is far from unusual during a time in which "medicine without doctors . . . was a necessity for many and a preference for some."[16] Throughout the remainder of the novel, Bramble writes about his pain, lodges complaints, and tries out an array of medical treatments as he attempts to allay the excruciating symptoms of gout and rheumatism. Bramble's chronic condition is a formidable problem that both letter writer and doctor might diagnose and treat, though Bramble has the distinct advantage of holding forth through his numerous letters, while the doctor's voice is omitted entirely from the novel.[17]

Through his use of the epistolary genre, Smollett offers a unique, first-person perspective about gout's impact on the body and on social relations generally. The letters that provide the structure for the narrative—especially those written by Bramble—represent a hybrid form that joins medical case history with narrative. Much of *Humphry Clinker*'s satirical force derives from Bramble's acerbic correspondence with Dr. Lewis, which frames the patient-doctor relationship as a charged site for the speculative treatment of chronic disease. In the Georgian period, patients' letters to their physicians played a vital role in the medical diagnostic process. In fact, doctors often preferred written letters to face-to-face consultation. Given the paucity of medical instruments (such as stethoscopes) and the difficulty of diagnosing physical symptoms, doctors often relied on written sources for evidence of family history and detailed descriptions of patients' physical states.[18] Through the epistolary details of his discomfort, Bramble offers insights into a variety of treatments for chronic conditions, including bathing in and drinking the waters of Bath, cold bathing in the sea, taking herbal remedies, and using smelling salts. In this way, Bramble's letters permit readers to participate in a sorting out of viable medical practice from common forms of quackery that prescribe ineffective treatments to gout sufferers.

Scholars have discussed how profoundly contemporary medical discourse informs *Humphry Clinker* but overlook Bramble's sexuality when doing so. Smollett portrays the vexing physical and psychological symptoms that aging gentlemen suffer as a consequence of the "hot blood and unrestrained libertinism" of their youth (319). Bramble's letters advance a causal link between the pursuit of sensual pleasure and the enduring chronic pain that was thought to follow. Gout attacks were viewed as a stark reminder of what happens to unregulated appetites even as, paradoxically, the visible symptoms of gout—inflamed toes, wrapped feet, the wearing of flannel—were lauded as badges of honor, as indicators of a life well lived. Bramble's prior indulgence in food, drink, and sex illuminates the tension between the immediacy of pleasure and the eventual pain to follow.[19] Besides Bramble's grumbling over his body, another consequence of his previous pleasure-seeking appears in the form of his estranged, illegitimate son, Humphry Clinker. Crucially, Bramble's epistolary representations of his body and progeny indicate a measured call to modify libertine excess for medical rather than moral reasons. In this, *Humphry Clinker* diverges from other libertine-reform narratives, notably Samuel Richardson's *Pamela*, which, as I argued in the previous chapter, cultivates Mr. B.'s reform through the virtuous example and writings of Pamela and the surrogate body of Mrs. Jewkes. Earlier plays from the turn of the eighteenth century often sentimentalized the libertine, a reflection of ongoing calls to expunge sexual excess from cultural consciousness.[20] In *Humphry Clinker*, young gentlemen should be wary of indulgence not for moral reasons, nor for a virtuous heroine's chastity, but because of the impact that pleasurable pursuit will have on their bodies in the long run.

Because gout was so widespread among this class of men, physicians during the period wrote about it extensively as a gentleman's disease. Gout was regularly attributed to men who ate and imbibed freely, but it could also be viewed as a repercussion for the sating of their sexual desire.[21] Debates over this point had circulated in Europe as far back as the Renaissance. In 1534, for example, Dominicus Burgawer, a German physician, resuscitated Hippocrates's classical teachings about gout: "The disease also comes from . . . excessive venery, especially after meals, for Hippocrates and other philosophers say eunuchs and those who have nothing to do with women do not get it."[22] During the eighteenth century, physicians such as Blackmore and Hill contested this claim, extolling the virtues of exercise that passionate lovemaking granted men.[23] George Cheyne, one of the most influential of early eighteenth-century physicians due in part to his pioneering work on sensibility, assumed that sex was a given for gentlemen, but at the same time, he warned of its deleterious consequences. In the fourth edition of *An Essay on the True Nature and Due Method of Treating the Gout* (1722), Cheyne identifies infertility as a serious problem for genteel and aristocratic couples, arguing that "the Liberties Men take beyond Women, the Riot they run into, their continu'd Debauches" are ultimately responsible for the lack of offspring that was supposedly rampant during the time.[24] Cheyne's preoccupation with reproduction speaks to larger questions surrounding the system of primogeniture. Men from landed families, incapable of procreation due to alcoholic fervor and various forms of indulgence, eventually come to Bath in search of relief for their gout. For Cheyne, then, the individual body and the social body both suffer due to sexual and sensual indulgence, though he also accepts these as the predictable life course for wealthy gentlemen. *Humphry Clinker* appears to adhere to Cheyne's model for understanding gout. Smollett's narrative conveys that sensual pleasures run rampant among men of polite society, and it also explores the corporeal and social sanctions for men who have sex outside of marriage. Bramble embodies this medical truth. His gout and impoverished bastard son, Humphry Clinker, are problems in need of narrative resolutions, and yet these problems are precisely what makes Bramble's story a compelling narrative.[25] Perfect health and other such orderly representation would be "nonnarratable elements" characterized by their "incapacity to generate a story," as D. A. Miller might argue.[26]

Gout is as likely to be discussed as other medical problems in a Georgian context, given that it was such a prevalent chronic disease and the subject of so much controversy. Cheyne's ideas about gout were influential throughout the eighteenth century, but it was William Cadogan's *A Dissertation on the Gout*, published the same year as *Humphry Clinker*, that sparked intense debate in the early 1770's. Due to their almost simultaneous release, scholars often put Smollett and Cadogan into conversation with one another.[27] Though in many ways, Cadogan repackaged Cheyne's ideas, Cadogan stoked controversy because he argued that gout was a consequence of one's own doing and totally unrelated to heredity. Moreover, Cadogan reversed previous thinking about the relationship between an imbalance among the four humors (blood, black bile, yellow bile, phlegm) and the mind: whereas an imbalance of the humors was often considered to be the cause of mental distress, Cadogan assumes that a troubled mind could be responsible for an imbalance of the humors.[28] These startling (for the time) claims disavowed to some extent the "honorable reputation" of those that had gout; after all, Cadogan insisted that men incur the symptoms of that chronic illness from their "indolence, intemperance, and vexation."[29] Like Cheyne, Cadogan believes that men give way to their appetites too freely, indulging "the luxuries of the table, wine, music, women, and every sensuality," but he condemns these actions in a much more severe manner than Cheyne.[30] For Cadogan, luxury facilitates all manner of sensual indulgence, which he presents as existing in an intertwined fashion. The problem with pleasure, for Cadogan, is that the human body has only a limited capacity to process such mixed sensory signals: "Pleasure is not infinite, and our sensations are limited: we can bear but a certain measure, and all urging beyond it, infallibly brings pain in its stead."[31] Critics decried Cadogan's prescription for puritanical restraint because he argued that gentlemen cause their own corporeal misery through epicurean indulgence.[32] Cadogan's punitive view of gout entails that if one falls prey to the disease, then one may just as readily pull oneself out of it. To do so, Cadogan argues, the patient needs to eat simply, to exercise, to abstain from alcohol, and to get out of the city to spend time in open, natural settings.

Bramble gradually adheres to these health imperatives as the narrative of *Humphry Clinker* develops. He learns to eat well, for example, and his seeming lack of interest in sex reverses the indulgences of his earlier libertine life. This is all part of the most natural progression, as *Humphry Clinker* suggests: once the pleasures of the city have run the libertine aground, he may find a restoration of health in bucolic retirement far from the disarray of city life. Bramble arrives at this conclusion in a sure-footed manner when he visits an old friend from his university days, Charles Dennison. Like Bramble, Dennison once indulged in pleasure but has now retired to the country to his utmost benefit: "The objects he had in view, were health of body, peace of mind, and the private satisfaction of domestic quiet, unallayed by actual want, and uninterrupted by the fears of indigence. . . . He required nothing but wholesome air, pure water, agreeable exercise, plain diet, convenient lodging, and decent apparel" (322). The cure for the excesses of city living for wealthy gentlemen is in modest country retirement, where one may find the air "so healthy, that the natives are scarce ever visited by any other disease than the small-pox, and certain cutaneous evils" (250–251). The pastoral, open settings of Wales and Scotland counteract the infection-carrying miasmas characteristic of Bath and London because they contain a mostly disease-free atmosphere and afford a sanitary, restful lifestyle. Yet, while Dennison's retirement includes his peaceful coexistence with wife and family, Bramble has no wife of which to speak. In this, the novel offers two possible kinship outcomes for aging libertines: either nuclear familial retirement or bachelorhood. In either case, the libertine's journey is one of sexual and sensory indulgence, and the dues must be paid through painful symptoms that appear on the body. To alleviate such discomfort, Smollett suggests, the aging gentleman should remove himself from the *bon ton* to bucolic environs, for the city and spa towns that typically serve as the libertine's playground only perpetuate an unceasing cycle of pleasure and pain, as the Bath-based letters from *Humphry Clinker* make clear.

BATH: THE MAKING OF A MEDICAL AND CULTURAL CENTER

In the opening chapters of *Humphry Clinker*, Bramble seeks medical intervention for his bodily distress as he and his family travel from spa town to spa town, eventually arriving to Bath. Instead of experiencing diminished pain, Bramble finds in Bath an especially pernicious environment for his beleaguered body. Bath is one of the primary targets of Smollett's biting satire; he finds it a cesspool in which disease proliferates and the classes intermingle in indecorous ways. The most popular of late eighteenth-century British resort towns, Bath, with its public engagements and promises of health and pleasure, plays a substantial role as a setting in establishing the narrative's fraught relationship between impaired bodies and failed relationships.

During the eighteenth century, Bath became a culturally and medically vibrant center. By the time that *Humphry Clinker* appeared in print in 1771, Bath attracted large numbers of people seeking health and leisure. With its theater, balls, public walks, shops, gardens, and architecture that declared an affinity for Greek and Roman design, Bath became a travel destination or home for those that considered themselves part of an "international cultural elite."[33] Due to its fashionable reputation, and the promise of health that supplemented the various entertainments it afforded, Bath grew from a small town of 2,000 inhabitants in 1700 to a bustling municipality of 30,000 by 1800, at which point it became one of Britain's ten most densely populated cities.[34] Some years after the publication of *Humphry Clinker*, *The Original Bath Guide* (1811) would advertise Bath's recreational and salutary possibilities in the same breath: "As a place of public resort for the affluent, the gay, and the invalid, the city of Bath is become one of the most distinguished spots in the kingdom."[35] The dual aims of health and leisurely pursuits distinguished Bath in significant ways from London by offering a healthy alternative to the supposedly dissipating pastimes of the capital. A verse that appears in a number of works about Bath throughout the eighteenth and nineteenth centuries makes a seductive claim about the unblemished, disease-free character of Bath:

> When fevers bore an epidemic sway
> Unpeopled towns, swept villages away
> While death abroad dealt terror and despair
> The plague but gently touch'd within their sphere[36]

Such adulatory lines imagine Bath as a space in which the "terror and despair" of plague times become distant concerns. Beyond advocating one's safety from the ravages of incurable maladies, Bath promoters insisted that pleasure and health would accompany residents and visitors. Such promises reinforced a classed heteronormative order, or, as Peter Borsay puts it, a "context in which the ruling order was able to produce and reproduce itself."[37] As Borsay implies, cultural production and biological reproduction reinforced one another in Bath. At their most potent, the cultural endeavors of Bath shaped class-based ideologies, bringing heterosexual couples of the same or similar social standings together at the marriage altar. At the same time, however, Bath was a destination for those with chronic illness and disability seeking respite from what ailed them. This fusing of the improbable (perfect health, disease-free living) with the ostensibly inevitable (successful heterosexual courtship) is precisely what Smollett found worthy of his satire.[38]

EPISTOLARITY AND COURTSHIP FAILURE IN *HUMPHRY CLINKER*

The novel form, with its musings over love, embodiment, and the quotidian, allows Smollett to theorize chronic disease and resort town life in ways that the medical writing of the likes of Cadogan and Cheyne could not. Smollett's use of the epistolary genre in particular facilitates shifting points of view, with various characters revealing their desires, bodily turmoil, and wavering psychological states. Evan Gottlieb views this "multiplicity of voices" as an early example of Mikhail Bakhtin's *heteroglossia*, the novel's egalitarian representation of "competing voices, none of which is finally dominant."[39] There is little question, though, that the male voices in *Humphry Clinker* dominate, both in terms of the number of letters written, as well as the length of those letters. The limited space dedicated to the thoughts of the female characters, Lydia and Win, often represent the vicissitudes of women's embodiment, and in Tabitha's case, a professed desire for the accrual of money through parsimonious means. In spite of the dominance of men's writing, the novel's panoply of voices establishes early on the intertwined concepts of illness and courtship failure, especially in Bath, but also in London and other resort towns in South Britain.

The foremost of the letter writers, Matthew Bramble, pens "intolerably acrimonious" epistles from Bath to represent his absolute disgust with that town for its alienation of the very visitors it purports to serve (33). Among its many defects, Bramble relates, are Bath's streets, which are inaccessible to people with mobility impairments. Bramble describes a recently built portion of the city center, The Square, as "pretty well laid out" though "the avenues to it are mean, dirty, dangerous, and indirect" (34). The Circus, another recent addition to Bath, has an entrance that is "difficult, steep, and slippery" (35). Bramble's detailed account of the disabling effects of the streets' layout indicates Smollett's awareness of the ways in which a community's structural design can act as a barrier to people with impairments. Moreover, Bramble describes Bath's air as problematic for the "delicate and infirm" who, "like so many spunges," are exposed to the "moisture of the atmosphere . . . a charming check to the perspiration of a patient, piping hot from the Bath, with all his pores wide open" (35). The air itself, riddled with effluvia, is a source of impurity, while the cold humidity of Bath outstrips any good that might be gained from bathing in the hot springs. Bramble emphasizes the environmental inconveniences that only deepen the plight of the people that would benefit from their time in town. If gout is a disorder that one may overcome on one's own, as Cadogan suggests, then Bath, despite its promises of sociability and wellness, is the wrong place for such improvement to take place. For Smollett, Bath provides fodder for satirical scrutiny in part because it aggravates the maladies of the aged and disabled. There is no viable future for people like Bramble because the streets and environment actively work against them.

But the aged are not the only ones to suffer in Bath. *Humphry Clinker* portrays women, both young and old, as constituting a powerless group in Bath due to their precarious place in the marriage market. Gary Kelly views a yawning chasm between Smollett's last novel and what Sarah Scott imagines in *Millenium Hall*, in that Smollett "purports to show the urgent need to master the dangerous presumption and desire of the subaltern, especially women."[40] Such a reading of Smollett's assumed patriarchal premise, convincing though it may be, neglects to do justice to the attention that *Humphry Clinker* calls to women's vulnerability in public spaces, or to the ways in which that vulnerability is tied to a critique of the social conditions under which disabled and aging bodies suffer. According to the

Bath-based epistles, for example, compulsory heterosexuality is both sustained and compromised by the risks that women run of public exposure. In this, *Humphry Clinker* highlights unresolvable contradictions inherent in women's sociability. Though attending the social activities tied to the baths is an integral part of social life for women, Smollett's narrative suggests that to indulge in these activities is to invite body shaming as well as physical and psychological harm.

In Bath's public, therapeutic spaces, women are subjected to the exacting, impossible demands of modesty and chastity. This is apparent in one of Lydia's Bath epistles, in which she reveals the extent to which bathing serves the dual purpose of treatment and fashionable display for women, who are expected to observe the season's sartorial norms while also sustaining an appearance of innocence. Lydia writes of Tabitha's adherence to such social demands: "My aunt, who says every person of fashion should make her appearance in the bath, as well as in the abbey church, contrived a cap with cherry-coloured ribbons to suit her complexion" (39–40). Tabitha, face flushed and dressed to the nines, obliges her maid, Win, to accompany her to the King's Bath, the largest and hottest of the springs, where one might "see patients up to their necks in hot water" and women in "jackets and petticoats of brown linen, with chip hats, in which they fix their handkerchiefs to wipe the sweat off their faces" (39). Underlying Lydia's letter is a view of the absurdity that women should spend so much time cultivating their appearance for an activity that elicits such an unsavory bodily function as sweat. Lydia, looking on from the pump-room, observes Win "who wore a hat trimmed with blue" before moving to a psychosomatic depiction of her that draws on romance conventions: "What betwixt her wan complexion and her fear, she looked like the ghost of some pale maiden, who had drowned herself for love. When she came out of the bath, she took assofetida drops, and was fluttered all day; so that we could hardly keep her from going into hysterics" (40). Win, who is here subjected to hysterical fits during her bathing experience gone-awry, becomes another unruly body in the King's Bath, and she reveals in the very next letter that she had dropped her petticoat while bathing, exposing her body above "the sin" (43). Win's loss of cover transforms her into a sexual object. As Win herself reveals in her letter, the onlookers take note, gazing at her with curiosity and amusement, though "they could see nothing" (43). *Humphry Clinker* indicates that soaking in the springs jeopardizes women because it potentially exposes their bodies in the male-dominated public domain. Lydia's and Win's letters illuminate the fraught connection between salutary instability and sexual indiscretion due to the way that they compare Win to an archetypal character—the forlorn, suicidal heroine of romances—at the very moment of her panic attack.

Other resort towns besides Bath facilitate troubling displays, and not just for women. Later in the narrative, while sea bathing in Scarborough, Bramble relates in a letter that he is rescued by Clinker, who mistakenly thinks he is drowning. Bramble writes of the trouble that occurs as he plunges from a bathing machine into the cold sea water, "I had swam out a few strokes, when hearing a noise, I turned about and saw the wildness of terror in [Clinker's] aspect—Afraid he would get out of his depth, I made haste to meet him, when, all of a sudden, he seized me by one ear, and dragged me bellowing with pain upon the dry beach, to the astonishment of all the people, men, women, and children there assembled" (184). This passage conveys the violent frenzy which so often attends water scenes in Smollett's novel.[41] In this case, Clinker leaves Bramble on the beach to be "pointed at, as the monster that was hauled naked a-shore upon the beach" until Bramble responds to his "disgrace" by striking Clinker down and then taking "shelter in the machine" where his clothes are stowed (184). Any benefits that might be gained by sea bathing are shown to be outstripped by the pain and social shame which attend the characters in each of the bathing scenes. Like Win Jenkins, Bramble disturbs the gaze of observant bystanders, who revel in the spectacle of his uncovered body. Win's and Bramble's parallel experiences suggest that women and invalid men alike should guard against public exposure for an activity that is entirely ineffective. As Bramble complains early on in the narrative, the typical bather "sacrifices his precious time, which might be employed in taking more effectual remedies and exposes himself to the dirt, the stench, the chilling blasts, and perpetual rains" (24). But almost as significant as the health hazards, bathers face the troubling possibility that they will deviate from decorum through the exhibition of their bodies. Such corporeal exposure is indicative of Smollett's tendency to use spa locales to critique the vulgar display of "diseased" or "deformed" bodies and supports contemporaneous critiques of bathing by the likes of Cadogan. What is more, these displays pinpoint a social ill in which body shaming is promoted by unscrupulous, voyeuristic onlookers who have no qualms with staring and pointing, imposing shame on the objects of their stare.

Tabitha is likewise subjected to uncertainty and harm in Bath as she searches out a male companion. Jery's epistles often make light of his Aunt Tabitha's quest "to avoid the reproachful epithet of old maid" (60). Tabitha is, as Jery describes her, "[a] maiden of forty-five. In her person she is tall, raw-boned, awkward, flat-chested, and stooping; her complexion is sallow and freckled; her eyes are not grey, but greenish, like those of a cat, and generally inflamed; her hair is of a sandy, or rather dusty hue; her forehead low; her nose long, sharp, and, towards the extremity, always red in cool weather; her lips skinny, her mouth extensive, her teeth straggling and loose, of various colours and conformation; and her long neck shrivelled into a thousand wrinkles" (60). Like Richardson's portrayal of Mrs. Jewkes, Jery's unflattering portrait of his aunt's features focuses especially on the contours and character of her face, and this passage in particular serves up a physiognomic indicator of her "temper": "she is proud, stiff, vain, imperious, prying, malicious, greedy, and uncharitable" and, as is often the case in such stock portrayals of old maids, her character "has been soured by disappointment in love" (60). Further, Tabitha's catlike eyes resonate with her nickname "Tabby." Cats in the eighteenth century were often associated with witchcraft, evil, and unregulated sexuality, and Tabitha's animalization here is clearly meant as a dig at the behavior of aging women who express sexual desire beyond their reproductive years.[42] Because of this, Tabitha is represented as physically and morally repugnant, a constant source of consternation to her brother, who abides her companionship due to the fact that she is his responsibility. Because her body is depicted as monstrous and hypersexual, it is fitting that she later becomes a Methodist, a religion that is widely viewed throughout the eighteenth century as excessive and objectionable.[43]

Throughout the narrative, Tabitha is subjected to highly physical forms of comedy, especially in Bath, where she eagerly pursues Sir Ulic MacKilligut. Tabitha makes her marital intentions clear to her housekeeper, Mrs. Gwyllim, in an early Bath letter, one of the few she writes throughout the novel: "Well, patience is like a stout poney; it bears a great deal, and trots a great way; but it will tire at the long run. Before its long, perhaps I may shew Matt, that I was not born to be the household drudge to my dying day" (44). Tabitha is aware of the burden she is on her brother and of her liminality as a single, never-married woman. In Sir Ulic Mackilligut, Tabitha finds an aged companion that could solve these problems. As Jery relates, Sir Ulic also has a distinctive body. He is a "poor Irish knight" who is "blind of one eye, and lame of one foot" (29, 30). When he first stumbles upon Sir Ulic, Jery laughs "to excess" at the spectacle of Sir Ulic leading a pupil that he is instructing on the finer points of dance (29). Sir Ulic's various disabilities are meant to make his interest in Tabitha all the more ludicrous given Tabitha's advanced years and her own physical constitution. Sir Ulic's presence in the narrative is short-lived, but his brief, thwarted courtship of Tabitha is a comic register of the impossibility of heterosexual romance in Bath, especially for the aging. Once he discovers that he has overvalued Tabitha's financial worth, Sir Ulic abandons his plans, taking the "first opportunity of incurring her displeasure decently" when he kicks Tabitha's beloved lapdog, Chowder, in the jaw while intervening in a chaotic scene at a ball, eliminating their potential union (63).[44] The various blunders that characterize this thwarted courtship contribute to the novel's critique of Bath as a locale that fails to make good on its promises

[115]

to promote the interests and well-being of consumers seeking pleasure, health, and marital prospects. The very same might be said of Tabitha's niece, Lydia, who suffers from headaches and melancholia as a mysterious "stroller" named Wilson seeks her acquaintance but is driven away by her overprotective brother, Jery. In this way, *Humphry Clinker* conveys that Bath harms the individual body while counteracting the advancement of the social body. In Bath, ill and disfigured bodies disrupt stability: single men and women become more desperate in their ploys for romance even as "stout" ponies "tire at the long run" (44). Such an alignment of disability and illness with heterosexual failure reinforces Smollett's gloomy view of crowded city spaces.

Another character that functions as an indicator of South Britain's disarray is Humphry Clinker, who appears as the group travels from Bath to London. Clinker's initial impression on the travelers is far from favorable due to an unsettling chronic illness that has altered his figure into something unsightly in Tabitha's eyes. His poverty is apparent in his partial nudity, another indicator of bodily vulnerability. Tabitha shrinks away from Clinker, whom she views as "a filthy tatterdemalion" (82). The group soon learns of the cause of his bedraggled state: he has been "taken ill of the ague, which disabled him from getting his bread" (82). Clinker, unable to labor, is at the point of starvation, but Bramble's characteristic sensibility takes hold, and he promptly hires Clinker as his driver. Diseased and exposed, Clinker fits right in with Win's naked appearance in the baths. These nude scenes align the two servants early on in the narrative. Like Win and the other characters, Clinker's body is a source of consternation that must be in some way resolved by the novel's closure. In fact, all of the major characters, with the exception of Jery, become ill while in South Britain. The narrative makes clear that these characters must become healthy for heterosexual romance to be viable. It is perhaps no surprise, then, that as illness and disability reign supreme in the Bath chapters of the novel, the possibility for other forms of connection that fall outside of the marriage plot are also given due consideration.

THE PROSPECT OF DISABILITY COMMUNITY

Beyond its exploration of youthful heterosexual courtship, *Humphry Clinker* also raises the possibility of intimate, male homosocial relationships among the aged and disabled. During the travelers' visit to Bath, for instance, two of Bramble's epistles explore disabled homosociability. Bramble relates to Dr. Lewis that he encounters a number of old friends, who have likewise become convalescents, in a coffee house: "We consisted of thirteen individuals; seven lamed by the gout, rheumatism, or palsy; three maimed by accident; and the rest either deaf or blind. One hobbled, another hopped, a third dragged his legs after him like a wounded snake, a fourth straddled betwixt a pair of long crutches, like the mummy of a felon hanging in chains; a fifth was bent into a horizontal position, like a mounted telescope, shoved in by a couple of chairmen; and a sixth was the bust of a man, set upright in a wheel machine, which the waiter moved from place to place" (54–55). Bramble perceives the assembly as linked by friendship, old age, and various forms of impairment—some caused by sensual indulgence, others by aging, and still others by unforeseen accidents. Bramble's grouping together of chronic disease with sensory and mobility impairment shows that elderly communities are forged in part by a shared experience of the body in pain. Whether these characters have had the misfortune of being crippled in war, or maimed during a fox hunt, or unduly exposed to the elements, they all gather at the coffee shop in fellowship to laugh at themselves: "The spirits and good-humour of the company seemed to triumph over the wreck of their constitutions. They had even philosophy to joke upon their own calamities; such is the power of friendship, the cordial of life" (56). Smollett's comic dehumanization of the various gentlemen is in line with contemporaneous accounts of self-deprecating men who deviate from physical standards. Through similes comparing the men to animals and a "mounted telescope," Smollett captures the supposed absurdity of the bodily postures that await those who live long enough to experience them. Here, Smollett invokes Richard Steele's proposition for the organization of ugly clubs in the early eighteenth century, in which variably-embodied or "ugly" men gathered together regularly in fellowship to ridicule each other and to make light of their bodies and visages.[45] As Steele's ugly club *Spectator* makes clear, ugly men were expected to find humor in their appearance, regardless of the cause. By learning to laugh at themselves, the men could make themselves more agreeable to peers and neighbors. Smollett's coffee shop passage, then, promotes the idea of a self-deprecating, disabled community of aging men.

Bramble, however, goes on to reveal that such gatherings are ill-suited to provide the necessary aid and succor for variable bodies. On the heels of the passage about good humor, Bramble finds each of the men "not without their moments, and even hours, of disquiet"; when he interacts with the men one-on-one, Bramble discovers that each of them "expatiated upon his own particular grievances; and they were all malcontents at bottom—Over and above their personal disasters, they thought themselves unfortunate in the lottery of life" (56). Bramble's letter suggests, then, that physical pain and impairment are felt entirely by the individual and that the formation of community cannot mollify the precarious conditions attributed to aging. In his essay about deformity, William Hay

(1754) uses a similar analogy of lottery-play to capture the shame one feels about bodily difference: "Bodily deformity is very rare: and therefore a person so distinguished must naturally think, that he has had ill luck in a lottery, where there are above a thousand prizes to one blank."[46] For Hay, most people "win" at the lottery because they fit the physical mold cast by social codes, but for those whose embodiment is so at odds as to stand out in a crowd, despair is inevitable. One feels rare, Hay affirms, a solitary loser. Like Hay, who finds ugly clubs deficient in a number of ways, Bramble uncovers the failures of the ugly club to root out despondence. The aged gentleman alone shoulders his condition, and disability in this context is imagined as occurring solely within the body of the individual, rather than in the built environment.

Subsequently, Bramble captures the deleterious effects of fashionable life on the mature population that forms a significant part of Bath's demographics, concluding that there is no cure or comfort for his solitary friends. Bramble writes that they have "long left off using the waters, having experienced their inefficacy" (56). The town as a whole has "become a mere sink of profligacy and extortion," driving these men and their families to remote, more affordable parts, such as the mountains of Wales or Exeter (57). Bramble believes that the "flood of luxury and extravagance" will follow them, however, obliging them to shift about from place to place until their dying breath (57). Some of Bramble's companions have long felt the sting of financial precariousness, whether through excessive living or decrepitude, or some combination of the two. Bramble imagines no courtship possibilities for these men, who "murder in private parties, among peevish invalids, and insipid old women" (57). Bramble's views reveal that the elderly were expected to remain autonomous as long as possible, which undermines our current widespread understanding that in the past, families were more willing to maintain an intergenerational household.[47] Such a scenario seems to be the case for these men. Alone and downcast, they seek what they ultimately cannot find in Bath: fellowship and the allaying of their pain. Through Bramble's letter writing, Smollett establishes the social and medical environments of Bath as ill-suited for the well-being of the elderly and the young alike, mocking the notion that Bath could be a respite for the aged, disabled, and chronically ill.

Smollett also explores the idea of disabled homosociability among younger individuals who perform disability for money. In London, Jery, who himself functions as a standard-bearer of genteel masculinity and health throughout the narrative, encounters a group of Grub Street authors, an "odd race of mortals" who pretend to be disabled as a way to "distinguish" themselves "by some oddity or extravagance" because they are "dull authors" in need of a compensatory personality (125). The distinction between this "odd race" and that of Bramble's companions is pronounced, given the performance of Jery's group. Jery describes one such writer that "made use of crutches, because, once in his life, he had been laid up with a broken leg, though no man could leap with more agility" (125) Another author feigns delicacy, though he is "the son of a cottager, born under a hedge, and had many years run wild among asses on a common," and another "affected distraction" in his sudden ejaculations of "dreadful oaths" and hissing serpent sounds (125). Still another of the men affects a stammer, which he at first "counterfeited" but cannot leave off because it has "become so habitual." (125). This authorial gathering is indicative of widespread anxieties surrounding the truth of disability—its susceptibility to be exploited by con men—another long-standing stereotype that *Humphry Clinker* reproduces. Public outcries against beggars that feigned blindness or disfigurement to solicit alms from charitably minded passersby reached full pitch during the eighteenth century.[48] These Grub Street authors, then, occupy a similar status to that of street mendicant. Jery writes that one of these writers, Tim Cropdale, uses a variety of disability disguises. He "literally lives by his wit, which he has exercised upon all his friends in their turns" (129). Jery reveals that Tim had once borrowed his horse only to sell it off for money. When Jery attempts to confront Tim in the street and physically beat him, "Cropdale metamorphosed into a miserable blind wretch, feeling his way with a long stick from post to post" to evade the beating (130). Cropdale performs blindness to evoke pity and thereby escape punishment. Jery imagines Grub Street authors in general as willing to do whatever it takes for a shilling. In Jery's damning description of these authors, disability becomes a potential site of affected idiosyncrasy and fraud, in which men desperately procure a living in a cutthroat industry. Their profession proves unappealing to Jery, for it "is at best but a desperate resource against starving, as it affords no provision for old age and infirmity" (133). Unlike Bramble's genteel friends in Bath, this class of men would have no monetary resources upon which to rely in old age.

As the congregations of Bramble's elderly companions and Jery's author friends make clear, homosociability among the disabled briefly materializes only to be dismissed as improbable or disingenuous. However, Smollett's capacious representation of bodily postures, abilities, and shapes indicates his investment in theorizing the meaning of chronic disease and disability. Bodies eventually waste away and fail, while potential relationships dissolve under the firm pressure of the cold humidity, crowded ballrooms, and stilted airs of Grub Street. There is no respite from such malignity unless one moves as far away from the effluvia as possible. In *Humphry Clinker*, Bramble and his family's flight from the fetid urban centers of

South Britain runs north to the idyllic countryside of Scotland and Wales, where hope for health and marriage becomes possible due in large part to clean air and culinary simplicity.

HUMPHRY CLINKER'S ROBUST MARITAL RESOLUTIONS

The letter writers that compose *Humphry Clinker* eventually shift their tone from despair over ongoing health concerns and courtship travails in Bath and South Britain to optimism for better salutary living to come, setting the stage for the felicitous concluding marriages characteristic of the comedy genre. A series of events mark this narrative transformation. Of paramount significance is the expedition itself: the group's travels to Scotland and Wales appear to have an overall positive effect on each of the characters.[49] For instance, as he readies to cross the Tweed River dividing England from Scotland, Bramble at last seems content, a drastic alteration from previous letters. While writing from Durham, Bramble remarks upon the pastoral beauty of Northumberland, "a fine country, extending to the Tweed, which is a pleasant pastoral stream" (202). Smollett's juxtaposition of urban disarray with bucolic beauty indicates the country's superiority. The food up north is also an improvement, a stark change from London's "deleterious paste" that is "destructive to the taste" (217). In Edinburgh, Bramble remarks upon the "good fish," "remarkably fine" bread, and "excellent water" (217). Bramble finds in the north what he could not find in Bath: delicious food and exercise, an amelioration of his corporeal distress, and the calming of his overstimulated nervous system. Travel and mobility have been the catalysts for Bramble's shift in disposition, and the painful symptoms of gout and rheumatism no longer saturate his epistles.

The letters also begin to highlight promising courtships, reflecting the novel's progression toward heterosexual romantic fulfillment. It is no coincidence, for example, that in the letter prior to the one in which he rejoices over his newfound health, Bramble speculates about the love interests of Tabitha and Win Jenkins, who fall for Captain Obadiah Lismahago and Humphry Clinker, respectively. However, these couplings are not without their obstacles. Win causes "a violent contest" between Clinker and Dutton, the former, a working-class hero, the latter of whom is Jery's servant and another would-be suitor for Win (207). Jery's intercession in the affair between Dutton and Clinker has "kindled the flames of discord in the family" (207). However, as Dutton is excised from the narrative, attitudes begin to shift. The sequence of these letters suggests that as the narrative's lasting relationships begin to take root, the characters' states of health improve, bodily manifestations of the order characteristic of the novel's concluding pages. In the following letter, Jery acknowledges that "Love . . . is resolved to assert his dominion over all the females of our family" (208). Love, it seems, has brought along with it strife, especially in the form of the inconsolable Lydia, who has not let go of Wilson, the suitor and "stroller" that seems to follow her everywhere she goes (208). Jery meanwhile continues to exist outside of the romance plot, never mentioning prospective mates. In short, there are still a number of narrative conflicts to be resolved at this point, but as the caravan moves north of the Tweed, the romantic couples begin to flourish at the same time that these characters achieve salutary stasis.

The restored health of Bramble is certainly one significant feature of the narrative's development, but the headaches, hysterical fits, and other maladies of the female characters continue until the end of the narrative. Lydia appears the most vulnerable to shifting bodily ailments of all of the women, alternating between good spirits and the melancholic symptoms of an inhibited lover. The rapidity with which she moves between divergent health states is not reconciled until one of the narrative's mysteries resolves itself: her love interest, Wilson, turns out to be George Dennison, the son of Charles Dennison, Bramble's old school mate. After repeated failures in tracking down Lydia, George returns home to his father's estate in the Scottish countryside where he is "seized with a dangerous fever, which overwhelmed his parents with terror and affliction" (329). George's restoration to full health and vivacious spirits occurs as he lays eyes on Lydia, now a guest in his father's home: "Is it possible, (cried he) that my senses do not play me false!—that I see Miss Melford under my father's roof—that I am permitted to speak to her without giving offence—and that her relations have honored me with their countenance and protection?" (330). As George's emotions seize him, the families go about writing up the documents for the impending marriage, achieving the narrative's ideal realization of marriage.

Another happy marriage that marks the novel's ending is that of Clinker and Win, whose union represents Smollett's attempt to account for the servant class and to remedy the wrongs of Bramble's youth. For his part Clinker undergoes a significant physical and spiritual transformation from the time of his initial appearance in the narrative as a starving and chronically ill vagrant. Soon after beginning his service to Bramble, Jery discovers Clinker "holding forth" on the virtues of religion to a Methodist congregation, singing psalms with "peculiar graces" (137). Bramble does not take well to this at first, especially considering his traditional view of Methodism as an insurgent belief system that threatens Anglican restraint.[50] Clinker's methodizing has an immediate impact on Tabitha and Win, who follow him into the fold. In time, Bramble comes around to his religious

[121]

practice. As Misty Anderson argues, Methodism comes to play a critical role in the cultivation of a unifying sociability for the family: "[Bramble]'s secular, sociable sympathy and Clinker's 'primitive Christianity' work well together as components of a dialogic cure for the chaos, luxury, and alienation of modern life."[51] Bramble is attracted to Clinker's "simplicity, warmed with a kind of enthusiasm," but there is clearly something more to their connection, and of course, the realization that they are estranged father and son becomes apparent by novel's end (153).

Clinker's physical strength is another means by which he and Bramble form an ideal partnership. Clinker demonstrates his vitality when he rescues both Bramble and Win Jenkins from certain destruction in a scene that marks a fundamental rebirth for Bramble.[52] As Bramble, Tabitha, and Win ford a river in their carriage, a rush of water from the previous night's storm breaks through a mill head, knocking the carriage over (313). After rescuing and safely depositing Win on the shore of the river, "he flew like lighting to the coach, that was by this time filled with water, and, diving into it, brought up the poor 'squire, to all appearance, deprived of life!" (313). Clinker takes Bramble "up in his arms, as if he had been an infant of six months, carried him ashore" (313). Clinker carries Bramble to safety, and in this transaction we observe contemporary, classed stereotypes of manhood: the working-class Clinker utilizes his robust body, while Bramble, a man of leisure, depends upon his servant/son for escape. After successfully saving Bramble from certain death, Clinker "danced about in such a distracted manner" (314). At this point, Clinker is a far cry from what was once his agued, emaciated form. There is evidence here of a viable future for him and his bride-to-be, Win, in addition to the matrimonial bliss soon to be attained by Lydia and Young Dennison. In each of these pairings, young, healthy bodies come together at the altar of marriage. Smollett's assertion of heterosexuality is thus contingent on the attainment of health.

LISMAHAGO, TABITHA, AND THE QUEERNESS OF AGED BODIES

The possibilities for marital bliss in *Humphry Clinker* include the union of aging characters. In its pairing of Tabitha with Captain Obadiah Lismahago, an aging gentleman, Smollett's novel registers its queerest articulation of kinship. Cynthia Port argues that, in the same way that *queer* reconceptualizes temporality, old age potentially undermines heteronormativity. For Port, the old and the queer both "have projected onto their bodies that which normative culture fears and represses within itself: the knowledge of eventual bodily failure and mortality."[53] Port sees in both the aged and the queer a potential insurgency against the promises of reproductive futurity, as each stand "outside mainstream temporalities" and resist "the promise of the future."[54] Jane Gallop concurs in her alignment of crip theory with aging studies, arguing that aged bodies refuse "worship of the future."[55] Such queer renderings of aging are useful for conceptualizing the body and temporality in *Humphry Clinker*. Through Tabitha and Lismahago, Smollett articulates a resistance to reproductive futures by imagining marriage as accessible to those in their advanced years. In this, *Humphry Clinker* offers a queerness that unsettles the pairing of the more youthful companions, and the novel's otherwise robust worship of the future is disturbed by the alternative temporalities raised by Tabitha and Lismahago.

In her search for a mate, Tabitha's propensity to "shoot at every sort of game" eventually pays dividends when the travelers cross paths with a physically impaired war veteran, Captain Obadiah Lismahago, who offers another dimension to the novel's rich canvas of physical disability and aging (190). Jery narrates his initial impressions of the Scotsman, who makes an unforgettable entrance to the novel as "a tall, meagre figure, answering, with his horse, the description of Don Quixote mounted on Rozinante" (188). Jery moves from quixotic descriptors to a distinctive physical description of Lismahago, who "stooped very much; was very narrow in the shoulders, and very thick in the calves of his legs. . . . As for his thighs, they were long and slender, like those of a grasshopper" (188). As is often the case with representations of physically disabled people of the time, Smollett imbues Lismahago's corporeality with animalistic dimensions. Lismahago's physiognomy is also noteworthy: "His face was, at least, half a yard in length, brown and shriveled, with projecting cheek-bones, little grey eyes on the greenish hue, a large hook-nose, a pointed chin, a mouth from ear to ear, very ill furnished with teeth, and a high, narrow fore-head, well furrowed with wrinkles" (188). Lismahago's facial features align him with Tabitha, whom Jery likewise describes in unappealing ways. His eyes, also greenish and gray, his physiognomy, sharp and animalistic, likewise link him to Tabitha.

As in his description of Tabitha, Smollett depicts Lismahago to aid in his decidedly physical form of comedy. When Lismahago first appears in the narrative, Jery represents him as a spectacle due to a series of comic errors that expose his body's imperfections. As Lismahago attempts to dismount from his horse, "The girth unfortunately gave way, the saddle turned, down came the cavalier to the ground, and his hat and periwig falling off" displaying "a head-piece of various colours, patched and plaistered in a woeful condition" (188). Lismahago's fall reveals an injured scalp, which immediately becomes an object of humor and concern to the inn's patrons: "For certain plebeians that were about the door, laughed aloud, in the belief that the captain had got either a scald head, or a broken head, both equally opprobrious." Meanwhile, "the ladies, at the window above, shrieked with affright, on the supposition that the stranger had received some notable damages in his fall" (188). The observers' different responses to Lismahago divide along gender lines, but regardless, his scalp draws stares. Lismahago finds himself in good company, though, since some of the other travelers in Bramble's party have distinctive embodiments of their own.

Because such visible difference requires an explanatory narrative, Lismahago's prominent head wound becomes the catalyst for a frame tale. Unlike Sir Ulic MacKilligut, whose corporeality is one-dimensional—a laughable, ridiculous counterpart to Tabitha—or even Bramble, whose chronic diseases are a consequence of his "unrestrained libertinism" and genteel privilege, Lismahago's condition is granted reverence due to his status as a military veteran. Lismahago justifies the state of his head wound: "The condition you saw it in, is neither the effects of disease, nor of drunkenness; but an honest scar received in the service of our country" (189). Lismahago's sorting out of "honest scars" from "disease" and "drunkenness" is suggestive of a hierarchy of impairment, in which some wounds or conditions cannot be morally justified while others are worthy of praise or dignity. The merit of a malady, Lismahago's inset narrative suggests, depends entirely on the circumstances surrounding the cause of the impairment in question. David Turner affirms the peculiar ways in which disabled ex-servicemen elicited the sympathy of nondisabled people by recounting their tales of "heroism and suffering" during the late eighteenth century, and this certainly is the case here.[56] Lismahago's aging is complicated by the traumatic wounds of military combat, while in the case of Bramble, the moral paucity of excessive living. *Humphry Clinker* assigns these scenarios significant class dimensions: Bramble is fortunate to enjoy the positive effects of travel to find the environment that is most suitable to the maintenance of his various conditions, while Lismahago's military service elicits moral feeling.

Lismahago's head wound becomes the talking point for a transatlantic captivity narrative, which converts Lismahago into an object of sympathy in the course of his fast-growing acquaintance with Bramble and his family. Lismahago gains further credibility with the group as he tells them of his various adventures during wartime in North America against the Miamis during the colonial battles between England and France during the Seven Years War. The group soon learns of his scalping at the hands of "a party of Indians" at Ticonderoga, who "broke his scull with the blow of a tomahawk, and left him for dead on the field of battle"

(189). As the group hears more about his captivity and subsequent hardships, they are overwhelmed by sentiment: "There is no hold by which an Englishman is sooner taken than that of compassion—We were immediately interested in behalf of this veteran—Even Tabby's heart was melted" (189). Their sympathy turns to outrage when they discover that, though he was born a gentleman, Lismahago has not had the financial means to rise in rank in a timely manner: "In the course of two sanguinary wars, he had been wounded, maimed, mutilated, taken, and enslaved, without ever having attained a higher rank than that of lieutenant" (189). Despite these injustices during two wars—the War of the Austrian Succession and the Seven Years War—Lismahago is reluctant to complain or make himself into an object of pity, "If I have not been lucky in the lottery of life, so neither do I think myself unfortunate" (190). Lismahago's unwillingness to feel sorry for himself provides a significant contrast to Bramble's company of aging men at Bath, who "thought themselves unfortunate in the lottery of life" (56). According to Turner, contemporary stock characterizations of ex-servicemen consisted in "a combination of modesty, courage, and refusal to blame others or make excessive claims on the emotions (or pockets) of . . . observers" and that this "confirmed [their] fitness as an object of compassion."[57] Unlike these popular portrayals, though, such as the 1799 account of a wounded soldier in G. M. Lewis's "The Disabled Seaman," who returns home having lost an eye and a leg only to then lose out on the love of his life, Lismahago enters the romance plot; he quickly gains the attention of Tabitha, who proclaims him "the prettiest gentleman" she has "ever seen" (198). Though this courtship is another manifestation of Smollett's relentless corporeal satire, it is noteworthy that Lismahago, aged and variably-embodied, is granted sexual subjectivity. Smollett offers in Lismahago a dynamic, three-dimensional register of variable embodiment in the context of war, masculinity, and aging.

Lismahago's part in the narrative serves a crucial function, for, like Bramble, he eventually acquires the physical agility that he lacks when he first appears in the narrative. Lismahago joins Bramble in the narrative trajectory toward corporeal rejuvenation. His newfound agility corresponds with his inclusion in the romance plot. By the end of the novel, Lismahago's vigor astounds the very people that he once disconcerted with his scalp wound. In a family celebration at Brambleton-Hall that marks the occasion of the impending marriages, Lismahago performs the part of Pierrot, the servant character from *Harlequin Skeleton*, and this performance is suggestive of his newfound vitality. As Lismahago flees the skeleton that represents death, "his horror became most divertingly picturesque, and seemed to endow him with such preternatural agility as confounded all the spectators" (346–347). Like Duncan Campbell, this passage is perhaps another eighteenth-century version of the supercrip: a disabled person who overcomes their impairment through seemingly impossible means. Lismahago's performance is indicative of his new disposition, which, like Bramble, has become sunnier: "From being reserved and punctilious, he is become easy and obliging. He cracks jokes, laughs and banters, with the most facetious familiarity; and, in a word, enters into all our schemes of merriment and pastime" (347). This is all to suggest that, though well advanced in years, Lismahago not only staves off death with his unexpected marriage to Tabitha, but that he finds health in doing so. The marriage between these two characters opens up the possibility for romance to rejuvenate aged partners.

The narrative further ensures that the relationship between Lismahago and Tabitha is consummated in a way that leaves little doubt as to the successful outcome. Lismahago soberly approaches the wedding night "with something arch and ironical" in his countenance (347–348). On the day following their matrimonial copulation, Jery remarks upon his vigor: "He sighs, and ogles, and languishes at this amiable object; he kisses her hand, mutters ejaculations of rapture, and sings tender airs. . . . In order to shew how little his vigour was impaired by the fatigues of the preceding day, he this morning danced a Highland saraband over a naked back-sword, and leaped so high, that I believe he would make no contemptible figure as a vaulter at Saddler's Wells" (349). From wounded war hero to athletic dancer and vigorous lover, Lismahago undergoes an incredible physical transformation. The narrative's concluding pages insist on his virility, transforming him into a healthy husband capable of complying with the strictures of marriage while upholding the significance of manly strength and bodily agility. However, despite his newfound virility and Tabitha's "fulsome . . . approbation of the captain's love," there is little doubt that this couple will not procreate given their advanced years (349). Tabitha and Lismahago, while in good health and spirits, offer an alternative to the reproductive futurity of the other marriages.

Bramble, on the other hand, remains firmly outside of the romance plot as he writes one last letter to his most intimate companion, Dr. Lewis. Bramble at last seems to have found the health he has sought throughout his journey. Finally, as he prepares to return to his estate at Brambleton Hall, Bramble relates to Dr. Lewis of his newfound health in Wales: "As I have laid in a considerable stock of health, it is to be hoped you will not have much trouble with me in the way of physic, but I intend to work you on the side of exercise" (351). In this, Bramble gestures toward the possibility of future visits in person from his "dear doctor." It is clear that at this stage in Bramble's life, male companionship is what he desires most. He has the foresight to maintain his active mind and body through hunting, giving up in the process all of his dormant activities: "I have got an excellent fowling-piece from Mr. Lismahago, who is a keen sportsman, and we shall take the heath in all weathers.—That this scheme of life may be prosecuted the more effectually, I intend to renounce all sedentary amusements, particularly that of writing long letters" (351). Bramble has staved off the symptoms of gout and rheumatism and intends to remain an active sportsman alongside his new brother-in-law. In a concluding metacommentary regarding the inactivity of writing, Bramble appears to have discovered something that Tobias Smollett himself could only dream of achieving: good health. However, the specter of gout attacks still looms, as Bramble relates to Dr. Lewis, "You must also employ your medical skill in defending me from the attacks of the gout" (351). Like Lismahago and Tabitha, Bramble, still susceptible to relapse, troubles the narrative's otherwise stout argument for heteronormative futures.

CONCLUSION

In establishing the novel's concluding marriages as physically and emotionally salutary, Smollett draws a connection between heterosexuality and health, emerging concepts during the eighteenth century in Britain that, as *Humphry Clinker* suggests, rely upon one another for coherence. The wide spectrum of embodiment that Smollett represents for so much of the novel, reflecting the vicissitudes of aging, disease, and hysteria, is finally narrowed to capture the novel's concluding fantasy of bodily health, happiness, and romantic fulfillment. Win and Clinker, the working-class component of the group, find happiness in one another's arms, with Win's hysterical fits and Clinker's ague distant memories. Lydia and Young Dennison overcome their highly sensitive nervous constitutions when they receive the endorsement of their families to marry. The odd men out of coupledom, Bramble and Jery, have their own felicitous endings: Bramble has finally been relieved of his chronic pain by eating healthy foods and traveling through the country, while Jery appears to be primed to marry a friend of Lydia's, reworking the old-guard, solitary libertine model espoused by Bramble. Of all of the characters, Lismahago and Tabitha's marriage indicates the novel's queerest displacement of heteronormative and ableist futures. That Tabitha is finally granted the sexual and emotional intimacy she has long sought is the novel's most notable exception to reproductive futurity. In all of these characters' embodied conflicts, *Humphry Clinker* remarks upon the vulnerability of certain bodies, but unlike Scott's *Millenium Hall*, it neglects to critique or question the social systems that are responsible for said vulnerability. Rather than celebrate the possibilities raised by variable embodiment, as Scott does, Smollett shapes his characters into ideal health by novel's end. Despite such an ending, I read the bodies in Smollett's novel not as signs which finally "dissolve," as Douglas does, but rather as three-dimensional representations of health, as fictions of embodiment that are still front and center despite the novel's regulating tendencies.[58] The major characters are in such a physical state as to be capable of the rigors of lovemaking, housekeeping, and labor but are still susceptible to the inevitability of corporeal distress, as Bramble's lasting wariness over future gout attacks intimates.

Throughout their travels, the variably-embodied characters from *Humphry Clinker* attract the attention of curious spectators. Smollett's repeated portrayals of amused onlookers gazing at their bodies indicate that the act of staring plays a key part in defining social relationships in public spaces. Win Jenkins's wardrobe malfunction at the King's Bath, Matt Bramble's nude display on the beach, and Obadiah Lismahago's humiliating fall from his horse draw attention to the spectacle that surrounds female, diseased, and aging bodies in the Georgian period. Smollett uses this unilateral social relationship for comic purposes, but he also depicts crowded public spaces as pernicious sites for people with variable bodies due to the risk they run of mortifying exposure. And to be sure, Smollett never critiques the one-way looking that occurs throughout his novel; rather, he takes for granted that people will stare at that which seems unusual. Perhaps women writers would have been more sensitive to this topic than Smollett due to their own firsthand experience of visual objectification. Whatever the case, by the end of the eighteenth century, during the period of political instability marked by the French Revolution, two British authors theorized feminism through ocular relationships that developed around variable bodies. In Frances Burney's *Camilla* (1796) and Maria Edgeworth's *Belinda* (1801), staring is likewise a troubling experience for female characters who are repeatedly objectified. However, Burney and Edgeworth also explore the consequences of starees that return the gaze, opening up possibilities for alternative avenues of expression and being when starer and staree are engaged in mutually consensual, ocular relationships. In their novels, Burney and Edgeworth rework the connections between mind and body, rearranging the shape and feel of intimate relationships. Their works explore an array of performed kinship models that are suggestive of unconventional ways for women to exist in the world. The lengths to which these writers go to explore the varied consequences of visual, embodied relationships is the subject of the next chapter.

NOTES

1. According to Linker, disability history and the history of medicine are not "rival siblings" or "conjoined twins" but instead contain a set of "family resemblances." Linker argues that we must overcome our disciplinary and methodological barriers to get a more nuanced portrait of both disability and disease and to conceptualize how these histories intersect with one another. Linker, "On the Borderland of Medical and Disability History," 500, 502, 535.

2. Ibid., 500, 502.
3. Ibid., 503, 534–535.
4. Stanback, *The Wordsworth-Coleridge Circle*, 3–5.
5. The phrase "journey to health" refers to William West's classic essay on *The Expedition of Humphry Clinker*. West, "Matt Bramble's Journey to Health," 1197–1208. Other studies that examine the medical dimensions and narrative structure of *Humphry Clinker* include Boucé, *The Novels of Tobias Smollett*; Douglas, *Uneasy Sensations: Smollett and the Body*; Erickson, "On the External Uses of Water in *The Expedition of Humphry Clinker*," 94–114; Ingram, "Dear Dick," 115–129; Reid, "Smollett's Healing Journey," 549–570.
6. Douglas, *Uneasy Sensations*, 167.
7. Smollett, *The Expedition of Humphry Clinker*, 82. All future references to the novel will appear in parenthetical citations.
8. Mitchell and Snyder, *Narrative Prosthesis*, 48.
9. Ibid., 49.
10. Porter, *The Greatest Benefit to Mankind*, 248.
11. Erickson, "On the External Uses of Water," 95–96.
12. The seismic shift in epidemiology that Gerald N. Grob identifies as happening in the early twentieth century, in which the dramatic decline in infectious disease–related deaths allowed more individuals to live long enough to experience chronic disease, does not account for the substantial amount of interest given to such incurable ailments as gout and rheumatism among aging people in the eighteenth century. Grob, *The Deadly Truth*, 217–218.
13. Boucé, *The Novels of Tobias Smollett*, 209.
14. Davis, *Enforcing Normalcy*, xv.
15. Susannah R. Ottaway argues that genteel and aristocratic men of advanced years were capable of an autonomy not granted to women or people from lower classes. Ottaway, *The Decline of Life*, 14–15.
16. Porter, *Greatest Benefit*, 281.
17. For more on the implications of the absence of Dr. Lewis's voice, see Ingram, "Dear Dick."
18. Ingram, 119.
19. Today, medical specialists understand gout to be a hereditary condition in which a buildup of uric acid crystals causes arthritic discomfort in the joints of the feet (especially the big toe), hands, ankles, and other parts of the body. The consumption of red meats and alcohol may exacerbate these conditions. Gout is now a highly treatable disease thanks to recent medical advancements, but this is far from the case in the eighteenth century.
20. Among these, Colley Cibber's *Love's Last Shift* (1696), John Vanbrugh's *The Relapse* (1696), and William Congreve's *The Way of the World* (1700).
21. Porter and Rousseau, *Gout*, 23.
22. Quoted in Porter and Rousseau, *Gout*, 23.
23. Ibid., 23–24.
24. George Cheyne inserts this statement on epicurean excess into the fourth edition of 1722 (it is not found in the earlier editions). Cheyne, *An Essay on the True Nature and Due Method of Treating the Gout*, 108.
25. Boucé, *The Novels of Tobias Smollett*.
26. Miller, *Narrative and Its Discontents*, 5.
27. See West's "Matt Bramble's Journey to Health," or Porter and Rousseau, *Gout*, for example.
28. West, "Matt Bramble's Journey to Health," 1198–1202.
29. Porter and Rousseau, *Gout*, 109; and Cadogan, *A Dissertation on the Gout, and All Chronic Diseases*, 16.
30. Cadogan, *A Dissertation on the Gout, and All Chronic Diseases*, 49.
31. Ibid., 49.

32. Porter and Rousseau, *Gout*, 109.
33. Borsay, "New Approaches to Social History," 874.
34. Ibid., 873.
35. *The Original Bath Guide*, 3.
36. See for instance, Chandler, *The Description of Bath*, 7; Wood, *An Essay Towards a Description of the City of Bath*, 57; Anstey, *New Bath Guide*, 8; *The Original Bath Guide*, 5.
37. Borsay, "New Approaches to Social History," 873.
38. In mocking this idealistic advertising, satirists such as Smollett skewered Bath for falling short of the mark. Smollett's *Humphry Clinker* and his earlier novel *The Adventures of Peregrine Pickle* (1751) belong to this tradition, though Smollett was certainly not alone in his derision of Bath—nor was he the first. In a 1737 verse satire "The Diseases of Bath," an anonymous author sees the resort town as a purveyor of contagious disease, facilitated by the filthy waters of the pump room and the grimy shops lining the streets. The moral shortcomings of Bath's visitors and residents mirror this disarray. Throughout the piece, the speaker derides the old maids and beaus that congregate in noisy, smelly rooms to socialize while soliciting the service of quacks who are happy to take their money. The speaker of the poem, one of the many "hoodwinked" seekers of health, achieves only "Two long Months at Bath . . . in Pain" by the end of the satire. Smollett's fiction would later join this line of critique. In *The Adventures of Peregrine Pickle*, the physicians at Bath are "a class of animals who live . . . like so many ravens hovering about a carcass." For Smollett, Bath is a magnet for avaricious doctors who prey on ill patients that have the means at their disposal to cover hefty medical bills. As in *Peregrine Pickle*, in which the titular hero employs a number of tactics to disrupt the inhabitants of Bath, *Humphry Clinker* portrays Bath as colossal failure in both medical and marital terms. "The Diseases of Bath," 13, 19; and Smollett, *The Adventures of Peregrine Pickle*, 203.
39. Gottlieb, *Preface* to *The Expedition of Humphry Clinker*, xi.
40. Kelly, "Introductory Note," in *Bluestocking Feminism*, xvi.
41. Erickson, "On the External Uses of Water."
42. Lawrence, "Feline Fortunes," 623–635.
43. Anderson, *Imagining Methodism*.
44. Part of the comic force of this passage is derived from Tabitha's extravagant closeness with Chowder. The lady-lapdog relationship is a convention of eighteenth-century literature meant to signify an "immoderate intimacy" that impedes men from physical intimacy with women. See Brown, "The Lady, the Lapdog, and Literary Alterity," 31–34.
45. Steele, "On Personal Defects; Proposals for an Ugly Club," from *Selections from the Tatler, Spectator, and Guardian*, 172–173.
46. Hay, *Deformity*, 13.
47. Ottaway, *The Decline of Life*, 8–9.
48. Turner, *Disability in Eighteenth-Century England*, 60–80.
49. Douglas, *Uneasy Sensations*, 175; West, "Matt Bramble's Journey to Health," 1206.
50. For more about *Humphry Clinker*'s representation of Methodism, see Anderson, *Imagining Methodism*, 200–220, 230–231.
51. Ibid., 208.
52. Erickson, "On the External Uses of Water," 109.
53. Port, "No Future?," 3.
54. Ibid., 3.
55. Gallop, "The View from Queer Theory," 327.
56. Turner, *Disability in Eighteenth-Century England*, 76.
57. Ibid., 75.
58. Douglas, *Uneasy Sensations*, 84.

4

GENDERED DISFIGUREMENT AND QUEER OCULAR RELATIONS IN FRANCES BURNEY'S *CAMILLA* (1796) AND MARIA EDGEWORTH'S *BELINDA* (1801)

THE FINAL CHAPTER OF THIS book examines literary representations of staring in order to conceptualize the gendering and queering of visible bodily difference at the turn of the nineteenth century in Britain. In the previous chapter, I identified passages from Tobias Smollett's *The Expedition of Humphry Clinker* in which characters gawk—sometimes in fascination, other times in disgust or derision—at variable bodies. Typically, in *Humphry Clinker*, such incidents incur shame in those at whom the stare is directed. In these scenes, bodies are a source of tension and absurdity, and their gradual regulation is a way for Smollett to create and resolve narrative conflict. In a similar fashion, Frances Burney's *Camilla* (1796) and Maria Edgeworth's *Belinda* (1801) stage encounters between characters that stare and characters at whom the stare is directed. However, rather unlike in *Humphry Clinker*, representations of sustained looking in these novels reveal a dynamic, relational set of cultural signifiers that situate disabled embodiment as vital for women's education, and as having consequences for gender mobility and queer relations. In these novels, when staring becomes a two-way affair, impaired characters transform themselves by accessing new sources of knowledge.

In thinking about staring as a potentially transformative act rather than as one that is limiting or oppressive, I depart from critical traditions that inform eighteenth-century studies (including those to which this book is indebted). For instance, Michel Foucault's *Discipline and Punish* is one of the dominant critical models for understanding looking in the later eighteenth century. In it, Foucault argues that Jeremy Bentham's prison design facilitates a form of "panoptical surveillance" that stands in for the way that disciplinary norms regulate social behaviors and attitudes during the Enlightenment. Crucially, this is also a model that allows a few individuals to surveil the multitudes, who never know when they are actually being watched.[1] Another of Foucault's frameworks for understanding looking is the "clinical gaze"—his term for the way that physicians and medical experts interact with their patients. In a departure from the kind of patient-led relationship that we observed between Matthew Bramble and Dr. Lewis, in the late eighteenth and nineteenth centuries physicians began to wield their expertise to unilaterally diagnose and treat their patients' bodies.[2] In each of these models, Foucault understands ocular relations to be fundamentally shaped by power relations that discipline the non-normative. The male gaze is another one-way visual dynamic, in which patriarchal order is consolidated through men's objectification of women, who are positioned as the subordinate other to male desire and control.[3] However, staring in this period is not only attributable to such mechanisms of domination and subordination; it can also be the means by which women experience growth in the public sphere.[4] Staring between women, for example, may bring about novel ways of being in the world that exceed the constraints of the private, domestic sphere. I examine in this chapter such expansive possibilities in the embodied and affective representations of watched women who dare to return the gaze of interrogative eyes.

To capture the dynamic interplay between mutually-consensual staring subjects, I use the term *queer ocular relations*. This expression draws from queer modes of being, in which same-sex desiring and gender nonconforming subjects find one another in environments that are hostile to their very existence. But of course, the act of cruising is not new to modern queer life. Reports of cruising grounds in early eighteenth-century London exist in historical records, leaving one to speculate about the gestures, looks, and pick-up lines that queer people used to connect with one another.[5] As in other kinds of interactive relationships, one may examine the social norms that govern queer staring. Ocular norms in general vary according to time and place, and thus the act of staring is shaped by cultural forces and has a rich, varied history. Rosemarie Garland-Thomson argues that "staring is a conduit to knowledge."[6] She writes, "An encounter between a starer and staree sets in motion an interpersonal relationship, however momentary, that has consequences. This intense visual engagement creates a circuit of communication and meaning-making. Staring bespeaks involvement, and being stared at demands a response."[7] Besides creating opportunities for personal interaction, the stare, for Garland-Thomson, creates the kind of visual uncertainty that facilitates new stores of information and experience that are crucial for personal growth, as well as the growth of a society. In Burney's and Edgeworth's novels, the act of staring at women's variable bodies and the mutual stare between women function as critical narrative moments that punctuate the development of characters such as Eugenia (from *Camilla*) and Lady Delacour (from *Belinda*). Instances of staring in each of these works amount to new ways of inhabiting the world for women. These novels indicate that women with variable bodies not only confronted the violence of the male, panoptical, and clinical gazes, but also engaged in the sorts of prolonged looking that betoken curiosity and wonder, stimulating opportunities for women to be educated and to connect with one another in creative ways that sidestep or undermine narrow domestic standards. Such facilitative forms of staring also serve to underscore the embodied contours of feminist thought in women's writing during the Age of Reform. Both Burney's *Camilla* and Edgeworth's *Belinda* call attention to prescriptive gender roles regarding a woman's intellect and appearance, and yet they also conceptualize the gaze that comes from their extraordinary female characters as auspicious for the growth of the self.

In *Camilla*, for instance, Eugenia Tyrold is a highly educated, physically disabled young woman who comes of age along with her sister, the eponymous Camilla. Like her sister, Eugenia has the misfortune of being under the care of her neglectful and immature uncle, Sir Hugh, who is a baronet and the head of Cleves, a prominent country estate. When in his good humor, Sir Hugh takes Eugenia and her siblings and cousins to a fair where he exposes Eugenia to the smallpox virus. The illness merges shortly thereafter when Sir Hugh drops Eugenia from the top of a teeter-totter, and her grave injury gives way to a high fever. She subsequently becomes feverish, and soon it is clear that smallpox is working its way through her.[8] Eugenia endures a long, rough, and feverish bout with the disease before she recovers, at which point she is left with a scarred face and "one leg shorter than the other . . . her whole figure diminutive and deformed."[9] For Eugenia, as the aforementioned smallpox and teeter-totter incidents might attest, one major obstacle to her maturation consists of learning how to navigate public spaces while her disfigurements are so visible to the spectating other. Maria Edgeworth's *Belinda* offers a contrasting understanding of the connections among staring, embodiment, and gender identity for women. While in *Camilla*, Eugenia performs genteel femininity despite her philosophical education, Harriet Freke embodies almost all of the terms of otherness available in *Belinda* and is a catalyst and regular disruptor of the heterosexual conduct plot. Rather unlike Eugenia, Harriet delights in being stared at for assuming a male identity in public spaces. In characterizing the relationship between Harriet and Lady Delacour as consisting in a shifting two-way dynamic, Edgeworth imbues their daring rapport with outrageous public performances of queer gender and kinship that are ultimately marked by agonizing bodily symptoms. Through their drastically different portrayals of women's embodiment, Burney and Edgeworth convey that feminism, women's education, and gender are shaped in part by staring eyes.

OF MONSTERS AND GENIUSES

In considering the possibilities that staring opens up for women in this period, I do not intend to downplay the ways in which it could subject women to highly precarious or dangerous circumstances. In a letter written in 1753, Lady Mary Wortley Montagu discusses the dire social implications of hypervisibility for young women of fashion when she counsels her daughter, the Countess of Bute, to teach her own daughter "to conceal whatever learning she attains, with as much solicitude as she would hide crookedness or lameness: the parade of it can only serve to draw on her the envy, and consequently the most inveterate hatred, of all he and she fools, which will certainly be at least three parts in four of her acquaintance."[10] Lady Mary's letter calls attention to the rigid social barriers imposed on women's education, of course, but it also makes a compelling analogy between a young woman's intelligence and her body. Just as bodily difference incurs unwanted attention, she implies, a young woman who possesses and demonstrates intelligence is bound to invite hostility from ignorant, gawking peers. Moreover, as her analogy insinuates, "crookedness" and "lameness" might actually be an advantage to young women in developing their intellects, something which might bring about "envy" and "hatred" in others. In Lady Mary's estimation, a young woman's mind should function, and her body appear, in socially sanctioned ways if the "he and she fools" are to be kept at bay. Lady Mary likewise assumes that staring has negative consequences, reflecting contemporaneous injunctions against staring by both men and women.[11] In *Camilla*, Eugenia is sometimes viewed as an unfortunate victim of circumstance, or as a monster. However, it is precisely because of her body that she becomes the most educated of her siblings through a thorough training in the classics. In this manner, Burney explores the mind-body connection in relation to feminism.

Before considering the relationship between Eugenia's academic formation and physical disabilities, I would like to examine a few examples of intellectual men who were "deformed." Helen Deutsch identifies and explores the mind-body problem as it relates to Samuel Johnson, who, she argues, "was both a monument and a monster."[12] Known on the one side for his tics and physical disabilities, and on the other for his brilliant conversation, influential writing style, and profound literary mind, Johnson exemplifies the monster-genius dichotomy in eighteenth-century England. His contemporaries considered him "as both Great

Cham (tartar monarch) and Caliban of Literature."[13] This coupling of brilliance and defect, for Deutsch, sheds light on a moment in British history in which the mind and body are tightly bound to each other "through the complex workings of sensibility."[14] Deutsch's work on Alexander Pope, considered the greatest English poet of the age (and, like Johnson, a physical curiosity), further illustrates that this monster-genius trope is pervasive in the eighteenth-century literary imagination.[15] Significantly, these writers occupy exalted places as the most prominent and influential men of letters from this era. Deutsch's argument that their writings and literary style are informed in significant ways by their physical attributes illuminates the enormous significance of the mind-body connection to literary culture in the later eighteenth century. It also speaks to fundamentally gendered forms of staring. If Lady Montagu's granddaughter must hide her intelligence and physical flaws, then the likes of Pope and Johnson may parade their brilliance and physical peculiarities to incur the wonder and admiration of their contemporaries. As these examples attest, one's experience of embodiment and agency are inevitably shaped by gender norms.

Class also determines one's experience of physical disability and intellectual achievement. William Hay—a physically disabled aristocrat who served in the House of Lords—is on record as being one of the first English thinkers to consider physical disability an advantage. In his 1754 tract *Deformity: An Essay*, Hay contests Sir Francis Bacon's argument that individuals with physical defects are "void of natural affection" and that they have "a perpetual spur . . . to rescue and deliver" themselves "from scorn."[16] Hay contends that far from making one "bold" or vengeful, as Bacon argues, physical defect "tends to the Improvement of the Mind" since one "that cannot shine in his Person, will have recourse to his Understanding: and attempt to adorn that Part of him, which alone is capable of Ornament."[17] Lack of standard superficial beauty or bodily ability entices one to develop character and intellect because, unable to win favor through superficial means, that person is left with no other way to impress than to become more virtuous or learned. The latter of these characteristics is of interest to Hay, who argues that "the time which others spend in Action" is time which the deformed individual "will pass in Study and Contemplation: by these he may acquire Wisdom, and by Wisdom fame."[18] Hay argues that having physical impairments and infirmities facilitate the development of an individual's intellectual capabilities since they cannot actively engage in physical activity as other people do.

For its time, *Deformity: An Essay* makes bold claims about the potential advantages that a person with impairments might have over someone with no noticeable defects. But before he does this, Hay compares himself to famous men in order to familiarize himself to his audience. In particular, he mentions Æsop, the fabulist, alongside some other prominent men from English and classical history: "In person I resemble Æsop, the Prince of Orange, Marshal Luxemburg, Lord Treasurer Salisbury, Scarron, and Mr. Pope: not to mention Thersites and Richard the Third."[19] Æsop's place on this list would be fitting and recognizable to his eighteenth-century audience. Hay, like Æsop, has a humpback and a disfigured body, but he does not want pity. Also like Æsop, he is perfectly capable of rational thought despite the corporeal difficulties which ostensibly beset him. Further, as Hay demonstrates, these bodily impairments actually strengthen his intellect.

Hay's argument that an impaired body may be the ideal host of a brilliant or learned mind seems to have existed throughout the eighteenth century in the figure of Æsop, whose cultural impact on this time period is significant. Though originating in antiquity, Æsop's moralistic tales did not appear in Europe until the advent of the printing press in the fifteenth century, and his cultural impact on England did not flourish until the Restoration and eighteenth century.[20] During this period, Æsop's fables were popular in England, with some of the versions of these tales including biographies of the fabulist himself. In 1793, for example, *The Fables of Æsop, With a Life of the Author*, an edition containing Samuel Croxall's early eighteenth-century interpretation of the fables, depicts Aesop as having an extraordinary appearance: "All agree that his person was uncommonly deformed. . . . His head was long, nose flat, lips thick and pendent, a hump back, and complexion dark . . . large belly, and bow legs: but his greatest infirmity was, that his speech was slow, inarticulate, and very obscure."[21] Æsop's various disabilities are all indicators of his physical, intellectual, and racial otherness. And yet the biographer indicates that Æsop's variable body functions as a ruse to his interlocutors: "As Nature often sets the most refulgent gems where they are least expected, so she endowed this extraordinary man with an accomplished mind, capable of the most sublime and elevated ideas."[22] As this passage indicates, Æsop's body serves to mask the brilliance of his mind and to break down assumptions before he introduces his fables.[23]

Despite Æsop's pleas to not be judged for his physical figure (he says at one point, "Ye should not only view the front of the house, but the tenant also; for frequently an upright and understanding soul dwells in a deformed and disordered body"), the narrative reveals that Æsop's body is both facilitator and demonstrator of his genius.[24] Many of Æsop's encounters with his fellow slaves and slave owners emphasize his corporeality, as these plot developments use illness or physical violence as the foregrounding tension to, and occasion for, Æsop's intelligence. Take for example a section in which Æsop is wrongly accused by some of his fellow slaves of having stolen their master's figs. Upon being condemned of having eaten the fruit, Æsop is unable to "answer readily in his defence" due to his "inarticulate" speech.[25] He is, however, able to prove to his master that he is not the culprit by swallowing a large amount of warm water and making himself vomit. When the liquid comes up clear—evidence that he had eaten nothing that day—the master recognizes Æsop's innocence and applies this test to the accusers, whose vomit reveals the content of the figs they had consumed. These other servants are then lashed for their misdeed.[26] In this case, Æsop circumvents his speech impediment by using his body as evidence of his innocence. Though Æsop's biography implores the reader to not judge one's mind by one's appearance, the story of the figs—along with several other inset narratives—illustrates the central importance of Æsop's abject bodily performance. In fact, the reader is frequently reminded that Æsop has a variable body, but it is this body that confounds and educates his interlocutors when they discover his extraordinary mind.

SCOTT, AUSTEN, AND WOLLSTONECRAFT: THE GENDERING OF THE MONSTER-GENIUS TROPE

The inability of Æsop's 1793 biographer to overlook Æsop's corporeality in favor of his intellectual brilliance is reflected in Burney's *Camilla*, published just three years later. Due to *Camilla*'s grappling with the mind-body problem that eighteenth-century cultural representations of Æsop are unable to overturn, Burney joins a small sorority of eighteenth- and early nineteenth-century women writers who portray physically variable women as being especially intelligent and morally upright. In her 1754 novel *Agreeable Ugliness*, Sarah Scott creates a heroine whose plain looks enable the development of virtue and intellect. In the narrative, the heroine-narrator describes her appearance as one of "native Ugliness," while her older sister, the Fair Villiers, is the most attractive female character throughout Paris and the areas surrounding the country seat where their family resides.[27] While the Fair Villiers aligns herself with her mother, and in the process learns to be vain and selfish, the narrator receives an education from her father, and consequently this masculine tutoring allows her to impress upon her potential suitors that she would be an ideal spouse.[28] This privileged masculine education and its virtuous fruits prove to be a result of the narrator's appearance: "As I had continually been told I was a Monster, I really believed it; and had employed my utmost Endeavors to cultivate some natural Talents, and acquire such Accomplishments, as might make me endured in Society."[29] Scott's narrative endorses Hay's argument that an extraordinary appearance or weak constitution facilitates intelligence and a strong sense of morality. Scott also conveys a proto-feminist ethos by marrying the heroine off to the man whom she desires throughout the novel once her initial arranged marriage comes to an end with her first husband's untimely death. *Agreeable Ugliness* thus stipulates that the fulfillment of female desire is to be explored and celebrated in relation to the narrator's "shocking" body, which, though initially an object of ridicule, finally becomes a key component of her vigorous passion and bold will.[30]

Jane Austen employs a similar depiction of physical disability and mental acuity in *Persuasion* through the figure of Mrs. Smith, Anne Elliot's former school companion. During Anne's visits to Mrs. Smith's humble lodgings in Bath, Anne learns that Mrs. Smith has undergone hard times since their school days as a consequence of a spendthrift husband who has left her widowed and in financial disarray. To compound matters, after her husband's death, Mrs. Smith contracts rheumatic fever, which impinges on her ability to walk. Though her financial and social status are precarious, and though she is confined to a modest living arrangement in Bath that she is unable to leave due to her impaired state, Mrs. Smith is credited with having an "elasticity of mind" and "that power of turning readily from evil to good" (174–175). Moreover, Mrs. Smith's intellectual and social intelligence allow her to play a key role in Anne's epiphany regarding William Elliot, Anne's would-be suitor, when she reveals to Anne that Mr. Elliot's intentions to marry her are likely based on selfishness and not out of love. Mrs. Smith's perceptiveness is the catalyst for Anne to make herself available to Frederic Wentworth, the novel's hero and Anne's eventual husband. *Persuasion*'s portrayal of Mrs. Smith as physically disabled and intellectually and socially aware likens it to Scott's *Agreeable Ugliness* and Burney's *Camilla*.

The most radical of women writers on behalf of women's rights during the Age of Reform, Mary Wollstonecraft, wrote a searing indictment of inequality among the sexes in *A Vindication of the Rights of Woman*. In her understanding of the inextricable connection between educated mind and normative body, she diverges from Scott and Austen. In *Rights of Woman*, Wollstonecraft argues that education for young girls and boys, along with the proper upbringing, will lead to a perfection of the body that is not often to be found in Britain. In the midst of her chapter titled "On National Education," in which she argues for mixed-sex education to establish young women and men on equal intellectual footing, Wollstonecraft expostulates on the beauty of Grecian statues, illustrating the ways in which the classed, lavish comforts of British living have impacted modern bodily form and function. She speculates that Grecian peoples must have been "far more beautiful" than the people of Britain of her day due to the latter's "extreme indolence, barbarous ligatures" and a "luxurious state of society" which all "forcibly act on" the body, causing so many British people to become "deformed."[31] After recognizing the impact of cultural and physical pressures on shaping the body, Wollstonecraft goes on to reify the connection between sound minds and bodies, but she also insinuates that one's physiognomy can be improved with the proper moral and educational foundation. For Wollstonecraft, an education that allows women to engage in the male-centric domains of scientific and literary endeavors can bring about such improvement: "To render the person perfect, physical and moral beauty ought to be attained at the same time; each lending and receiving force by the combination. Judgment must reside on the brow, affection and fancy beam in the eye, and humanity curve the cheek, or vain is the sparkling of the finest eye or the elegantly turned finish of the fairest features; whilst in every motion that displays the active limbs and well-knit joints, grace and modesty should appear."[32] For Wollstonecraft, physical and moral beauty reach their pinnacle when they develop alongside one another through a thorough education that goes beyond the mere celebration of typical female "accomplishments." It is the combination of "physical and moral beauty" that will be reflected in the outward features of young women. To conceive of education differently, then, is to improve the form, appearance, and function of British bodies. Equal education for young girls and boys will bring grace to "active limbs and well-knit joints" and yield beautiful bodily forms. In this way, Wollstonecraft crafts an argument about the importance of female education to an audience that was wary of the effects of a "masculine education" on young women's appearance, among other things. Wollstonecraft thus uses a rhetorical strategy to connect to the likes of Locke in formulating education as a valuable tool to help women improve themselves and by extension British society as a whole. Wollstonecraft is, of course, of vital importance to early feminist thought in Britain, and in her very reliance on the concept of ideal forms of embodiment for her argument, we see how deeply embedded ableism is in even the most radical of late eighteenth-century thought in Britain.

ENABLING EUGENIA TYROLD'S MIND

Burney's representation of Eugenia reworks Wollstonecraft's argument about education, embodiment, and physiognomy. In a similar fashion to Scott and Austen, Burney creates a physically disabled female character in Eugenia Tyrold whose sharp intellect and moral compass enable her to come of age in praiseworthy fashion. While Eugenia must confront her social reality as a public spectacle and, like Æsop and William Hay, prove to those whom she encounters that she is not just a "little lame thing" to be mocked and denigrated, her intellectual development is often attributed to, or contingent upon, her variable body (77). Where Eugenia also breaks relatively new ground, insofar as the genre of the novel is concerned, is in her development into a classical scholar and philosopher, highly unusual for a young woman in this era.[33] Eugenia's coming-of-age is based on the assumption that an impaired body and philosophical mind are an ideal match, and the fact that she is ultimately granted her sexual desire through her eventual marriage to Frederic Melmond underscores this novel's endorsement of female desire and agency in a late eighteenth-century context.

Despite Eugenia's remarkable maturation, strengthened as it is by her various impairments, the novel implies that her physical disabilities may have been avoided if not for the carelessness of her uncle, Sir Hugh, whose negligence draws attention to the medical context out of which *Camilla* emerges. *Camilla*'s publication in 1796 registers the impending closure of a century of unprecedented growth for "popularized medicine," which benefits from Enlightenment's emphasis on circulating knowledge about the body, the rise of print culture, and the emergence of a consumer society.[34] Increased awareness of foreign medical treatments also contributes to this trend in England. During her travels through Turkey in the 1720's, Lady Mary Wortley Montagu observed the widespread practice of smallpox inoculation, and her social influence brought about the establishment of this practice in England. Smallpox inoculation became commonplace in England throughout the remainder of the eighteenth century, especially in the countryside where mass treatments were more effective than in densely populated cities and towns.[35] In preparation for writing *Camilla*, Burney conducted extensive research on the contagious nature and disfiguring potential of the smallpox, which she uses as a plot device to mark Eugenia as a victim of Sir Hugh's neglect.[36] At the beginning of the novel, Sir Hugh justifies his shortsighted decision to take the children to the fair despite young Eugenia's not having been inoculated: "She will be sure to have it when her time comes, whether she is moped up or no; and how did people do before these new modes of making themselves sick of their own accord?" (23). Sir Hugh's anachronistic perspective in this scene is startling given that inoculation was so widely considered an effective treatment at the time of this novel's publication. Hence, Eugenia's suffering is shown to be especially needless, and the blame for her facial disfigurement can be placed squarely on the shoulders of her uncle, whose misunderstanding of such a prevalent practice underscores his naïveté and lack of education. Given the later eighteenth century's ever-increasing orientation toward these sorts of elite medical practices, and given the coalescence of Western Europe's investment in normalizing concepts such as wellness and illness, Burney's depiction of Eugenia's physical appearance is meant to make her stand out from the more conventional, healthy bodies which surround her.[37]

Sir Hugh's decision to make Eugenia the heiress of the Cleves estate exacerbates the spectacle attached to Eugenia's person and has important ramifications throughout the novel. Sir Hugh's largess, however, lends Eugenia an agency that would otherwise be unattainable. As Katherine Binhammer suggests, Eugenia's allowance, significantly more substantial than her siblings' allowance, liberates her from many of the concerns Camilla faces.[38] Camilla, for example, is run into debt due to her brother Lionel's insistent demands for money and the sartorial pressures exerted upon her by Mrs. Mitten. For Eugenia, meanwhile, these particular kinds of stress are absent: her social status and fortune facilitate her education in the classics and allow her to build cultural forms of capital without financial duress. And yet it is also the case that money and inheritance eventually become sources of distress for Eugenia. While her allowance affords her so much, it is precisely her position as heiress to Cleves that sets her up to be abducted and forcibly married to Alphonso Bellamy. Thus, even while Eugenia's tutoring is supplied by her wealth, her inheritance attracts Bellamy's mercenary intentions.

Just as money and inheritance provide Eugenia with the paradoxical effects of agency and vulnerability, Eugenia's body causes her pain even as it is the catalyst for her intellectual achievement. Eugenia's facial and physical disfigurements, though the subject of spectacle in public spaces, prove to be vital for her development into a classical scholar. And yet the extent to which Burney is making an explicit feminist political statement through Eugenia's education is certainly up for debate.[39] Burney's gender politics, which vacillate between being feminist in the critical attention her fiction calls to the ill effects of patriarchy, and conservative in the reinforcement of the very social fabric that perpetuates these problems, may best be understood as moments of textual contradiction. Kristina Straub argues that, for Burney, "ideological gaps and contradictions . . . seem the result of simple honesty about her cultural circumstances as woman and writer rather than a deliberate attempt to subvert."[40] In this same vein, Claudia Johnson labels Burney an "equivocal being" because of her public status as a woman writer in the 1790's, a time period in which British fiction is "bizarre and untidy."[41] Straub and Johnson both make important points about the ambiguity inherent in Burney's writing, a characteristic that is readily apparent in other women's fiction of this period, too. I would add, however, that Eugenia's story, at the very least, reveals anxiety about the ways that disabled women are treated. At its most politically potent, *Camilla* undermines assumptions about prescriptive gender roles and the ways in which they intersect with the lived reality of disabled women in the late eighteenth century.

In *Camilla*, Eugenia's physical reality and its impact on her coming-of-age cannot be overstated. Her growth into a young woman consists of a series of corporeal mishaps and public mortifications in which she, like Æsop, attracts the contemptuous stare of ignorant, derisive spectators. The psychological torment that Eugenia experiences as a consequence of these encounters consists of a melancholy that is always associated in some way with her body. Burney's violent, comic approach to novel writing, a rarity among her contemporaries, allows for this mind-body connection to be imagined in the first place. As Margaret Doody notes, Burney employs elements of farce in her writing, with conventions such as violent horseplay and an exaggerated emphasis on the body making their way into her first novel, *Evelina*, while her subsequent novels *Cecilia*, *Camilla*, and *The Wanderer* also rely on these same tropes to varying degrees.[42] As Doody remarks, Burney's fiction is "insistently physical," and *Camilla* is no exception to this rule.[43] Eugenia is perhaps the best example of this: at the very beginning of the novel, she becomes the victim of her uncle's lack of circumspection—represented, true to farce, in comical terms—and bodily pain and impairment are the immediate and long-term consequences for her. What is more, *Camilla*'s use of farce places Eugenia's disfigurement in the foreground of the novel's many plots and subplots, thereby making Eugenia, though just one character among many to populate Burney's sweeping domestic epic, an immensely important figure to scrutinize. Burney's unique writing style, with its emphasis on physicality and its allowance for interiority, allows for the development of Eugenia's keen intellect that eventually permits her to challenge long-standing assumptions about gender and the body.

In order for Burney to eventually make this critique, she depicts Eugenia's education as a philosopher. It is Eugenia's bodily impairments that make her the most capable of her numerous family members to take on the lessons in the classics from the family tutor, Dr. Orkborne. In his hiring of Dr. Orkborne, Sir Hugh originally plans to make up for his stunted education by taking lessons alongside his nephew, Lionel, but his efforts fall short due to his own intellectual torpor and Lionel's insistent mockery of his uncle's fruitless attempts to retain the material that Dr. Orkborne teaches to them. After forfeiting his and Lionel's lessons, Sir Hugh sends Indiana, Eugenia's exceedingly fair cousin, to take lessons in their stead. However, Indiana's education never takes flight as a consequence of her fatuousness. With Sir Hugh, Lionel, and Indiana all having proven to be failures for a serious education due to their various ineptitudes, Eugenia's physical lassitude, along with her intellectual potential, mark her as the ideal candidate for the lessons: "The little girl," Burney writes, "who was naturally of a thoughtful turn, and whose state of health deprived her of most childish amusements, was well contented with the arrangement" (49). Here, Burney implies that Eugenia's inability to partake in typical childhood activity designates her as the perfect student, since her mind was inherently of a "thoughtful turn" anyway. In this way, Eugenia learns to use her body for intellectual achievement, thereby making Eugenia a young woman with agency and not just a victim of her impairments.

Eugenia's education aids her decidedly difficult maturation process as she undergoes psychological agony due to others' crude perceptions of her body's irregularities. When Eugenia's insipid cousin, Clermont Lynmere, rejects Sir Hugh's arrangement for him to marry Eugenia, her education rescues her from melancholia: "This view of her unfortunate appearance cast her, at first, into a train of melancholy ideas, that would have fast led her to unhappiness . . . had not the natural philosophy of her mind come to her aid; or had her education been of a more worldly sort" (630). Eugenia's serious and insular education, Burney implies, edifies Eugenia in the face of her cousin's critique of her body. Eugenia later laments to her sister that Frederic Melmond, the young man whom she truly loves, is attracted to Indiana despite his discovery of Eugenia's passionate feelings for him: "Is it possible I could ever—for a moment, for a single moment, suppose Melmond could willingly be mine! could see his exquisite susceptibility of every thing that is most perfect, yet persuade myself, he could take, by choice, the poor Eugenia for his wife! the mangled, deformed,—unfortunate Eugenia!" (722–723). Camilla calms Eugenia in this instance by reminding her of her "intrinsic worth," and once again Eugenia has the intellectual perspective to pull herself out of her melancholia. Felicity Nussbaum remarks that Eugenia's body allows her "opportunities to negotiate sexual difference" including her ability to escape the "usual trivial" ordeals that beset women with ordinary bodies.[44] Nussbaum's analysis is apt because the narrative repeatedly draws the reader's attention to Eugenia's disfigurements, and yet the reader is also made aware of the ways in which her mind enables her to overcome the difficulties which result from the social stigma attached to those irregularities.

Eugenia's education, it has been argued, is not without its drawbacks. As Claudia Johnson points out, Eugenia's grounding in the classics forms "the basis of [her] virtue and at the same time really does deform her."[45] Here, Johnson addresses some of the problems that would result from a young woman learning only the classics. For one thing, since Eugenia has not been exposed to novels, a frivolous pursuit in Dr. Orkborne's eyes, no doubt, she "cannot anticipate the machinations of fortune hunters."[46] Thus, Eugenia is not able to read between the ostensibly lovesick lines of Bellamy's letters so that she can avoid subjecting herself to his dangerous advances. Perhaps, as Johnson suggests, if Eugenia were to have the chance to pursue the feminine realm of novels, she would be able to correctly read Bellamy's iterations of love for exactly what they are: the proclamations of an emotionally unstable and violent gold digger. But because Eugenia views everything in sweeping, epic terms—a product of her focus on the classics—she cannot accurately perceive Bellamy's avaricious pursuit of her. Her inability to read Bellamy's letters and actions places Eugenia in an unstable position, and Bellamy takes advantage by abducting her from a theater and taking her up to Gretna Green where he forces marriage upon her. Because of her epic virtue, Eugenia refuses to break her forced vows with Bellamy.[47] And yet despite these shortcomings, Eugenia is, by the end of the novel, able to view her social abjection in relation to the epic narratives that she has read. Rather than view her education as problematic, I read it as that which, along with money, gives Eugenia agency.

Though Eugenia's body plays a significant role in her education, the narrative at times privileges mind over body. This is apparent, for example, when Eugenia's father, Mr. Tyrold, takes her and her sister on a guided field trip to show her a madwoman. In this curious passage, Mr. Tyrold hopes to lift Eugenia's spirits by getting her to see her deformities as relatively moderate tribulations compared to what an intellectually impaired woman might endure. Upon arriving to the woman's front gate, all Eugenia enviously observes is that the woman is beautiful, at which point Mr. Tyrold starts his lesson to her about how beauty is short-lived: "The happiness caused by personal attractions pays a dear after-price. . . . To be wholly disregarded, after engaging every eye . . . to be unheard after monopolising every ear—can you, indeed, persuade yourself a change such as this demands but ordinary firmness?" (308). This initial lesson does not convince Eugenia, however, who responds, "I would purchase a better appearance at any price . . . the world could impose!" (308). It is not until Eugenia notices that the woman is intellectually impaired, as Johnson argues, that this lesson convinces her to not lament her state.[48] After "turning round with a velocity that no machine could have exceeded," uttering frantically for a shilling, and "unresisting the scratches which tore her fine skin" from a cat that she tries to "twine . . . round her neck with great fondling," the madwoman makes sounds "that resembled nothing human" (310). Eugenia is finally convinced of her father's "awful lesson": the madwoman's "shocking imbecility" convinces her to "submit, at least with calmness, to [her] lighter evils and milder fate" (310–311).[49] George Haggerty argues that Mr. Tyrold gives Camilla "advice that works against her self-interest time and time again," and the same thing can be said about his counsel to Eugenia in this instance. Beyond being insensitive and unrealistic, Mr. Tyrold is unable to "understand . . . the torments of . . . female youth," and much less the torments of physically disabled female youth.[50] However ineffective Mr. Tyrold's advice may be, Eugenia's witnessing of the woman's incoherent speech seems to make her see the relative ease of her own life, physical deformities and all. Here is an instance of the novel's ostensible endorsement of a sound mind over a beautiful body.

This lesson, however, does not prove to stick with Eugenia, who by the end of the novel is still very cognizant of, and vocal about, her body. At this point in the novel, Eugenia finally stares back at her detractors and tormentors. Her ability to articulate her abjection comes after Bellamy accidentally kills himself, which places Eugenia in a position of power as a widow.[51] Mrs. Arlbery, a relatively young fashionable widow who acts as mentor to the heroine, Camilla, is for the majority of the novel the only character to critique the hero, Edgar Mandlebert, because he consistently misreads Camilla and holds her to impossible standards. By extension, Mrs. Arlbery's critique is aimed at the patriarchal structure which repeatedly impacts Camilla and Eugenia in such appalling ways. But Eugenia eventually becomes the other widowed social critic, and her education allows her to evaluate her various, terrible life experiences and to write her memoirs with such sensibility, insight, and persuasion:

> Ye, too, O lords of the creation, mighty men! Impute not to native vanity the repining spirit with which I lament the loss of beauty; attribute not to the innate weakness of my sex, the concern I confess for my deformity; nor to feminine littleness of soul, a regret of which the true source is to be traced to your own bosoms, and springs from your own tastes: for the value you yourselves set upon external attractions, your own neglect has taught me to know; and the indifference with which you consider all else, your own duplicity has instructed me to feel. (905).

This passage contains allusions to the sufferings of Helen at the hands of Homer, demonstrating Eugenia's personal and critical response to Helen's supposed narcissism.[52] Hence, Eugenia's critique calls attention to the classical reading that she has undertaken in her schooling. Eugenia's message in this passage indicates her proto-feminist ethos. Eugenia uses her education as a means to self-empowerment through her trenchant critique of the male gaze to which she has been so harshly and unfairly subjected throughout the novel. Eugenia, at long last, recognizes that the burden of not fitting in, of being perceived as a "lame duck" in public, is not her fault. The source of the guilt, she proclaims, is the "value" which men place "upon external attractions," which is another way of saying that she is not vain for being self-conscious, as Richard Steele or even her own father would argue.[53] Since men have set the social terms by which women are to be evaluated, the blame for Eugenia's social and psychological abjection is to be directed at the staring men that have either ridiculed or acted violently toward her. After all, Mr. Tyrold's lesson about beauty is not taken to heart, and his intention of making Eugenia overlook her own embodiment does not resonate with her.

Another aspect of this passage that I would like to emphasize is the manner in which Eugenia's formal and experiential forms of education have allowed her to express this powerful critique. Eugenia's sexual terror at the hands of Bellamy, her endurance of the taunts of strangers, and her cousin Clermont's rejection of his arranged marriage with her, are all traumatic life experiences for which her formal education never could prepare her. Eugenia's education does, however, enable her to pen her critique of her own liminality. Eugenia is capable of discerning that the "duplicity" of men—whose overvaluing of female beauty and repudiation of extraordinary female bodies—is that which has "instructed" her to "lament" her situation. Her interrogation of this oppression reveals that the true culprit in all of this is men, whose sexualizing gaze has turned her into a spectacle in public places. The fact that Eugenia's portrait is to appear in her autobiography further underscores the connection between the workings of her mind and body. There she would appear, staring back at readers who might wonder at her extraordinary visage and body. In this way, Eugenia, like Scott's agreeably ugly narrator, employs her body, which moves from being an object of scorn, ridicule, and sexual aggression to a staring subject that condemns men's marginalization of physically disabled women.

To further complicate the novel's concluding take on deformity and its relationship with the mind, Burney marries Eugenia off to Melmond as one of the novel's several happy marital endings. Burney subsequently describes Eugenia's various physical impairments as being invisible to her interlocutors, a description that flies in the face of Eugenia's writings. While Eugenia's marriage to Melmond appears a favorable one to her on a number of levels (Melmond is, after all, the young man whom she has desired throughout much of the novel) there is a sense in which the narrative abandons its criticism of the male gaze. Burney writes of Eugenia on the penultimate page of the novel, "Where her countenance was looked at, her complexion was forgotten; while her voice was heard, her figure was unobserved; where her virtues were known, they seemed but to be enhanced by her personal misfortunes" (912). Here, Burney implies that it is up to visibly impaired individuals to overcome their tribulations through their development of virtue and intelligence, attributes which will supposedly help those with ordinary bodies to overlook unusual physical appearances. Burney also suggests that the male gaze is something that can be sidestepped, an idea which Eugenia's autobiography roundly dismisses. And yet again, the novel is making a concerted effort to disassociate the mind from the body, with Eugenia's voice and virtue overriding her various defects. The ending contradicts other parts of the novel (most notably Eugenia's memoirs, quoted above), and this inconsistency leaves us to wonder at the likes of Eugenia's happiness and place within aristocratic society. The fact that Eugenia is married off to Melmond, who is often "enfeebled . . . by a tender sensibility" just as Eugenia is "enfeebled" by her various physical disabilities, suggests that Burney may be discomfited leaving her as a young, wealthy widow, instead opting to marry her off to a highly sentimental young man (699). Might this pairing of variably-embodied characters reveal that, for Burney, a possible solution to the crisis of gender in the 1790s—characterized by the lack of "a distinct gender site" for women—is both a return to sentimentalized masculinity and a movement toward a more advanced form of education for women?[54]

Camilla's contradictory concluding take on Eugenia, however, muddles any coherent answer to this question because it registers uncertainty over the mind-body connection and the roles of gender and sensibility in the Age of Reform. Though *Camilla* often seems to value Eugenia's mind and disregard her body, it also reveals at various points that Eugenia's mind and body in fact work in tandem—her disabled body enabling her apt mind. Eugenia's writings demonstrate that she finally comes of age by calling attention to and critiquing a very real and harrowing social plight faced by women who were visibly physically impaired in one way or another at the time that Burney wrote this novel, and yet this critique is subsequently softened by Eugenia's marriage and her "forgotten" and "unobserved" defects. After considering this and other textual inconsistencies from *Camilla* and *The Fables of Æsop,* we might take note of the cultural uncertainty over physical disability in the late eighteenth century that is marked by an attempt to celebrate the virtuous, intellectual, and philosophical mind while looking past the crippled body, but also by an inability—for Frances Burney and Æsop's biographer, anyway—to adequately satisfy this endeavor.

QUEER OCULAR RELATIONS IN EDGEWORTH'S *BELINDA*

Burney typically portrays staring in *Camilla* as a one-sided action: young men gaze upon Eugenia's body, and Eugenia does not return their hard glares until the end of the novel, when she begins her autobiography. Through Eugenia's character, Burney poses a challenge to contemporaneous views about women's education and variable bodies. However, Eugenia is not exactly a subversive character; by novel's end, she puts aside her feminist writings in favor of marriage, at which point her various forms of physical difference are said to no longer be visible. *Belinda*, conversely, depicts the stare between Harriet Freke and Lady Delacour as a two-way affair, in which curiosity and awe become the catalysts for a queer relationship that disrupts the romance- and conduct-oriented plot that would seem to drive the narrative. Staring between these characters represents a gateway to queer kinship, even if such intimacy gets coded as spectacularly exotic and dangerous. Harriet stands at the nexus of these prospects due to a consistent, public exhibition of maleness that is at odds with the heterosexual romance plot.[55] Harriet at last experiences crural disfigurement when stepping in a man trap during one of many "frolics" that cause scandal and domestic unrest.[56] Far from shying away from terms of difference, as Eugenia often does when she is in public spaces, Harriet exults in them. This enduring iconoclasm could be said to signpost the contours of proper femininity. And yet, in wanting above all to be seen, Harriet reworks such conduct limitations for women and gender nonconforming people through the spot-on presentation of male rakish revelry. Harriet's character in turn reveals the elasticity of gendered, classed, and sexed codes at the dawn of a new century. The various romps that Harriet pursues aid in the novel's trenchant critique of heterosexuality and gender normativity. In the character of Harriet, Edgeworth aligns physical disability with gender mobility to establish the queer social conditions out of which the heteronormative ending at last asserts itself. The compelling, multifaceted interplay between private domesticity and public transgender subjectivity in *Belinda* reveals the mutability of optical perspectives as well as the limitations of arbitrary gender norms. In flouting such norms publicly, Harriet and Lady Delacour offer a model of intimacy in which spectating queer bodies rework the logics (and limits) of classed heterosexual domesticity.

A dynamic, tacitly agreed upon staring relationship flourishes between Harriet and Lady Delacour. The scenes in which the two stare upon one another in mutual fascination, attraction, and, finally, abnegation, flout polite decorum and detract considerably from the corrective, heteronormative plot. As Lisa L. Moore argues, Edgeworth's representation of Harriet as a "warning to women readers" indicates a very real possibility that "such representations might exceed their intended effect, allowing women readers access to the indecent behaviors they read about and to those (perhaps different) that are produced by the act of reading independently for pleasure itself."[57] This tension between dangerous and pleasurable outlets outside of the domestic sphere animates the high-spirited rapport that develops between Lady Delacour and Harriet. Harriet first appears in the novel in an inset narrative, which Lady Delacour relates to Belinda to account for her enigmatic breast wound. Lady Delacour recounts the significant moments leading up to the wounding incident—a cross-dressed pistol duel gone awry—by detailing her life of dissipation as a rich heiress who revels in all manner of extravagance. She meets Harriet in the midst of ongoing domestic troubles with her husband and various maternal failures, and describes her initial attraction to Harriet in these terms:

You see I had nothing at home, either in the shape of husband or children, to engage my affections. I believe it was this 'aching void' in my heart which made me, after looking abroad some time for a bosom friend, take such a prodigious fancy to Mrs. Freke. She was just then coming into fashion—she struck me the first time I met her, as being downright ugly; but there was a wild oddity in her countenance which made one stare at her, and she was delighted to be stared at—especially by me—so we were mutually agreeable to each other—I as starer, and she as staree. (43)

This passage indicates the manner in which Lady Delacour is instantly enthralled by Harriet, who becomes a most captivating substitute for ongoing domestic strife. The "aching void" of Lady Delacour's heart—that empty space where, according to Christian principles, domestic bliss and spiritual harmony must reside—needs to be occupied by someone, and Harriet comes to fill that void.[58] Lady Delacour describes the "prodigious fancy" that she immediately takes to Harriet, characterizing the incipient bond between them as that of "starer" and "staree" (43). Edgeworth's use of *staree* to describe Harriet's "wild oddity" speaks to an implied agreement between the two characters and is utterly innovative for the history of the written English language. According to the *Oxford English Dictionary*, Edgeworth's use of *staree* is the first in the written records available, directing attention to her creative use of language and to the subversive relationship that she depicts between mutually engaged characters. In staring upon one another in such a fashion, Lady Delacour and Harriet Freke deviate from conduct manuals that warn against a "wanton Eye," which, as Hannah Woolley had written over a century earlier, "is the truest evidence of a wandring and distracted mind."[59] The eye, according to Woolley, should not behold "the comeliness of any Creature" but should be drawn instead "up to Heaven" to behold the majesty of god.[60] The utter delight which Harriet and Lady Delacour take in one another's company culminates in a series of escapades in which their inquisitive eyes, far from beholding the majesty of the heavens, are set firmly upon one another to behold one another's "comeliness." Harriet's body often attracts the gaze of women such as Lady Delacour who seek something different from the narrow, prescriptive conduct norms that define their livelihoods. By characterizing the relationship between Lady Delacour and Harriet as that of starer and staree, Edgeworth imbues their rapport with a visible queer eroticism that persists through the narrative, even after their mutual falling out. Their relationship also indicates a set of narrative coordinates in which physical disability and transgender bodies co-exist in sensorial ways that are especially visual in orientation.

The visual terms of the starer-staree relationship that binds Lady Delacour to Mrs. Freke is a vivid literary instance of what Rosemarie Garland-Thomson calls "baroque staring."[61] According to Garland-Thomson, baroque staring is a two-way form of prolonged looking that opposes "proper" forms of staring, the latter of which are typically characterized by "decorous, selective looking."[62] Garland-Thomson describes baroque staring as "flagrantly stimulus driven" and as a "rogue looking that refuses to be corralled into acceptable attention.... It is gaping-mouthed, unapologetic staring."[63] Based linguistically on the seventeenth-century artistic style of the same name, in which the artist revels in sensory detail and disregards emergent forms of scientific rationality, baroque staring marks a meeting between two individuals in which there is "unrepentant abandonment to the unruly, to that which refuses to conform to the dominant order of knowledge."[64] In literary representation, I would add, a baroque stare might be accompanied by chaotic representations of sights and sounds that capture the unruliness of the novel world represented therein, for looking is often tied to the other senses, with the visual, aural, and haptic working together in especially interconnected ways. The baroque stare thus entertains possibilities that might seem alien, shocking, or downright dangerous.

The indecorous hazards of the baroque stare are also instructive for conceptualizing queer relationships in homophobic and transphobic settings, such as the one that Edgeworth represents in such memorable terms in *Belinda*. The connection between Harriet and Lady Delacour is supremely invested in visual, aural, and haptic representations of outrageous behavior, especially on Harriet's part. As a high-ranking person of fashion and proud "staree," Harriet is accompanied by the chaotic sights and sounds that invoke irrationality in Edgeworth's narrative. Lady Delacour uses a colorful metaphor to capture this, referring to herself here in the third person: "Lady Delacour's sprightly elegance was pale—not to say faded pink, compared with the scarlet of Mrs. Freke's dashing audacity" (43). Harriet, according to Lady Delacour, "is downright brass—but of the finest kind—Corinthian brass" (43). Harriet's imperviousness to shame—her resolute impudence—takes on the metaphorical hardness and fineness of the best of the bronze metals available in the period. With her colorful and fashionable brazenness always on display, Harriet emboldens Lady Delacour to take enormous social risks that would compromise her reputation. Such risks range from Lady Delacour's highly public flirtation with Colonel Lawless, with all of the trappings of an extramarital affair, and culminate in Lady Delacour's cross-dressed pistol duel with Mrs. Luttridge, her sworn enemy. In the latter of these episodes, Lady Delacour sustains a breast injury from the recoil of the pistol shot that she fires into the air. The frenzied sounds that follow the pistol misfire likewise ring out in the passage: "a loud shout" accompanies the mob of townspeople that attempt to corral and punish the participants for their cross-dressed frolic. The sound of a "large herd of squeaking, grunting pigs" that run "squeaking from one side of the road to the other" is accompanied by the shouts of the townsmen, who yell, "Shame! Shame! Shame!—duck 'em, duck 'em—gentle or simple—duck 'em!" (58). The sonic and visual chaos of this scene—a transphobic, peasant-led riot in the midst of a novel about women's conduct—marks the baroque style that Lady Delacour and Harriet embody. The stare that initially brings the two together is that which brings about the narrative disorder of grunting pigs and flailing bodies. So, while the prevailing plot of the narrative is Lady Delacour's conversion from intractable socialite to domestic-bound wife and mother, the inset narrative that Lady Delacour relates to Belinda represents in detail a series of public displays of public female and transgender agency that fly in the face of the novel's established order of heterosexual patriarchy (always precarious in any case). The ocular relationship between Lady Delacour and Mrs. Freke thus represents rogue, queer modes of being that resist visual and aural coherence and gesture toward the unassimilable.

The intimacy that builds between Lady Delacour and Harriet poses further uncertainty to an already unstable set of gendered codes that, as we saw previously in this chapter with regard to *Camilla*, mark the Age of Reform.[65] The baroque stares that they share open up experiential possibilities that exceed the bounds of the two-sex system—a seemingly natural arrangement that could not account for the array of gender identities that existed in the eighteenth century.[66] In Lady Delacour and Harriet's ocular relationship, they accept gender mobility as a given by repudiating the Enlightenment tendency toward a rational organization of gender categories, insisting instead upon wonder, which, as Garland-Thomson writes, "places starer and staree in dynamic relation" and is the catalyst for new modes of thinking and being.[67] What Harriet brings to the narrative, beyond the "harum scarum manners" that attract so many, is a public performance of masculinity that utterly fascinates Lady Delacour and that undermines binary thinking about sex and gender. As "*man-woman*," as she is derisively called, Harriet shows gender binaries to be untenable (219). Take for instance Lady Delacour's description of Harriet's ability to pass as male: "Harriet had no conscience, so she was always at ease; and never more so than in male attire, which she had been told became her particularly. She supported that character of a young rake with such spirit and *truth*, that I am sure no common conjurer could have discovered anything feminine about her" (47). Harriet's ability to embody the "truth" or seeming essence of classed masculinity in such a convincing fashion speaks to the ways in which gender is permeable, performative, and not tied to biological sex. Edgeworth poses this very possibility in a number of passages, including one in which Lady Delacour remarks upon Harriet's "bold masculine arms" (49). Because Harriet is never once represented in women's clothing, Harriet's embodying of gender is undeniably stable: always dressed as a man, Harriet assumes male masculinity in word and deed, and is a transgender character. Harriet is regularly remarked upon as occupying a third (or "unsexed") gender. Lady Delacour, for instance, muses that "though [Harriet] had laid aside the modesty of her own sex, [she] had not acquired the decency of the other" (47–48). In the gendered terms of sensibility and virtue, Harriet is relegated to the blank space of an unnamed gender category.

Moreover, Harriet is typically accounted for in transphobic ways in the narrative, but these passages also serve to underscore the visibility of transgender embodiment at the turn of the nineteenth century. As Belinda accompanies Mr. Vincent and Mr. Percival on a country excursion, for instance, the group approaches an inscrutable form in the distance that turns out to be Harriet. Noteworthy in this passage is the uncertainty that accompanies the dialogue among the three with respect to Harriet's gender identity. Mr. Percival asks, "What is that yonder on the top of one of the great rocking stones?" The passage which follows this query is quoted at length, with my own emphasis on gender and object pronouns:

> "*It* looks like a statue," said Vincent. "*It* has been put up since we were here last."
> "I fancy *it* has got up of *it*self," said Belinda, "for *it* seems to be getting down of *it*self. I think I saw *it* stoop. O! I see now, *it* is a man who has got up there, and *he* seems to have a gun in *his* hand, has not *he*? *He* is going through his manual exercise for *his* diversion—for the diversion of the spectators below, I perceive—there is a party of people looking at *him*."
> "*Him*!" said Mr. Percival.
> "I protest *it* is a *woman*!" said Vincent.
> "No, surely," said Belinda: "*It* cannot be a *woman*!"
> "Not unless *it* be Mrs. Freke," replied Mr. Percival.
>
> In fact, it was Mrs. Freke, who had been out shooting with a party of gentlemen, and who had scrambled up on this rocking stone.... As they rode nearer to the scene of action, Belinda heard the shrill screams of a female voice, and they descried amongst the gentlemen a slight figure in a riding habit. (250)

Harriet is placed upon a kind of pedestal for all to gaze upon, a staree whose intention is to incite astonishment in the marveling onlookers. The excursionists' initial protracted stare at what appears to be a statue has the makings of a baroque stare, in the form of "gaping, open-mouthed staring."[68] Soon, however, their stares become stares of mastery, in which they seek to identify, to categorize, and to ultimately dominate through the authoritative language of gender pronouns. The language of the passage shifts from the inhuman to the human, and then to a breakdown of language altogether. At first, Mr. Vincent believes that they gaze upon a statue, perhaps because of Harriet's imposing height and placement atop the rocking stone. Harriet is thus, from first appearance in the passage, already dehumanized. In what remains of the conversation, Belinda further degrades Harriet. In her response to Mr. Vincent, Belinda ascertains that the figure is indeed *not* a statue due to that figure's movement, and yet in her seeming inability to codify the figure as male or female opts for a third term: "I think I saw *it* stoop." *It* renders Harriet as nonhuman and monstrous in the way that transgender subjects are often subjected to violence through blatant misgendering. But in the following sentence, Belinda switches pronoun registers from *it* to *he*, from "it is a man" to "he seems to have a gun in his hand." The phallic quality of the held gun is so obvious as to hardly require comment, but Belinda's attempt at masterful staring breaks down: Harriet is neither *he* nor *she*—and especially not *it*—none of these pronouns adequately capture Harriet's gender, and Belinda's masterful stare is confounded. The fact that Harriet is once again reveling in the role of "staree," with a multitude of witnesses observing a thrilling performance of military exercises, indicates a recalcitrant resistance to the masterful optics of naturalized gender binaries.

The final dominating impulse of the excursionists is to come to a conclusive statement about Harriet's body. Mr. Vincent insists that the figure in the distance is a woman, but Belinda responds with incredulity, and Mr. Percival insinuates that neither gender properly applies to Harriet when he says, "Not unless it be Mrs. Freke." Here, Harriet's name becomes its own gendered term: Harriet is both exception and rule. In the end, none of the gawking party can adequately justify or rationalize Harriet's display of military ability. The group's vexed exchange and prolonged stare at what they deem an impenetrable figure are interrupted by the "shrill screams of a female voice" which come from "a slight figure in a riding-habit" (250). Then, as the group approaches the rocking stone, they hear Harriet "laughing loud as she rocked this frightened girl upon the top of the stone" (250). Is Harriet symbolically dragging the "slight figure," who turns out to be young Miss Moreton, to the brink of social destruction by encouraging her to don "men's whole boots" instead of the "half boots" customary of young women? Mr. Percival thinks so, and Belinda concurs: "What a lesson to young ladies in the choice of female friends" (252). Now, according to Belinda's "proper" or masterful staring that the novel appears to sanction, such a statement might seem persuasive. The virtues and pitfalls of female friendship, after all, are among the most explicit lessons of the novel. However, Harriet's regularly articulated bombshells, whether intended to scorn female delicacy or to speak out for women's rights ("I hate slavery! Viva la liberte! . . . I'm a champion for the Rights of Women") disrupt the flow of the narrative, rendering the queer subplot an ongoing source of productive tension with the heteronormative main plot (229). As Ula Klein argues, Harriet's vocal interjections about women's empowerment, though perhaps of a reductive nature, are a clear reminder that radical ideas from the likes of Wollstonecraft imagine the world differently for women.[69] The tension between proper and baroque staring and the jarring auditory cues that disorder the narrative situate Harriet on the fringes of the decorous society that *Belinda* in many ways endorses. However, Harriet's visual and auditory interruptions represent that which cannot be properly codified or written off as mere foolishness. Harriet is a recalcitrant subject who, like the ladies of *Millenium Hall*, signals exceptional ways of being in the world.

The baroque optics that characterize Harriet's relationship with Lady Delacour operate in an ebb and flow manner, with Lady Delacour switching roles to become *staree* and Harriet functioning as *starer* at critical moments of the narrative. During these dynamic acts of mutual staring, Harriet dares Lady Delacour to break with the propriety that governs women's actions in polite society. The cross-dressed pistol duel that Harriet incites is, of course, one of these moments, but a night carriage ride to a conjurer's dimly lit home serves as yet another example of transgressive behavior incited by Freke's intense gaze. As she is readying to depart from a night of gambling and "high spirits" with her "coxcomb" companion, Colonel Lawless, Lady Delacour is apprehended by what she at first thinks is "a smart-looking young man" that "stared [her] full in the face . . . and jumped into the carriage after [her]" (45). Harriet's penetrating stare is the means by which a chaotic adventure begins. When Colonel Lawless demands to know who the unknown man is, Harriet laughs and declares, "Who am I! Only a Freke!" Harriet follows this pronouncement with a manifesto: "Fun and Freke for ever, huzza!" (46). Harriet's frantic, fast-paced speech serves as the catalyst for the nocturnal adventure that follows. Lady Delacour relates her full absorption in Harriet as they embark on a carriage ride to an unknown part: "Harriet was mad with spirits, and so noisy and unmanageable that, as I told her, I was sure she was drunk. . . . I was so taken up with her oddities, that, for some time, I did not perceive we were going the Lord knows where" (46). Harriet's unwieldy queerness occupies an unorthodox, nocturnal temporality that guides Lady Delacour down unlit streets. After a mortifying visit to a dimly lit conjurer's home, where Lady Delacour learns that her fortune is to divorce Lord Delacour and marry Colonel Lawless, Harriet abandons Lady Delacour in the carriage with Colonel Lawless, who attempts to take sexual liberties with her. As catalyst to the late-night carriage ride and disruptor to one of the enduring pillars of heteronormativity—women's monogamous commitment to their husbands—Harriet subverts the established order of normative domesticity and subjects Lady Delacour to the possibility of male sexual violence, which Lady Delacour appears to casually dismiss as par for the course. The baroque staring that marks the ocular relationship between Harriet and Lady Delacour threatens to overturn completely Lady Delacour's already weakened nuclear family. As the final volume of *Belinda* reveals, the reconciliation of Lady Delacour's family is marked by the severing of her ocular relationship with Harriet, though Lady Delacour applies what she has learned in this relationship to her familial arrangement.

STAGING THE STARE: EDGEWORTH'S PERFORMATIVE RESOLUTION

The culmination of the ocular relationship between Harriet Freke and Lady Delacour is an encounter that, as Garland-Thomson would put it, "redefines both" in decidedly corporeal ways.[70] In a critical passage, Edgeworth imposes a dramatic narrative shift by bringing the queerness of their shared relationship to bear on their bodies. As a physician, Dr. X., attends to her seeming mortal breast injury, Lady Delacour is gravely affected by nightly visits from what appears to be an apparition in the form of Colonel Lawless (who has at this point in the narrative already been killed in a duel with Lord Delacour). Lady Delacour, under the influence of opium and Methodist tracts, believes that her ghostly stalker is there to announce her imminent demise. From her vantage point, Lady Delacour witnesses the visits in "forms that flit before my eyes when I am between sleeping and waking" (307–308). The unknown visitor turns out to be Harriet Freke, on a spy's mission (and in male spy's clothing) to uncover compromising information about Lady Delacour. Lady Delacour's incessant staring at the stalker deprives her of her will to live and she soon gives up all hope of recovery. Lady Delacour's inability to countenance the true identity of the intruder induces a fatal fear in her, and this is also the point in the narrative at which her breast injury appears most fatal. The wound and the visitor, then, function as parallel mysteries which must be deciphered. This scene also underscores the widening rift between Lady Delacour and Harriet, who are no longer in cahoots, but who still rely on one another for the shaping of their public and private identities.

In a last-ditch effort to save her friend from destruction, Belinda, all pluckiness and skepticism, endeavors to solve the mystery with her own inquisitive stare. As she beholds the "apparition" herself, her eyes once again fail her: "The figure stood still for some moments. [Belinda] advanced a few steps nearer to the window, and the figure vanished. [Belinda] kept her eye steadily fixed upon the spot where it had disappeared, and she saw it rise again and glide quickly behind some bushes" (309). As in the rocking stone scene, Harriet eludes Belinda's stares of dominance for a period of time. Belinda's inability to countenance Harriet's identity from a distance exposes the chasm between the infallibly decorous sentiment that guides Belinda's comportment and the dangerous liminality that surrounds Harriet. The true identity of the ghostly visitor eludes Belinda until Harriet cries out in distress when stepping in a spring-trap. Subsequently, as Belinda approaches what at first appears to be a strange man, she is struck by the figure's "wonderful resemblance to Harriet Freke" (310). Harriet, now injured, soon learns of the severity of the leg's cuts and bruises, "that the beauty of her legs would be spoiled, and that she would never be able to appear to advantage in man's apparel" (312). Harriet consequently feels ashamed of the failed mission and is finished as Lady Delacour's staree; their rapport has officially terminated: "The dread of being seen by Lady Delacour in the deplorable yet ludicrous situation . . . operated next upon her mind, and every time the door of her apartment opened, she looked with terror towards it, expecting to see her ladyship appear" (312). At last, a disciplinary gaze is levied upon Harriet due to the spring-trap mishap. The ocular relationship between Lady Delacour and Harriet thus marks both characters' bodies in unmistakable ways, with Lady Delacour finally recovering from the bruise on her breast and Harriet left ailing with a badly disfigured leg. Despite the leg injury, Harriet's insistent resistance amounts to an evasion of social subjugation that serves as a reminder of the possibilities for women and gender nonconforming people in the public and private spheres, even if this reminder is in the form of a warning. The character of Harriet, while perhaps intended as a cautionary tale, also probes and reworks the gender/sex system in ways that the narrative's staged closure fails to regulate.

Because she summarily dismisses Harriet from the plot to focus on Belinda and Clarence Hervey's circuitous courtship and to put the final touches on Lady Delacour's domestication, Edgeworth might appear to abandon the air of unruly queerness and impairment that, throughout volumes one and two, mark the ocular relationship between Lady Delacour and Harriet. However, Harriet's transgender embodiment, while nonexistent in volume three, is not at odds with the narrative's decidedly staged denouement in which Lady Delacour invites the reader to visualize ideal domesticity as theatrically performed. In this scene, virtuous characters are rewarded with a happy ending of harmonious coupledom and nuclear family reconciliation. These worthy remaining characters grasp one another affectionately in a culminating gesture that grants one last look at the construction of standard domesticity in Edgeworth's novel. As she positions each of the characters, Lady Delacour tells them, "Let me place you all in proper attitudes for stage effect. What signifies being happy, unless we appear so?" (478). Through Lady Delacour, Edgeworth reveals that the generic expectations of novel closure are tied directly to the *appearance* of household tranquility, personal reform, and health, all of which work together to confer legitimacy to reproductive futures and, relatedly, to households free of illness and deformity. And what better way to "show" these facets of a desirable conclusion than through allusion to stage performance, which, as Terry F. Robinson points out, allows Edgeworth to demonstrate Lady Delacour's spiritual and physical transformation, rather than merely describe it?[71] Notably absent from this last scene is Harriet, who has been corporeally punished for "wild oddity" (43). But even if Edgeworth's concluding scene does not portray the kind of subversive baroque staring that Harriet promulgates, there is still ambiguity in Edgeworth's commentary on the shape of the healthy nuclear family. In showcasing some characters in this scene and omitting others, Edgeworth makes explicit the heteronormative and ableist contours of the novel form, but does not leave these fictional standards unchallenged.

By bringing the performative orientation of theater to the last pages of the novel, Edgeworth exposes the discursive apparatuses that undergird the novel. As Michael Gamer argues, Edgeworth's brand of fiction mediates between the realism often attributed to other novels from her contemporaries (such as Burney) and the romances that were said to pre-date and contrast with said realism.[72] In what Gamer calls Edgeworth's "romance of real life," I would argue, Edgeworth also shows the fictional quality of healthy heteronormative domesticity through adoption of dramatic technique.[73] The concluding lines of the performance draw directly from theatrical convention, with Lady Delacour delivering the epilogue:

> Now, Lady Delacour, to show that she is reformed, comes forward to address the audience with a moral—a moral!—yes,
> Our *tale* contains a moral, and, no doubt, You all have wit enough to find it out. (478)

Rather than announce in a direct manner the moral of the novel, Lady Delacour invites readers to speculate for themselves what it might be. Moreover, Lady Delacour is the one to deliver these lines in order "to show that she is reformed" (478). By insinuating that Lady Delacour's newly acquired morality is in need of proof, and by leaving the moral up for grabs to readers with "wit enough to find it out," Edgeworth implies that the gendering of maternal and wifely roles within the nuclear family are as much about presentation—or more to the point, *re*presentation—as it is anything else (478). The shifting optical dynamics of this scene position the reader as the ultimate, privileged starer, with Lady Delacour once again assuming the role of staree. In this way, Edgeworth makes visible the organization of the nuclear family, which is formally at center stage and carefully arranged for the reading public to consume and adopt. Given that all of the characters' bodies on stage are, by this point, in good health, the denouement also gestures toward the pivotal role that an ideal physical constitution plays in the formation of domestic bliss.

However, such an ending suggests that *all* relationships—from the utterly conventional to the queer—are performed for the spectating other and that, relatedly, one's health must also be confirmed through exhibition. As Lady Delacour's orchestrated scene attests, the demonstration of one's health has the effect of substantiating heterosexual romance and securing the nuclear family's primacy. Edgeworth's deliberate staging of healthy heterosexuality speaks to the empiricist orientation of Enlightenment thought, in which one arrives at truth through the senses. This dramatization also applies the tenets of the ocular relations between Harriet and a once-ailing Lady Delacour. Their relationship is a visual performance of its own, a staged version of kinship that is queer, disruptive, embodied—even if, in the end, it is concealed from the reader's view, it is too vibrant throughout the narrative to dismiss. In this way *Belinda*, like *Camilla* before it, contains a contradiction of its own: though it registers queer excess through deleterious symptoms on the body that function as physiognomic indications of depravity, it also offers an affective blueprint for women and gender nonconformists that threatens to undermine the core values of the British domestic sphere. Lady Delacour and Harriet's history is narrated to readers who would have been accustomed to narratives about adventurous stage actresses, but their story is also one that imagines queer relationships through the very kind of hypervisible display that Lady Mary Wortley Montagu considers dangerous for young women.[74] Given the tension between that inset narrative and the main plot, *Belinda* offers insight into how people look at one another and therefore how they look at difference. The act of staring, for Edgeworth, is at its most subversive when it is grounded in consensual ocular relationships between queer subjects. Edgeworth also shows that the social boundaries secured by the healthy nuclear family are maintained in part by the very act of staring that defines queer relationships. As Edgeworth's final narrative staging suggests, even the most normative of healthy heterosexual arrangements are performed and are therefore malleable and unnatural.

CONCLUSION

In concluding the novel in a theatrical manner, Edgeworth affirms that heterosexual domesticity has to be performed and seen by observant bystanders to be granted its social ascendency. Lady Delacour's health in the final scene is likewise made visible to the reader, and would seem to secure the most desirable future for her nuclear family, now reconciled and together. However, the very establishment of these corresponding principles is obscured to some degree by the colorful hypervisibility of the queer ocular connection that ties Lady Delacour's ailing body to Harriet Freke's rapscallion maleness. The inset narrative dedicated to their starer-staree relationship, and the disorderly manner in which it spills over into the heterosexual courtship drama beyond that inset narrative, establishes a binary between normative embodiment and queer eroticism that is eventually dismantled in the gestural, performed ending. *Belinda* thus offers a story in which normative and queer sexualities are not in competition with one another for narrative coherence, but are, on the contrary, complementary schemas that aid in the shaping of the novel. *Belinda* establishes health as a symptom of heterosexual domesticity, only to destabilize this fiction with a staged ending that announces the elastic performativity of all bodily orientations and forms of unions. In *Camilla*, Burney relies upon another popular genre of the day—the autobiography—which, like drama in *Belinda*, underscores the polymorphous character of the variegated novel form. Eugenia's employment of autobiography enables her to respond to the viciousness of the men (such as Bellamy) who have made her life miserable. *Camilla* likewise ends with matrimonial bliss and glosses over the subject of Eugenia's variable body by claiming that her defects are no longer observable in the context of social relations. This bodily erasure is in line with the tenets of narrative prosthesis but is also suggestive of the ways in which heterosexuality must be flexible enough to encompass properly classed and gendered forms of physical difference.

When Eugenia dares to stare back at the men of her social circles through her incisive autobiography, she offers one of *Camilla*'s most probing critiques of men who would ensure women's virtue through surveillance. In this way, Eugenia critiques conformity to a gendered status quo that is ultimately inhospitable to variably-embodied women. In *Belinda*, the gaze between Lady Delacour and Harriet is only decipherable to them and is narrated in an inset narrative that seems to be set apart from the main plot, but which has lasting narrative implications. When Belinda, the conduct model for young women, tries to participate in the staring that connects Lady Delacour and Harriet, she is utterly confounded, and though she is validated by the narrative for her virtue and disciplined mind, she can never be said to impose dominance on the variable body that is Harriet's. Both Edgeworth's *Belinda* and Burney's *Camilla* end with assertions of heterosexual romance, but because they also include vast social canvases, in which an array of character types, bodies, and desires appear, those endings are hardly neat in their containment of bodily or sexual difference. Scenes such as the one in which Harriet appears majestically atop the rocking stone, presenting maleness and leading young women astray from the narrow confines of socially acceptable womanhood, or Eugenia's decision to take up the pen and critique the society of which she is part, make visible an array of social outlets for women. The act of staring at variable bodies is what makes these possibilities viable. In *Camilla*, staring forecloses possibilities for young women's development, as is the case with Eugenia when she is surrounded by ogling men, but ends with the declaration that women ought to stare back; in *Belinda*, staring opens up paths to expression and understanding that gesture toward the affirmation of, and intimacies between, queer bodies. While both novels conclude with conventional heterosexual marriage, health, and normative domestic arrangements, these endings hardly eradicate the social and political possibilities raised by transformative, mutually consensual ocular relationships. These novels show that heteronormativity and able-bodiedness are systems upon which narratives often rely for closure, but also that these systems are shaped in significant ways by the very bodies that fall short of their impossible demands. The futures promised by these novels, in other words, are circumscribed by the queer and variable bodies that make them possible. In the characters of Eugenia Tyrold, Harriet Freke, and Lady Delacour, we observe imaginative and expansive ways of thinking, and transformative models of being, for women and all those who do not fit neatly in the two-sex system.

NOTES

1. Foucault, *Discipline and Punish*, 195–230.
2. Foucault, *The Birth of the Clinic*.
3. See for instance, de Beauvoir, *The Second Sex*; and Mulvey, "Visual Pleasure and Narrative Cinema," 833–844.
4. Jessica A. Volz explores the ways in which British women writers at the turn of the nineteenth century use literary representations of visuality to probe and challenge patriarchal constraints. Volz argues for the significance of visual cues in fiction of the era: "Visuality, more than free indirect discourse, provided women writers with a discreet means of shifting views and viewpoints in order to show that even if their heroines conformed outwardly, they were beginning to see and think in ways that called appearances and patriarchal authority into question." See Volz, *Visuality in the Novels of Austen, Radcliffe, Edgeworth and Burney*, 22.

5. Rictor Norton writes about the various cruising grounds of London, such as "The Sodomites' Walk" in Moorfield, among many others. See Norton, *Mother Clap's Molly House*, 70–91.
6. Rosemarie Garland-Thomson, *Staring*, 15.
7. Ibid., 3.
8. Felicity Nussbaum cites extraordinary uses of the teeter-totter, or seesaw, at the turn of the nineteenth century in England. It "was . . . sometimes curiously prescribed as treatment for patients to correct . . . deformity of the back." Curiously, as Nussbaum points out, Burney uses the seesaw as the means by which Eugenia's back is disfigured in the first place. Nussbaum, *Limits of the Human*, 121–123.
9. Burney, *Camilla*, 33. Further references to the novel will appear parenthetically in the text.
10. Montagu, *Letters and Works of Lady Wortley Montagu, Volume 2*, 162.
11. The *Spectator* often warns against men staring at women, but there is also an example from No. 492 in which the letter writer, Matilda Mohair, complains of a woman named Dulceorella who has "a peculiar Art of staring at a young Fellow, till she sees she has got him, and inflam'd him by so much Observation." In this instance, staring is assumed to be an inappropriate way of interacting between the sexes, and particularly so because it is a sign of a young woman's sexual assertiveness. Addison and Steele, "Spectator No. 492" in *The Spectator*, 91.
12. Deutsch, *Loving Dr. Johnson*, 71.
13. Ibid., 71.
14. Ibid., 72.
15. Deutsch, *Resemblance and Disgrace*.
16. Bacon, *Essays Moral, Economical, and Political*, 201–203.
17. Hay, *Deformity*, 68.
18. Ibid., 69.
19. Ibid., 4.
20. Lewis, *The English Fable*.
21. Croxall, *The Fables of Æsop*, x.
22. Ibid., x–xi.
23. Though the 1793 biography I have been citing makes a point of aligning itself with Sir Roger L'Estrange's view that Æsop was physically distinctive in appearance, there is another 1793 collection about Æsop—*The Life of Esop*—in which R. Dodsley's narrator sides with Samuel Croxall's perspective that "Esop was of a handsome countenance and shape" rather "than ugly and deformed." In Dodsley's version, there is an implied unwillingness to accept such an influential Western thinker as Æsop as appearing in such an atypical fashion. Dodsley instead insists on assigning the deformed body in question to an Arabic fabulist, Lokman, thereby imagining deformity as non-white and non-European. This dispute over Æsop's physical aspect demonstrates that the cultural anxiety over the visibly distinctive body had implications for English/Western identity and its investment in classical literature and philosophy throughout the century. See Dodsley, *Select Fables of Esop and Other Fabulists*, xi.
24. Ibid., xlvi.
25. Croxall, *The Fables of Æsop*, 4.
26. Ibid., 5.
27. Scott, *Agreeable Ugliness*, 13.
28. Gonda, "Sarah Scott and 'The Sweet Excess of Paternal Love,'" 511–535.
29. Scott, *Agreeable Ugliness*, 57.
30. Ibid., 13. *Agreeable Ugliness* ends with the narrator using her body as a defense against patriarchal mandate, much in the same way that Eugenia uses her body as a means of self-representation and critique against the male gaze in *Camilla*.

31. Wollstonecraft, "A Vindication of the Rights of Woman," 257.
32. Ibid., 257.
33. The Bluestockings are notable exceptions to this rule. Elizabeth Montagu, Sarah Fielding, and Elizabeth Carter (who translated all of the works of Epictetus, the Stoic philosopher), among others, had profound understandings of the classics and were apt translators of Greek texts to modern English. For more on the these remarkable women, see for example, Rizzo, *Companions Without Vows*, as well as Nussbaum, *The Limits of the Human*. Burney herself (along with her close friend Hester Thrale) learned some Greek from Samuel Johnson. However, Burney's insecurities learning language skills deemed inappropriate for women caused her to regard a classical education as something which she "would always dread to have known." See Doody, *Frances Burney*, 240–243.
34. Porter, "Spreading Medical Enlightenment," 215–216.
35. In Georgian England, inoculation was extremely important because smallpox was such an enormous public health threat: excessively contagious, it could either cause death or leave a patient with permanent facial scarring (the latter of these scenarios, as we have seen, is the case for Eugenia). See, for example, Porter, *Disease, Medicine and Society in England, 1550–1860*, 41.
36. See Bloom and Bloom's "Explanatory Notes" pertaining to page 22 from *Camilla*, 931–932.
37. As Michel Foucault reminds us, "abnormality is still a form of regularity." Western Europe's medical discourse of the late eighteenth and nineteenth centuries firmly establishes the Enlightenment notion that the study of anomalous bodies offers insight into the workings of the natural world. Foucault, *The Birth of the Clinic*, 35, 102.
38. Binhammer, "The Economics of Plot in Burney's *Camilla*," 1–20.
39. The fiction of Sarah Scott, as I have already suggested in chapter 2, also grants a fulfillment of desire for women with variable bodies. See, for instance, *Millenium Hall* (1764), which like *Agreeable Ugliness* explores female desire and deformity, though in less conventional ways, with female-female companionship considered a viable, pleasurable, and socially reformist alternative to heterosexual romance.
40. Kristina Straub is less interested in creating a "coherent, consistent or political statement" about Burney and more concerned with "how literature makes and reflects cultural ideology." See Straub, *Divided Fictions*, 3.
41. Johnson, *Equivocal Beings*, 1.
42. Doody, *Frances Burney*, 48.
43. Ibid., 49.
44. Nussbaum, *Limits of the Human*, 126.
45. Johnson, *Equivocal Beings*, 152.
46. Ibid., 152.
47. As Doody points out, this is a "heroic view, but perhaps the wrong one" since Eugenia could have legally gotten out of the marriage. Doody, *The Life in the Works*, 243.
48. Johnson, *Equivocal Beings*, 154–155.
49. This scene has been the speculation of much criticism which my reading of Eugenia does not account for here. For examples of these readings, see McDonagh, *Idiocy: A Cultural History*, or Doody, *Frances Burney*.
50. Haggerty, *Unnatural Affections*, 138.
51. The wealthy English widow could occupy a privileged place within eighteenth-century society. Widows often had control over the estates and money that their deceased husbands left them, and consequently these women had a great deal of autonomy and exercised social power. *Camilla*'s Mrs. Arlbery is a fine example of this eighteenth-century social phenomenon. For more, see Froide's *Never Married* and Vickery's *Behind Closed Doors*.

52. Doody, *Frances Burney*, 240–243.
53. Steele's "Ugly Club" entry reinforces this point. See Steele, "On Personal Defects; Proposals for an Ugly Club." Also, Mr. Tyrold tells Eugenia that "a too acute sensibility of personal defects, is one of the greatest weaknesses of self-love," though he mistakenly cites Addison, not Steele (302). Steele, "On Personal Defects; Proposals for an Ugly Club," from *Selections from the Tatler, Spectator, and Guardian*, 172.
54. Claudia Johnson has identified the 1790's as a time period in which a "crisis of gender" results from the French Revolution. This watershed moment, for Johnson, had the effect of disrupting socially sanctioned gender roles leaving women, in particular, "without a distinct gender site." Johnson, *Equivocal Beings*, 11.
55. I refrain from assigning gender pronouns to Harriet Freke due to the way that the narrative represents Harriet's consistent inhabiting of a male identity, but the narration repeatedly switches between "he" and "she" (and the dehumanizing "it") in reference to Harriet.
56. Edgeworth, *Belinda*, 66. Further references to the novel will appear parenthetically in the text.
57. Moore, *Dangerous Intimacies*, 85.
58. Terry F. Robinson points out that this is a reference to William Cowper's poem "Walking with God." But, given Lady Delacour's Methodism, this could also be a reference to John Wesley's hymnal verse: "No good thing in me resides, / my soul is all an aching void, / Till thy Spirit here abides, / And I am fill'd with God." John Wesley, *A collection of hymns, for the use of the people called Methodists*. See Robinson, "'Life Is a Tragicomedy!,'" 156.
59. Woolley, *The gentlewomans companion*, 39.
60. Ibid., 40.
61. Garland-Thomson, *Staring*, 50–51.
62. Ibid., 50.
63. Ibid., 50.
64. Ibid., 50.
65. Johnson, *Equivocal Beings*, 11.
66. Female husbands and mollies offer eighteenth-century examples of transgender embodiment.
67. Garland-Thomson, 51.
68. Ibid., 50.
69. Klein, "Bosom Friends and the Sapphic Breasts of *Belinda*," 1–13.
70. Garland-Thomson, 50.
71. Robinson cites Edgeworth's praise for Elizabeth Inchbald's *A Simple Story*, which shows rather than tells: "Writers of inferior genius waste their words in describing feeling." Robinson, "'Life Is a Tragicomedy!'"
72. Michael Gamer argues that Edgeworth's fiction mediates between the "realism" attributed to the novel form and the "romance" of gothic tales through a brand of didactic fiction called "romances of real life." Gamer, "Maria Edgeworth and the Romance of Real Life," 232–266.
73. Ibid., 235.
74. Robinson, "'Life Is a Tragicomedy!,'" 158–160.

CODA

Hypochondria and the Implausibility
of Heterosexual Romance in
Jane Austen's *Sanditon* (1817)

THROUGHOUT *NOVEL BODIES*, I HAVE investigated the richness of eighteenth-century British literary depictions of disability and queerness, the joint appearance of which often signals an authorial impulse to write social reform into narrative. A range of eighteenth-century novels, from the canonical to the lesser known, represent variably-embodied characters as imaginative vessels for cultural transformation. Through Duncan Campbell's embodying of an otherworldly queerness, for instance, *The History of the Life and Adventures of Mr. Duncan Campbell* invites readers to ponder the viability of deaf education; through Mrs. Jewkes's monstrous sapphism, Samuel Richardson converts Mr. B. into a man of feeling; through the sapphic and disabled characters that populate *Millenium Hall*, Sarah Scott remedies the patriarchal degradation of society; through Matthew Bramble's gradual attainment of health, Tobias Smollett exposes healthy heterosexuality as both narrative objective and unsustainable fantasy; and through the queer ocular relationship that develops between Harriet Freke and Lady Delacour, Maria Edgeworth envisions forms of gender mobility, bodily variability, and intimacy that exceed the constraints of the two-sex system. These works—in addition to the other novels that I have examined—conceptualize non-normative bodies and desires as mutually sustaining fictions that shape kinship frameworks and social relations generally. Burgeoning constructions of heteronormativity and able-bodiedness in the Enlightenment anticipate by a century or more the establishment of eugenics as an official science. Such a proto-eugenics orientation notwithstanding, deformity and other forms of physical difference in the eighteenth century are often depicted as embodied forms of queerness that cannot be contained or eradicated, even by the regulatory tendencies of novels. As a whole, these works reveal that, while disability can be a one-dimensional catalyst for plot development, it can also stand in for larger sociopolitical discussions and serve as a transformational force in the representational landscape of the period.

Such themes are at the heart of British fiction even if we move forward in time ever so slightly from the period under consideration in this book. Jane Austen's novels, for instance, reveal that intersections of bodily variability and sexuality are at the very heart of the British canon. Before bringing this book to a close, then, I would like to briefly discuss how these literary themes materialize in her oeuvre—particularly in her final work, the unfinished *Sanditon* (1817). In Austen's works, the ideal version of genteel romance typically squares individual choice with economic and class-based interests. Moreover, they represent a healthy constitution in young women as a prerequisite for marriage. In the final pages of *Sense and Sensibility*, for example, Marianne is overcome by a terrible illness but recovers to marry Colonel Brandon; in *Mansfield Park*, Fanny Price is delicate and prone to headaches, but when Sir Thomas Bertram returns from Antigua, he finds her improved "in health and beauty," and she eventually marries her cousin, Edmund Bertram; in *Persuasion*, Anne Elliot gains a second youth—evident in the "bloom and freshness of youth restored . . . on her complexion"—before marrying Frederic Wentworth; and in *Pride and Prejudice*, the physically vigorous Elizabeth Bennet captures the notice of Darcy when she marches through the mud to attend to her ill sister, Jane. Ann de Bourgh, whose "sickly constitution" sets her up as foil to Elizabeth, at last loses out to Elizabeth in marriage to Darcy despite the arranged union that her powerful mother, Lady Catherine de Bourgh, had always promoted.[1] As these examples attest, Austen's heroines either have or acquire visible manifestations of health by the time they marry, aligning them to some degree with the narrative trajectory of Smollett's *The Expedition of Humphry Clinker*.

Sanditon, however, is a departure of sorts for Austen, particularly in the way that she divests the narrative of the urgency of heterosexual coupledom and reproductive futurity. Like her other novels, *Sanditon* contains a host of characters under either real or imagined corporeal distress, but a certain vagueness obscures the romance angle of the narrative: who is to marry whom? Which of the characters would Austen have written into budding heterosexual romance? Even if we take into account that Austen only completed a draft of one volume of *Sanditon*, her indifference to the romantic prospects of the central character, Charlotte Heywood, diverges from her completed works. Unlike other Austenian heroines—who from the beginning of their respective narratives seem meant for marriage because of their economic vulnerability (Elizabeth Bennet, Elinor and Marianne Dashwood, Fanny Price), guarded despondence at the loss of love (Anne Elliot), need of improvement (Emma Woodhouse), or metafictional orientation (Catherine Morland)—Charlotte appears far less in want, or need, of a husband. Rather than write the trappings of early courtship into Charlotte's character, Austen portrays her as an astute observer who discerns the truth behind the hypochondria and unseemly personal interests that run rampant among the characters of a seaside resort town. As in the other novels that I have examined throughout *Novel Bodies*, the act of *discerning*—in this case, Charlotte's infallible perspective—plays a crucial role in defining the contours of corporeality and sexuality. Moreover, Austen's acerbic portrayal of hypochondria and invalidism reveals an embodied queerness in characters who are remote from heterosexuality. What is Austen up to in *Sanditon*, then? The uncertainty which saturates the narrative, I argue, inheres not only in its fragmentary nature, or in the tenuous speculation of the resort town's primary investor, Mr. Parker, but also in the ill and queer bodies that confound and rework the standard heterosexual romance plot for which Austen is known. *Sanditon*'s sustained attention to the condition of characters' bodies, in other words, occupies narrative space and inhibits early courtship possibilities from taking root. In their stead, Austen imagines networks of *aromantic* characters who are much more readily imagined easing themselves from bathing machines into the sea than appearing at a marriage altar.

In Charlotte, Austen creates a heroine who is in no apparent way dependent upon marriage for future security, despite the considerable size of her family. The matchmaking compulsion that dictates Mrs. Bennet's every action in *Pride and Prejudice*, for instance, is notably absent in *Sanditon*. While Mr. and Mrs. Heywood take every opportunity to get Charlotte and her siblings out of the home and into the wider world of genteel sociability, marriage does not seem to be a primary concern of theirs. When they decide to send Charlotte with Mr. and Mrs. Parker to Sanditon for a visit, their objectives in doing so are clear: "Charlotte was to go,—with excellent health, to bathe and be better if she could—to receive every possible pleasure which Sanditon could be made to supply by the gratitude of those she went with—and to buy new parasols, new gloves and new brooches for her sisters and herself at the library, which Mr. P. was anxiously wishing to support."[2] Through her characteristic use of free indirect discourse, Austen conveys Mr. and Mrs. Heywood's reasoning in sending their favorite daughter to Sanditon: Charlotte is to sea bathe, to improve upon her already "excellent health," to enjoy the various "pleasures" afforded by the resort town, and to go shopping. Given this rather specific list of objectives, it is striking that meeting a young man of means is entirely omitted. The Heywoods, it would seem, simply want their daughter to enjoy the "pleasure" of a seaside vacation without the pressure of finding a spouse. Adding to the overall impression of this un-marriage plot is that, unlike Catherine Morland, Charlotte does not see herself as a fictional heroine. During her first shopping trip at Sanditon, Charlotte distances herself from Camilla Tyrold: "She had not Camilla's youth, and had no intention of having her distress; so, she turned from the drawers of rings and brooches, repressed further solicitation and paid for what she had bought" (316). With this intertextual reference to Camilla's debt to Mrs. Mitten, Austen establishes Charlotte's maturity and self-reliance, further indications of her ability to navigate potential pitfalls on her own terms.

Also unlike Camilla, who is beleaguered by an array of suitors, Charlotte is short on romantic prospects. In lieu of adhering to the norms of compulsory heterosexuality, as Camilla is compelled to do, Charlotte becomes a kind of "medical Man," a post which Mr. Parker had coincidentally been seeking to fill when he and his wife originally came to Willingden (301).[3] This is evident in Charlotte's amusing exchange with Arthur Parker, "an invalid" who is "so delicate that he can engage in no Profession" (312). When the two sit down for tea (along with Arthur's hypochondriac sisters), the narrator remarks that Mr. Parker, Arthur's older brother, feels "considerable pleasure" in observing Charlotte and him conversing, presumably because they might make a suitable couple (336). Rather than build toward courtship, however, the scene details Charlotte's diagnosis of Arthur's assorted issues: his "Broad made and Lusty" frame (which, to her relief, shields her from the heat of an unnecessary fire), his highly stimulated nerves, and his love of heavily buttered toast are indications of an injurious life of luxury, which could ultimately be overcome through fresh air and exercise (335). After listening to Arthur's listing of various ailments, Charlotte says to him, "As far as I can understand what nervous complaints are, I have a great idea of the efficacy of air and exercise for them:—daily, regular exercise;—and I should recommend rather more of it to you than I suspect you are in the habit of taking" (337). Arthur opposes Charlotte's recommendations, insisting that he walks enough in his short turns about the house and terrace. A constellation of medical debates dominate this passage, while any hint of romance between the two is lacking. In this comic rapport, Austen draws a clear distinction between what would be expected of two similarly aged, single people of the opposite sex and what ensues instead: an utterly aromantic doctor-patient conversation. Charlotte ultimately ascertains that Arthur possesses "no Disorders but such as called for warm rooms and good Nourishment" (339). Through Arthur, Austen demonstrates that hypochondria is, among other things—a "malady of interpretation," as George Grinnell would argue—a condition which Charlotte appears to interpret correctly.[4] For Grinnell, hypochondria of the sort that Arthur exhibits is a common object of inquiry in the Romantic period due to its very mutability, for its multivalent manifestations in unique individuals who trouble distinctions between illness and health (a distinction which becomes increasingly important in medical discourse of the Romantic period).[5]

Besides obscuring the line between illness and health through his hypochondria, Arthur also blurs the distinction between male heterosexuality and what D. A. Miller calls "unheterosexuality."[6] According to Miller, unheterosexuality is evident in Robert Ferrar's flagrant disregard for Elinor Dashwood in *Sense and Sensibility*. Robert compromises male heterosexuality when he becomes an enemy to the marriage plot through his unabashed adoption of an orientation that "would prevent it from ever getting started."[7] His lingering interest in something so trivial as a toothpick case underscores his unsentimental indifference toward Elinor and for the opposite sex generally. Robert is, for Miller, a "self-fertilizing flower" whom Austen uses to surprise the reader in his eventual marriage to Lucy Steele.[8] The toothpick case itself is antithetical to the jewelry that proliferates in Austen's work, which typically functions as currency within the dominant social landscape of family and marriage. Like Robert's toothpick case, Arthur's toast rack provides Arthur with something that distracts from romance: in this case it is the means by which Arthur makes the perfect slice of heavily buttered toast, which he consumes with a delight that is otherwise wanting in his exchange with Charlotte. As he boasts to her, "'I never burn my toasts, I never put them too near the fire at first. And yet, you see, there is not a corner but what is well browned'" (338). Arthur's toast rack is, like Edward's toothpick case, a gratuitous object which directs one not toward marriage but toward the sating of a ravenous appetite. In his fussy attention to the details of the toasting session, Arthur jettisons possible courtship with Charlotte in favor of the rich food that contributes to his own delicacy. Thus, Arthur shows an orientation for unheterosexuality while also serving as a corporeal locus of Austen's satire.

Admittedly, *Sanditon*'s unfinished draft form is one of its queerest features: the likes of Arthur trouble any coherent division that might exist between health and illness—not to mention heterosexuality and unheterosexuality—but the open-endedness of the novel also means that there is no opportunity for Austen to regulate his body, nor to cast him aside for a conventional, heteronormative dénouement. The same goes for the many other invalid and hypochondriacal characters who populate Austen's narrative fragment. On that note, I would be remiss not to mention that a potential companion for Charlotte appears in Arthur's older brother, Sidney, whose discernment, "handsome" features, "lively countenance," and "decided air of Ease and Fashion" bring him to Charlotte's notice in the final chapter of volume 1 (345). Perhaps in Sidney, Austen intended to fashion a husband for her heroine, and it seems likely that the narrative would have eventually detailed the building of their relationship in the chapters to come. If *Sanditon* had been completed, invalid and hypochondriac characters like Arthur would likely serve as sources of comic relief and unrest to make a healthy marriage between Charlotte and Sidney all the more satisfying for readers. Of course, one can only speculate.

Without an ending, and without the plot development to generate that ending, Austen's *Sanditon* provides a spectrum of bodies and desires that exist for their own sake, rather than as superficial devices to propel heroic characters toward the inevitable: heterosexual domesticity. In allowing for such a flexible rendering of variable and queer bodies, *Sanditon* reminds us that illness (whether perceived or imaginary) and bodily difference are otherwise often represented as barriers to heterosexual romance, something to be vanquished or sidestepped for happiness to be obtained. *Sanditon* also reminds us of how dependent narrative closure is upon either excising or curing certain kinds of bodies and bodily states to establish the alleged primacy of cross-sex romance. In its own disordered representation of bodily difference, *Sanditon* corresponds thematically with other novels that I have examined throughout *Novel Bodies*. In their varied depictions of deformity, deafness, chronic disease, illness, and gender and sexual variability, these works simultaneously harness emerging intersections of heteronormativity and able-bodiedness for narrative purpose and rearrange these seemingly natural alliances to create unforeseen social worlds that still resonate with us today. Our ability to identify the ways in which variable bodies have informed normative desire can enable us to think more expansively about what has counted as intimacy and who has been deemed deserving, or undeserving, of affection. With its capacious representations of bodies and desires, Enlightenment era authors have much to teach us about nascent configurations of disability and queerness, as well as their afterlives. In grappling with these affiliations—and in reconstituting them to create vibrant, novel worlds—these authors confront impasses at the core of pressing social and political issues of their time, and they have plenty to tell us about our own as well.

NOTES

1. For the quotations in this sentence, see Austen, *Mansfield Park*, 139; Austen, *Persuasion*, 132–133; and Austen, *Pride and Prejudice*, 50. John Wiltshire has written the most authoritative work on the moral and narrative significance of Austen's representations of illness and embodiment. See Wiltshire, *Jane Austen and the Body*.
2. Austen, *Northanger Abbey, Lady Susan, The Watsons, Sanditon*, 303. All future references to *Sanditon* will appear in parenthetical citations.
3. Amy Mallory-Kani astutely observes that, in Charlotte Heyword, Austen establishes a "viewpoint" that "replaces the perspective of the (male) doctor figure" and that Austen gives Charlotte "the same ironical stance that the author herself employs through the use of free indirect discourse." Through Charlotte, Austen establishes proper medical authority. See Mallory-Kani "'What Should We Do with a Doctor Here?,'" 313–326.
4. Grinnell, *The Age of Hypochondria*, 7.

5. Ibid., 3–5. In my reading of the weighty significance of hypochondria in *Sanditon*, I adopt a different perspective from that of D. A. Miller, who views Austen's representations of hypochondria as indications that health remains an "ancillary theme" in her fiction, "in a docile relation to the traditional social order on which the novel is respectfully based." Miller, "The Late Jane Austen," 55–79.
6. Miller, *Jane Austen, or The Secret of Style*, 16.
7. Ibid., 14–15.
8. Ibid., 15.

ACKNOWLEDGMENTS

I am eager to give thanks to the many gracious individuals who have helped me to bring this book to light. To begin, I would thank George Haggerty, who has instilled in me a love of reading eighteenth-century British novels for all of their delightful idiosyncrasies. With his steady mentorship and profound knowledge of the eighteenth century and queer theory in tow, George has accompanied me throughout this journey. My mentors in the Department of Literature at the University of California, San Diego (UCSD) have likewise been unwavering in their intellectual and emotional support. I give heartfelt thanks to Kathryn Shevelow for teaching me so much about eighteenth-century women writers and theater, and for supporting me throughout my coursework, dissertation, and beyond. Michael Davidson introduced me to disability studies and inspired me with the curiosity to apply its rich theoretical models to eighteenth-century literature. Margaret Loose, Lisa Lampert-Weissig, Meg Wesling, Jodi Blanco, Stephanie Jed, and Don Wayne offered stimulating seminars, cultivating my critical interests. Daniel Vitkus arrived during my last year at UCSD but quickly became a good friend and offered valuable professional guidance. I also want to thank Corrinne Harol for introducing me to the Restoration and eighteenth century in an unforgettable undergraduate course that I took with her at the University of Utah.

My colleagues in the Department of English at Texas A&M University–Corpus Christi (TAMUCC) extended to me steadfast support and warm collegiality during my time there. Kelly Bezio has read every chapter of this book and has given me exceedingly helpful feedback and encouragement; Kathryn Vomero Santos has likewise offered excellent input on chapters and articles and has helped me to believe in this project, and in myself; Dale Pattison, Jennifer Sorensen, Lucy Sheehan, Sarah Salter, and Kevin Concannon have all read portions of this book, offering keen insights. Sandrine Sanos has been a fabulous mentor and co-conspirator, and I thank her for all of the meals, conversations, drinks, and impromptu music listening parties we shared in her lovely home. Robin Carstensen, Molly Engelhardt, Isaac Hinojosa, Chrissy Lau, Andrea Montalvo-Hamid, Laura Muñoz, Susan Wolff Murphy, Sharon Talley, and Wendy Walker have been stalwart comrades in Women's, Gender, and Sexuality Studies. Brenton Day and the

ACKNOWLEDGMENTS

student workers at Bell Library helped me track down indispensible secondary sources. The many graduate and undergraduate students that I had the privilege to teach at TAMUCC, especially those who took my "History of Sexuality in British Literature" and "Strange Fictions" courses, helped me to envision this project in vitally new ways.

A generous two-year fellowship from the Miriam Wagenschein Endowment in Women's, Gender, and Sexuality Studies at TAMUCC gave me two course releases, in addition to funding for research trips to the British Library, Harry Ransom Center, and the Newberry Library. I also want to acknowledge the generosity of the Ransom Center and the Newberry for extending short-term fellowships to me to aid in the research component of this book. Thanks to the librarians, staff, and scholars at Chawton House Library, where I spent a beautiful spring month in 2013. Carla Zecher organized a marvelous four-week NEH Summer Institute at the Newberry Library in 2013, from which I gained valuable experience working in the archives. Since that time, I have made a number of visits to the Newberry, and I thank the librarians, staff, and scholars there for helping me to feel comfortable and included in such a vibrant scholarly community.

I am delighted to have recently joined the Department of English at Marquette University. I would like to thank my new colleagues for their support, especially Gerry Canavan, Melissa Ganz, Christine Krueger, Albert Rivero, Brittany Pladek, and Angela Sorby, whose comments and queries helped me to refine arguments for chapter 1. Elizabeth Angeli, Amy Blair, Cedric Burrows, Lilly Campbell, Leah Flack, Paul Gagliardi, Angelique Harris, Heather Hathaway, C. J. Hribal, Jodi Melamed, Gary Meyer, Elizaveta Strakhov, Sarah Wadsworth, Jenny Watson, and Amelia Zurcher have all extended warm welcomes, making me feel at home in Milwaukee. Taylor Ralph and the librarians at Raynor-Memorial Libraries assisted me in tracking down sources. A course release from Dean Richard C. Holz enabled me to finish this book.

It has been an absolute privilege to be a member of the American Society for Eighteenth-Century Studies (ASECS), a collaborative intellectual community that has always energized and inspired me. First and foremost, I want to recognize the inimitable Paul Kelleher, a beloved friend and trusted mentor who has been extraordinarily supportive of me since we first met in 2011. He has read every word of this book, and my writing has benefited from his steadfast support and feedback. I am also beyond lucky to have an outstanding mentor in Helen Deutsch, who has read my work, offered counsel, and written on my behalf on countless occasions. Misty Anderson has likewise been a brilliant mentor and dear friend. Jason Pearl gave me input on the coda of this book, and guided me through aspects of the marketing and production processes that were foreign to me. Ashley Cohen has been a treasured companion and has encouraged me since we first met at the Huntington Library as graduate students. Rebecca Shapiro introduced me to the editing team at Bucknell at her "The Doctor Is In" mentorship program. A shout-out goes to colleagues in the disability and queer caucuses and to peers from across the ASECS community, who have been supportive of me both personally and professionally, including Julie Beaulieu, John Beynon, Stan Booth, Jill Bradbury, Fiona Brideoake, Lisa Freeman, Corey Goergen, Caroline Gonda, Suvir Kaul, Declan Kavanagh, Ula Klein, Emily Kugler, Susan Lanser, Chris Loar, Devoney Looser, Travis Chi Wing Lau, David Mazella, Alice McGrath, Derrick Miller, Laura Miller, Lisa Moore, Chris Mounsey, Sal Nicolazzo, Danny O'Quinn, Alpen Razi, Jared Richman, Jamie Rosenthal, Emily Stanback, Kristina Straub, Madeline Sutherland-Meier, Mark Vareschi, Kathleen Wilson, and Jarred Wiehe. In the late stages of writing this book, I found support and encouragement on Twitter from scholars working on the eighteenth century and beyond. Kathleen Alves, Manu Samriti Chander, Rebecca Colesworthy, Zoë Eckman, Josh Epstein, Emily Friedman, Joey Gamble, Stephen Guy-Bray, Michael Haselton, Stephanie Insley Hershinow, Mark Kelley, Jacqueline Langille, Dylan Lewis, Sheila Liming, Kathy Lubey, Aiden Norrie, Nush Powell, Matthew Reznicek, Emily West, and Eugenia Zuroski, among many others, have repeatedly offered advice, signal-boosted my research, and cheered me to the finish line. I thank them for their powerful critical insights and wicked senses of humor.

I sharpened the arguments of this book by sharing portions of it in venues beyond ASECS, including at invited talks at the University of Southampton, the Newberry Library, the University of New Mexico, Emory University, Stony Brook University, and the Texas Medical Center. Thanks to the faculty, graduate students, staff, and administration at these excellent institutions—including Michael Kauth, Jess Libow, Mike Ryan, and Adrienne Unger—who organized and promoted the events, booked travel and lodgings, and took me out for meals and drinks.

I have long dreamed of publishing my book in Bucknell University Press's *Transits* series. Working with the series' team—Greg Clingham, Kate Parker, Miriam Wallace, and Pam Dailey—has been an absolute pleasure, and I thank them for their patience and support. Thanks especially to Miriam, who spearheaded this particular project. This book has benefited so much from her guidance. I also want to thank the two anonymous readers who offered incredibly helpful feedback in their attentive, eloquent, and thorough reports. Thanks to Helen Wheeler at Westchester Publishing Services for helping me through the production process, and to Catherine Mallon for the attentive, conscientious copyediting.

A number of friends, whom I think of as family in the queerest (and dearest) sense, have offered care and support in the form of shared meals and drinks,

ACKNOWLEDGMENTS

camping trips, dancing, and revelry. John Linkins has been a terrific partner and friend to me and was with me when this project was born. I also thank Lance Criley, Andy DeFuniak, Ted Gideonse, Chad Hermandorfer, Al Iverhouse, Tom Hutchings, Bryan Leigh, A. J. Mathews, Benjamin Olson, Stephen Stabile, Bryan Taft, and Mike Wolfe for their enduring love and friendship. Fred Carmean, Kevin Eastman, Jerome Fitzgerald, and David Mordini hosted me for weeks at a time in their beautiful homes while I worked at the Newberry, and I will never forget the many laughs and adventures we shared during those visits to Chicago.

My parents have always encouraged me to follow my heart, and I cannot thank them enough for believing in me and for supporting my education. My mother, Patricia Farr, taught me how to read when I was three years old, and I carry her boundless love with me everywhere I go. My father, David Farr, sparked my love of research and writing and is a model of expansive paternal kindness and love. My beloved husband, Alan Nyitray, has been a deeply caring and devoted companion. Our wide-ranging discussions touching on science, public health, medicine, politics, disability, and sexuality continue to open unforeseen intellectual horizons to me. He has helped me to work through a number of impasses in writing *Novel Bodies*, but most importantly, he loves me through thick and thin. My love for him is limitless, and it is to him that I dedicate this book.

An earlier version of chapter 4 appeared as "Sharp Minds/Twisted Bodies: Intellect, Disability, and Female Education in Frances Burney's *Camilla*" in *The Eighteenth Century: Theory and Interpretation* 55, no. 1 (Winter 2014): 1–17, University of Pennsylvania Press © 2014, and reprinted with permission.

BIBLIOGRAPHY

Adams, Rachel, Benjamin Reiss, and David Serlin, eds. *Keywords for Disability Studies*. New York: NYU Press, 2015.
Ahmed, Sara. *Queer Phenomenology: Orientations, Objects, Others*. Durham, N.C., and London: Duke University Press, 2006.
Alexander-Floyd, Nikol G. "Disappearing Acts: Reclaiming Intersectionality in the Social Sciences in a Post-Black Feminist Era." *Feminist Formations* 24, no. 1 (Spring 2012): 1–25.
Anderson, Misty G. *Imagining Methodism in Eighteenth-Century Britain: Enthusiasm, Belief, and the Borders of the Self*. Baltimore: Johns Hopkins University Press, 2012.
Anstey, Christopher. *The New Bath Guide: Or, Memoirs of the B-N-R-D Family, in a Series of Poetical Epistles*. Bath: Pope, 1762.
Armstrong, Nancy. *Desire and Domestic Fiction: A Political History of the Novel*. New York: Oxford University Press, 1987.
———. *How Novels Think: The Limits of Individualism from 1719–1900*. New York: Columbia University Press, 2006.
Austen, Jane. *Mansfield Park*. Edited by James Kinsley. Oxford: Oxford University Press, 2003.
———. *Northanger Abbey, Lady Susan, The Watsons, Sanditon*. Edited by James Kinsley and John Davie. Oxford: Oxford University Press, 2008.
———. *Persuasion*. Edited by Linda Bree. Peterborough, Canada: Broadview Press, 2000.
———. *Pride and Prejudice*. Edited by James Kinsley. Oxford: Oxford University Press, 2004.
Bacon, Francis. *Essays or Counsels, Civil and Moral*. Whitefish, Mont.: Kessinger, 2010.
———. *Essays Moral, Economical, and Political*. London: Bensley, 1798.
———. *The Works of Francis Bacon, Baron of Verulam, Viscount St. Alban, and Lord High Chancellor of England, in five volumes*. London: Millar, 1765.
Ballaster, Ros. *Seductive Forms: Women's Amatory Fiction from 1684–1740*. Oxford: Clarendon Press, 1998.
Bannet, Eve Tavor. "Life, Letters, and Tales in Sarah Scott's *A Journey through Every Stage of Life*." In *The Age of Johnson: A Scholarly Annual* 17 (2006): 233–259.
———. "Sarah Scott and America: Sir George Ellison, the Real Man of Sensibility, and the Squire of Horton." *Eighteenth-Century Fiction* 22, no. 4 (Summer 2010): 631–656.
Bearden, Elizabeth. "Before Normal, There Was Natural: John Bulwer, Disability, and Natural Signing in Early Modern England and Beyond," *PMLA* 132, no. 1 (January 2017): 33–50.
Beauvoir, Simone de. *The Second Sex*. Translated by Constance Borde and Sheila Malovany-Chevallier. New York: Vintage, 2011.
Bell, Christopher M., ed. *Blackness and Disability: Critical Examinations and Cultural Interventions*. East Lansing: Michigan State University Press, 2012.
Berlant, Lauren, and Michael Warner. "Sex in Public." *Critical Inquiry* 24, no. 2 (Winter 1998): 547–566.
Binhammer, Katherine. "The Economics of Plot in Burney's *Camilla*." *Studies in the Novel* 43, no. 1 (Spring 2011): 1–20.

BIBLIOGRAPHY

Bond, William. *The History of the Life and Adventures of Mr. Duncan Campbell, a Gentleman, Who, Tho' Deaf and Dumb, Writes down Any Stranger's Name at First Sight; with Their Future Contingencies of Fortune*. London: Curll, 1720.

———. *The History of the Life and Adventures of Mr. Duncan Campbell, Late of Exeter Court over-against the Savoy in the Strand. A gentleman, who, when living, tho' deaf and dumb, wou'd write down any stranger's name at first sight: with the future contingencies of their fortune*. The 3rd edition, corrected. London: 1739.

———. *The Supernatural Philosopher: or, the mysteries of magick, All exemplified in the history of the life and surprizing adventures of Mr. Duncan Campbell*. London: Curll, 1728.

Borsay, Peter. "New Approaches to Social History. Myth, Memory, and Place: Monmouth and Bath 1750–1900." *Journal of Social History* 39, no. 3 (Spring 2006): 867–889.

Boucé, Paul-Gabriel. *The Novels of Tobias Smollett*. Translated by Antonia White. London: Longman, 1976.

Branson, Jan, and Don Miller. *Damned for Their Difference: The Cultural Construction of Deaf People as "Disabled": A Sociological History*. Washington, D.C: Gallaudet University Press, 2002.

Brideoake, Fiona. *The Ladies of Llangollen: Desire, Indeterminacy, and the Legacies of Criticism*. Lewisburg, Pa.: Bucknell University Press, 2017.

Brown, Hilary. "Sarah Scott, Sophie von La Roche, and the Female Utopian Tradition." *The Journal of English and Germanic Philology* 100, no. 4 (October 2001): 469–481.

Brown, Laura. "The Lady, the Lapdog, and Literary Alterity." *The Eighteenth Century* 52, no. 1 (Spring 2011): 31–45.

Bulwer, John. *Chirologia: Or, The Natvral Language of the Hand. Composed of the Speaking Motions, and Discoursing Gestures Thereof. Whereunto Is Added Chironomia: Or, The Art of Manvall Rhetoricke*. London: T.H. and Tyton, 1644.

———. *Philocophus, Or, The Deafe and Dumbe Mans Friend Exhibiting the Philosophicall Verity of That Subtile Art, Which May Inable One with an Observant Eie, to Heare What Any Man Speaks by the Moving of His Lips: Upon the Same Ground . . . That a Man Borne Deafe and Dumbe, May Be Taught to Heare the Sound of Words with His Eie, & Thence Learne to Speake with His Tongue*. London: Moseley, 1648.

Burney, Frances. *Camilla*. Edited by Edward A. Bloom and Lillian D. Bloom. Oxford: Oxford University Press, 2009.

Cadogan, William. *A Dissertation on the Gout, and All Chronic Diseases, Jointly Considered as Proceeding from the Same Causes: What Those Causes Are; and a Rational and Natural Method of Cure Proposed. Addressed to All Invalids*. Philadelphia; London: William and Thomas Bradford, 1771.

Castle, Terry. "Matters Not Fit to Be Mentioned: Fielding's *The Female Husband*." *ELH* 49, no. 3 (Autumn 1982): 602–622.

Chandler, Mary. *The Description of Bath: A Poem . . . . With Several Other Poems. By Mrs. Mary Chandler . . . . To Which Is Added, A True Tale, by the Same Author*. The eighth edition. London: Leake, 1767.

Chen, Mel Y. *Animacies: Biopolitics, Racial Mattering, and Queer Affect*. Durham, N.C.: Duke University Press Books, 2012.

Cheyne, George. *An Essay of the True Nature and Due Method of Treating the Gout*. The fourth edition, revis'd, corrected, and enlarg'd to more than double of the former. London: Strahan and Hammond, 1722.

Cody, Lisa Forman. *Birthing the Nation: Sex, Science, and the Conception of Eighteenth-Century Britons*. Oxford: Oxford University Press, 2008.

Crenshaw, Kimberlé. "Mapping the Margins: Intersectionality, Identity Politics, and Violence against Women of Color." *Stanford Law Review* 43, no. 6 (July 1991): 1241–1299.

Croxall, Samuel. *Fables of Aesop and Others*. The second edition. London: Astley, 1728.
———. *The Fables of Æsop, With a Life of the Author; and Embellished with one Hundred Twelve Plates*. London: Stockdale, 1793.
Davidson, Michael. "Cripping Consensus: Disability Studies at the Intersection." *American Literary History* 28, no. 2 (April 2016): 433–453.
Davis, Lennard J. "Dr. Johnson, Amelia, and the Discourse of Disability in the Eighteenth Century." In *"Defects": Engendering the Modern Body*, edited by Helen Deutsch and Felicity Nussbaum, 54–74. Ann Arbor: University of Michigan Press, 2000.
———. *Enforcing Normalcy: Disability, Deafness, and the Body*. London; New York: Verso, 1995.
———. "Introduction: Disability, Normality, and Power." In *The Disability Studies Reader*. 4th ed., edited by Lennard Davis, 1–16. New York: Routledge, 2013.
———. "Who Put the 'The' in 'the Novel'? Identity Politics and Disability in Novel Studies." *Novel: A Forum on Fiction* 31, no. 3 (Summer 1998): 317–334.
Deutsch, Helen. "The Body's Moments: Visible Disability, the Essay and the Limits of Sympathy." *Prose Studies* 27, nos. 1-2 (April–August 2005): 11–26.
———. "Deformity." In *Keywords for Disability Studies*, edited by Rachel Adams, Benjamin Reiss, and David Serlin, 52. New York and London: NYU Press, 2015.
———. *Loving Dr. Johnson*. Chicago: University of Chicago Press, 2005.
———. *Resemblance and Disgrace: Alexander Pope and the Deformation of Culture*. Cambridge, Mass.: Harvard University Press, 1996.
Deutsch, Helen, and Felicity Nussbaum. "Introduction." In *"Defects": Engendering the Modern Body*, edited by Helen Deutsch and Felicity Nussbaum, 1–28. Ann Arbor: University of Michigan Press, 2000.
Dickie, Simon. *Cruelty and Laughter: Forgotten Comic Literature and the Unsentimental Eighteenth Century*. Chicago: University of Chicago Press, 2011.
———. "Deformity Poems and Other Nasties." *Eighteenth-Century Life* 41.1 (January 2017): 197–230.
The Diseases of Bath. A Satire. London: Roberts, 1737.
Dodsley, R. *Select Fables of Esop and Other Fabulists In Three Books*. London: Dodsley, 1793.
Doody, Margaret Anne. *Frances Burney: The Life in the Works*. New Brunswick, N.J.: Rutgers University Press, 1988.
Douglas, Aileen. *Uneasy Sensations: Smollett and the Body*. Chicago: University of Chicago Press, 1995.
Edelman, Lee. *No Future: Queer Theory and the Death Drive*. Durham, N.C.: Duke University Press, 2004.
Edgeworth, Maria. *Belinda*. Edited by Kathryn J. Kirkpatrick. Oxford: Oxford University Press, 2009.
Edwards, Paul, and David Dabydeen, eds. *Black Writers in Britain, 1760–1890*. Edinburgh: Edinburgh University Press, 1991.
Erevelles, Nirmala, and Andrea Minear. "Unspeakable Offenses: Untangling Race and Disability in Discourses of Intersectionality." *Journal of Literary & Cultural Disability Studies* 4, no. 2 (January 2010): 127–145.
Erickson, Paul. "On the External Uses of Water in *The Expedition of Humphry Clinker*." In *Tobias Smollett, Scotland's First Novelist: New Essays in Memory of Paul-Gabriel Boucé*, edited by O. M. Brack, 94–114. Newark: University of Delaware Press, 2007.
Farr, Jason S. "Attractive Deformity: Enabling the 'Shocking Monster' from Sarah Scott's *Agreeable Ugliness*." In *The Idea of Disability in the Eighteenth Century*, edited by Chris Mounsey, 181–201. Lewisburg, Pa.: Bucknell University Press, 2014.
———. "Libertine Sexuality and Queer-Crip Embodiment in Eighteenth-Century Britain." *Journal for Early Modern Cultural Studies* 16, no. 4 (Fall 2016): 96–118.

BIBLIOGRAPHY

Foucault, Michel. *The Birth of the Clinic*. London: Routledge, 2003.
———. *Discipline and Punish: The Birth of the Prison*. 2nd ed. New York: Vintage Books, 1995.
———. *The History of Sexuality, Volume 1: An Introduction*. New York: Vintage Books, 1990.
Frazer, John. *Deuteroskopia; Or, a Brief Discourse Concerning the Second Sight, Commonly so Called*. Edinburgh: Symson, 1707.
Freud, Sigmund. "The Uncanny." In *An Infantile Neurosis; and Other Works (1917–1919)*. London: Hogarth Press, 1986.
The Friendly Daemon or the Generous Apparition; Being a True Narrative of a Miraculous Cure, Newly Performed upon That Damous Deaf and Dumb Gentleman, Dr. Duncan Campbell, by a Familiar Spirit That Appear'd to Him. London: Roberts, 1726.
Froide, Amy M. *Never Married: Singlewomen in Early Modern England*. Oxford: Oxford University Press, 2005.
Gallop, Jane. "The View from Queer Theory." *Age Culture Humanities*, no. 1 (2016), http://ageculturehumanities.org/WP/the-view-from-queer-theory/.
Gamer, Michael. "Maria Edgeworth and the Romance of Real Life." *Novel: A Forum on Fiction* 34, no. 2 (Spring 2001): 232–266.
Garland-Thomson, Rosemarie. *Extraordinary Bodies: Figuring Physical Disability in American Literature and Culture*. New York: Columbia University Press, 1996.
———. "Staring Back: Self-Representations of Disabled Performance Artists." *American Quarterly* 52, no. 2 (June 2000): 334–338.
———. *Staring: How We Look*. Oxford; New York: Oxford University Press, 2009.
Gonda, Caroline. "The Odd Women: Charlotte Charke, Sarah Scott and the Metamorphoses of Sex." In *Lesbian Dames: Sapphism in the Long Eighteenth Century*, edited by John Beynon and Caroline Gonda, 111–126. Burlington, Vt., and Farnham, U.K.: Ashgate Publishing, Ltd., 2010.
———. "Sarah Scott and 'The Sweet Excess of Paternal Love.'" *Studies in English Literature, 1500–1900* 32, no. 3 (Summer 1992): 511–535.
Green, Francis. *Vox Oculis Subjecta: A Dissertation on the Most Curious and Important Art of Imparting Speech, and the Knowledge of Language to the Naturally Deaf, And, Consequently, Dumb*. London: White, 1783.
Grinnell, George C. *The Age of Hypochondria: Interpreting Romantic Health and Illness*. London: Palgrave Macmillan, 2010.
Grob, Gerald N. *The Deadly Truth: A History of Disease in America*. Cambridge, Mass.: Harvard University Press, 2005.
Guy-Bray, Stephen. "Fellowships of Joy: Angelic Union in Paradise Lost." *Early Modern Culture* no. 10 (May 2014): 1–20.
Haggerty, George E. *Men in Love: Masculinity and Sexuality in the Eighteenth Century*. New York: Columbia University Press, 1999.
———. *Queer Gothic*. Urbana: University of Illinois Press, 2006.
———. *Unnatural Affections: Women and Fiction in the Later 18th Century*. Bloomington: Indiana University Press, 1998.
Hall, Stuart. "The Work of Representation." In *Representation: Cultural Representations and Signifying Practices*, edited by Stuart Hall, Jessica Evans, and Sean Nixon, 15–29. London: Sage, 1997.
Hay, William. *Deformity: An Essay*. London: Dodsley, 1754.
Haywood, Eliza Fowler. *A Spy on the Conjurer Or, a Collection of Surprising and Diverting Stories, with Merry and Ingenious Letters*. London: Peele, 1724.
Hirschmann, Nancy J. "Freedom and (Dis)Ability in Early Modern Political Thought." In *Recovering Disability in the Early Modern Period*, edited by Allison P. Hobsgood and David Houston Wood, 167–186. Columbus: Ohio State University Press, 2013.

Ingram, Allen. "Dear Dick: Matthew Bramble and the Case of the Silent Doctor." In *Tobias Smollett, Scotland's First Novelist: New Essays in Memory of Paul-Gabriel Boucé*, edited by O. M. Brack, 115–129. Newark: University of Delaware Press, 2007.

James, Jennifer C. "Gwendolyn Brooks, WW2, and the Politics of Rehabilitation." In *Feminist Disability Studies*, edited by Kim Q. Hall, 136–158. Bloomington: Indiana University Press, 2011.

Johns, Alessa. *Women's Utopias of the Eighteenth Century*. Urbana: University of Illinois Press, 2003.

Johnson, Claudia L. *Equivocal Beings: Politics, Gender, and Sentimentality in the 1790s: Wollstonecraft, Radcliffe, Burney, Austen*. Chicago: University of Chicago Press, 1995.

Johnson, Samuel, and James Boswell. With introduction by Ian McGowan. *Journey to the Hebrides: A Journey to the Western Islands of Scotland & The Journal of a Tour to the Hebrides*. Edinburgh: Canongate Classics, 2001.

Joshua, Essaka. "Disability and Deformity: Function Impairment and Aesthetics in the Long Eighteenth Century." In *The Cambridge Companion to Literature and Disability*, edited by Clare Barker and Stuart Murray, 47–61. Cambridge: Cambridge University Press, 2018.

———. "Picturesque Aesthetics: Theorising Deformity in the Romantic Era." In *Disabling Romanticism: Body, Mind, and Text*, edited by Michael Bradshaw, 29–48. London: Palgrave Macmillan, 2016.

Kafer, Alison. *Feminist, Queer, Crip*. Bloomington: Indiana University Press, 2013.

Kavanagh, Declan. *Effeminate Years: Literature, Politics, and Aesthetics in Mid-Eighteenth-Century Britain*. Lewisburg, Pa.: Bucknell University Press, 2017.

Kelleher, Paul. "Defections from Nature: The Rhetoric of Deformity in Shaftesbury's *Characteristics*." In *The Idea of Disability in the Eighteenth Century*, edited by Chris Mounsey, 71–90. Lewisburg, Pa.: Bucknell University Press, 2014.

———. *Making Love: Sentiment and Sexuality in Eighteenth-Century British Literature*. Lewisburg, Pa.: Bucknell University Press, 2015.

———. "The Man Within the Breast: Sympathy and Deformity in Adam Smith's *The Theory of Moral Sentiments*." *Studies in Eighteenth-Century Culture*, 44 (2015): 41–60.

Kelly, Gary. "Introductory Note." In *Bluestocking Feminism: Writings of the Bluestocking Circle, 1738–1785*. Vol. 5, edited by Gary Kelly, xxxi–xliv. London: Pickering & Chatto, 1999.

King, Kathryn R. "Spying upon the Conjurer: Haywood, Curiosity, and 'the Novel' in the 1720s." *Studies in the Novel* 30, no. 2 (Summer 1998): 178–193.

King, Thomas A. *The Gendering of Men, 1600–1750*. Madison: University of Wisconsin Press, 2004.

Klein, Ula. "Bosom Friends and the Sapphic Breasts of *Belinda*." *ABO: Interactive Journal for Women in the Arts, 1640–1830* 3, no. 2 (November 2013): 1–13.

———. "Eighteenth-Century Female Cross-Dressers and Their Beards." *Journal for Early Modern Cultural Studies* 16, no. 4 (Fall 2016): 119–143.

Krentz, Christopher. "Duncan Campbell and the Discourses of Deafness." *Prose Studies* 27, no. 1–2 (April-August 2005): 39–52.

Lane, Harlan. *When the Mind Hears: A History of the Deaf*. New York: Vintage, 1989.

Lanser, Susan. "Bluestocking Sapphism and the Economies of Desire." *Huntington Library Quarterly* 65, nos. 1/2 (2002): 257–275.

———. "Befriending the Body: Female Intimacies as Class Acts." *Eighteenth-Century Studies* 32, no. 2 (Winter 1998–99): 179–198.

———. "'Queer to Queer': The Sapphic Body as Transgressive Text." In *Lewd and Notorious: Female Transgression in the 18th Century*, edited by Katharine Kittredge. Ann Arbor: University of Michigan Press, 2003.

———. *The Sexuality of History: Modernity and the Sapphic, 1565–1830*. Chicago: University of Chicago Press, 2014.

Lau, Travis Chi Wing. "Before the Norm." *Disability Studies Quarterly* 37, no. 3 (Summer 2017).

Lawrence, Elizabeth Atwood. "Feline Fortunes: Contrasting Views of Cats in Popular Culture." *Journal of Popular Culture* 36, no. 3 (Winter 2003): 623–635.

Lewis, Jayne Elizabeth. *The English Fable: Aesop and Literary Culture, 1651–1740*. Cambridge: Cambridge University Press, 1996.

Linker, Beth. "On the Borderland of Medical and Disability History: A Survey of the Fields." *Bulletin of the History of Medicine* 87, no. 4 (Winter 2013): 499–535.

Locke, John. *An Essay Concerning Human Understanding*. Tegg and Son, 1836.

———. *Some Thoughts Concerning Education:* Mineola, N.Y.: Dover Publications, 2007.

Lubey, Kathleen. *Excitable Imaginations: Eroticism and Reading in Britain, 1660–1760*. Lewisburg, Pa.: Bucknell University Press, 2014.

Mallory-Kani, Amy. "'What Should We Do with a Doctor Here?': Medical Authority in Austen's *Sanditon*." *Nineteenth-Century Contexts* 39, no. 4 (May 2017): 313–326.

McDonagh, Patrick. *Idiocy: A Cultural History*. Liverpool: Liverpool University Press, 2009.

McKeon, Michael. *The Origins of the English Novel, 1600–1740*. Baltimore: Johns Hopkins University Press, 2002.

———. *The Secret History of Domesticity: Public, Private, and the Division of Knowledge*. Baltimore: Johns Hopkins University Press, 2006.

McRuer, Robert. "Compulsory Able-Bodiedness and Queer/Disabled Existence." In *The Disability Studies Reader*, 4th ed., edited by Lennard Davis, 369–380. New York: Routledge, 2013.

———. *Crip Theory: Cultural Signs of Queerness and Disability*. New York: New York University Press, 2006.

Miles, M. "Signing in the Seraglio: Mutes, Dwarfs and Jestures at the Ottoman Court 1500–1700." *Disability & Society* 15, no. 1 (July 2000): 115–134.

Miller, D. A. *Jane Austen, or The Secret of Style*. Princeton, N.J.: Princeton University Press, 2003.

———. "The Late Jane Austen." *Raritan* 10, no. 1 (Summer 1990): 55–79.

———. *Narrative and Its Discontents: Problems of Closure in the Traditional Novel*. Princeton, N.J.: Princeton University Press, 1989.

Milton, John. *Paradise Lost and Paradise Regained*. London: Vintage Classics, 2009.

Mitchell, David T., and Sharon L. Snyder. *The Biopolitics of Disability: Neoliberalism, Ablenationalism, and Peripheral Embodiment*. Ann Arbor: University of Michigan Press, 2015.

———. *Narrative Prosthesis: Disability and the Dependencies of Discourse*. Ann Arbor: University of Michigan Press, 1997.

Montagu, Lady Mary Wortley. *The Letters and Works of Lady Mary Wortley Montagu, Volume 2*. Philadelphia: Carey, Lea & Blanchard, 1837.

Moore, Lisa L. *Dangerous Intimacies: Toward a Sapphic History of the British Novel*. Durham, N.C.: Duke University Press Books, 1997.

Mounsey, Chris. "Introduction: Variability: Beyond Sameness and Difference." In *The Idea of Disability in the Eighteenth Century*, edited by Chris Mounsey, 1–27. Lewisburg, Pa.: Bucknell University Press, 2014.

Mulvey, Laura. "Visual Pleasure and Narrative Cinema." In *Film Theory and Criticism: Introductory Readings*, edited by Leo Braudy and Marshall Cohen, 833–844. Oxford: Oxford University Press, 1999.

Nicolazzo, Sarah. "Henry Fielding's *The Female Husband* and the Sexuality of Vagrancy." *The Eighteenth Century: Theory and Interpretation* 55, no. 4 (December 2014): 335–353.

Norton, Rictor. *Mother Clap's Molly House: The Gay Subculture in England 1700–1830*. London: GMP Publishers Inc., 1992.

Nussbaum, Felicity A. *The Limits of the Human: Fictions of Anomaly, Race and Gender in the Long Eighteenth Century*. Cambridge: Cambridge University Press, 2003.

The Original Bath Guide, Considerably Enlarged and Improved, Comprehending Every Species of Information That Can Be Required by the Visitor and Inhabitant, Etc. London: Savage, Meyler & Son, 1811.

Ottaway, Susannah R. *The Decline of Life: Old Age in Eighteenth-Century England.* Cambridge: Cambridge University Press, 2007.

Port, Cynthia. "No Future? Aging, Temporality, History, and Reverse Chronologies." *Occasion* 4 (June 2012): 1–19.

Porter, Roy. *Disease, Medicine and Society in England, 1550–1860.* Cambridge: Cambridge University Press, 1995.

———. *The Greatest Benefit to Mankind: A Medical History of Humanity.* New York: W. W. Norton & Company, 1999.

———. "Spreading Medical Enlightenment: The Popularization of Medicine, 1650–1850." In *The Popularization of Medicine, 1650–1850*, edited by Roy Porter, 215–231. London: Routledge, 1992.

Porter, Roy, and G. S. Rousseau. *Gout: The Patrician Malady.* New Haven, Conn.: Yale University Press, 2000.

Powell, Manushag N., and Rivka Swenson. "Introduction: Subject Theory and the Sensational Subject." *The Eighteenth Century: Theory and Interpretation* 54, no. 2 (Summer 2013): 147–151.

Quillet, Claude. *Advice to New-Married Persons: Or, The Art of Having Beautiful Children. In Four Books. To Which Is Added, The Art of Bringing up Children, &c.* London, 1750.

Reeve, Clara. *The Progress of Romance, through Times, Countries, and Manners; with Remarks on the Good and Bad Effects of It, on Them Respectively; in a Course of Evening Conversations. By C. R. Author of the English Baron, the Two Mentors, &c. In Two Volumes.* Dublin: Price, Exshaw, White, Cash Colbert, Marchbank, and Porter, 1785.

Reeves, James Bryant. "Untimely Old Age and Deformity in Sarah Scott's *Millenium Hall.*" *Eighteenth-Century Fiction* 27, no. 2 (Winter 2014–2015): 229–256.

Reid, B. L. "Smollett's Healing Journey." *Virginia Quarterly Review* 41 (Autumn 1965): 549–570.

Reiss, Benjamin. *Theaters of Madness: Insane Asylums and Nineteenth-Century American Culture.* Chicago: University of Chicago Press, 2008.

Richardson, Samuel. *Pamela.* Edited by Thomas Keymer and Alice Wakely. Oxford: Oxford University Press, 2008.

Richman, Jared. "The Other King's Speech: Elocution and the Politics of Disability in Georgian Britain." *The Eighteenth Century: Theory and Interpretation* 59, no. 3 (Fall 2018): 279–304.

Rizzo, Betty. *Companions Without Vows: Relationships among Eighteenth-Century British Women.* Athens: University of Georgia Press, 1994.

Robinson, Terry F. "'Life Is a Tragicomedy!': Maria Edgeworth's *Belinda* and the Staging of the Realist Novel." *Nineteenth Century Literature* 67, no. 2 (September 2012): 139–176.

Samuels, Ellen. *Fantasies of Identification: Disability, Gender, Race.* New York: New York University Press, 2014.

Sanchez, Melissa E. "Libertinism and Romance in Rochester's Poetry." *Eighteenth-Century Studies* 38, no. 3 (Spring 2005): 441–459.

———. "'Use Me But as Your Spaniel': Feminism, Queer Theory, and Early Modern Sexualities." *PMLA* 127, no. 3 (May 2012): 493–511.

Sandahl, Carrie. "Queering the Crip or Cripping the Queer? Intersections of Queer and Crip Identities in Solo Autobiographical Performance." *GLQ* 9, no.1-2 (April 2003): 25–56.

Scott, Sarah. *Agreeable Ugliness: Or, the Triumph of the Graces. Exemplified in the Real Life and Fortunes of a Young Lady of Some Distinction.* London: Dodsley, 1754.

———. *The History of Sir George Ellison*. Edited by Betty Rizzo. Lexington: University of Kentucky Press, 2007.

———. *A Journey through Every Stage of Life, Described in a Variety of Interesting Scenes, Drawn from Real characters. By a Person of Quality. In Two Volumes*. London: Millar, 1754.

———. *Millenium Hall*. Edited by Gary Kelly. Peterborough, Ontario, Canada: Broadview Press, 1995.

Secret Memoirs of the Late Mr. Duncan Campbell, the Famous Deaf and Dumb Gentleman. London: Millan and Chrichley, 1732.

Sedgwick, Eve Kosofsky. *Between Men: English Literature and Male Homosocial Desire*. New York: Columbia University Press, 1985.

Shakespeare, Tom. "The Social Model of Disability: An Outdated Ideology?" *Research in Social Science and Disability* 2 (June 2001): 9–28.

Shapiro, Joseph P. *No Pity: People with Disabilities Forging a New Civil Rights Movement*. New York: Broadway Books, 1994.

Shea, Gerald. *The Language of Light: A History of Silent Voices*. New Haven, Conn.: Yale University Press, 2017.

Siebers, Tobin Anthony. *Disability Theory*. Ann Arbor: University of Michigan Press, 2008.

Smollett, Tobias. *The Expedition of Humphry Clinker*. Edited by Lewis M. Knapp and Paul-Gabriel Boucé. Oxford: Oxford University Press, 2009.

———. *The Expedition of Humphry Clinker*. Edited by Evan Gottlieb. New York; London: W. W. Norton & Company, 2015.

———. *Peregrine Pickle*. Edited by James L. Clifford. Oxford: Oxford University Press, 1983.

Stanback, Emily B. *The Wordsworth-Coleridge Circle and the Aesthetics of Disability*. London: Palgrave Macmillan, 2017.

Steele, Sir Richard. *Selections from the Tatler, Spectator and Guardian*. Clarendon Press, 1885.

Stoler, Ann Laura. *Race and the Education of Desire: Foucault's History of Sexuality and the Colonial Order of Things*. Durham, N.C.: Duke University Press, 1995.

Stone, Christopher, and Bencie Woll. "Dumb O Jemmy and Others: Deaf People, Interpreters and the London Courts in the Eighteenth and Nineteenth Centuries." *Sign Language Studies* 8, no. 3 (Spring 2008): 226–240.

Straub, Kristina. *Divided Fictions: Fanny Burney and Feminine Strategy*. Lexington: University of Kentucky Press, 1987.

———. *Domestic Affairs: Intimacy, Eroticism, and Violence between Servants and Masters in Eighteenth-Century Britain*. Baltimore: Johns Hopkins University Press, 2009.

———. "Men from Boys: Cibber, Pope, and the Schoolboy." *The Eighteenth Century* 32, no. 3 (1991): 219–239.

Sutherland, Alex. *The Brahan Seer: The Making of a Legend*. Bern; New York: Peter Lang, 2009.

Taylor, Gary. *Castration: An Abbreviated History of Western Manhood*. London: Routledge, 2002.

Traub, Valerie. *The Renaissance of Lesbianism in Early Modern England*. Cambridge: Cambridge University Press, 2002.

Turner, David M. "Campbell, Duncan," *Oxford Dictionary of National Biography Online*.

———. *Disability in Eighteenth-Century England: Imagining Physical Impairment*. New York: Routledge, 2012.

The Ugly Club Manuscript, 1743–54. Manuscript. From Liverpool Central Library, MS UGL 367.

Vermeule, Blakey. *Why Do We Care about Literary Characters?* Baltimore: Johns Hopkins University Press, 2011.

Vickery, Amanda. *Behind Closed Doors: At Home in Georgian England*. New Haven, Conn.: Yale University Press, 2009.

Volz, Jessica A. *Visuality in the Novels of Austen, Radcliffe, Edgeworth and Burney*. London and New York: Anthem Press, 2017.

Walpole, Horace. *The Castle of Otranto*. Edited by Nick Groom. Oxford: Oxford University Press, 2014.

Warner, William B. *Licensing Entertainment: The Elevation of Novel Reading in Britain, 1684–1750*. Berkeley: University of California Press, 1998.

Watt, Ian. *The Rise of the Novel*. Berkeley: University of California Press, 2001.

Weber, Harold. *The Restoration Rake-Hero: Transformations in Sexual Understanding in Seventeenth-Century England*. Madison: University of Wisconsin Press, 1986.

Wendell, Susan. "Unhealthy Disabled: Treating Chronic Illnesses as Disabilities." In *The Disability Studies Reader*, 4th ed., edited by Lennard J. Davis, 161–176. New York: Routledge, 2013.

Wesley, John. *A Collection of Hymns, for the Use of the People Called Methodists*. The seventh edition. London: 1791.

West, William. "Matt Bramble's Journey to Health." *Texas Studies in Literature and Language* 11, no. 3 (Fall 1969): 1197–1208.

Wheeler, Roxann. *The Complexion of Race: Categories of Difference in Eighteenth-Century British Culture*. Philadelphia: University of Pennsylvania Press, 2000.

Wiehe, Jarred. "No Penis? No Problem: Intersections of Queerness and Disability in Laurence Sterne's *The Life and Opinions of Tristram Shandy, Gentleman*." *The Eighteenth Century* 58, no. 2 (Summer 2017): 177–193.

Williams, Raymond. *Keywords: A Vocabulary of Culture and Society*. Oxford: Oxford University Press, 1985.

Wilmot, Earl of Rochester John. *Selected Works*. Edited by H. Frank Ellis. London; New York: Penguin Classics, 2004.

Wilson, Kathleen. "The Performance of Freedom: Maroons and the Colonial Order in Eighteenth-Century Jamaica and the Atlantic Sound." *The William and Mary Quarterly* 66, no. 1 (January 2009): 45–86.

Wiltshire, John. *Jane Austen and the Body: "The Picture of Health."* Cambridge: Cambridge University Press, 1992.

Wollock, Jeffrey. "John Bulwer and the Significance of Gesture in 17th-Century Theories of Language and Cognition." *Gesture* 2, no. 2 (January 2002): 227–258.

Wollstonecraft, Mary. *A Vindication of the Rights of Woman and A Vindication of the Rights of Men*. Edited by Janet Todd. Oxford: Oxford University Press, 2009.

Wood, John. *An Essay towards a Description of Bath: In Four Parts*. 2nd edition. London: Bettenham, 1738.

Woolley, Hannah. *The Gentlewomans Companion; Or, A Guide to the Female Sex: Containing Directions of Behaviour, in All Places, Companies, Relations, and Conditions, from Their Childhood down to Old Age*. London: Maxwell, 1673.

Wright, David. *Deafness: A Personal Account*. Rev. ed. London; Boston: Faber & Faber, 1991.

Wycherley, William. *The Country Wife*. In *Restoration and Eighteenth-Century Comedy: A Norton Critical Edition*, edited by Scott McMillin, 3–78. London: Norton Critical Editions, 1997.

INDEX

Italics indicate illustrations.

ability, 2, 153; to bear children, 20; boundary with disability, 11, 23–24; to communicate, 37, 53; health and, as order, 104–105; and labor, 92–93, 96–98; and patriarchy, 88; physical, 80–81, 87, 135; and racism, 94, 96–99; to reason, 6

able-bodiedness, 1, 3, 13, 30, 32n5, 164; compulsory, 11, 34n57; consolidation with heterosexuality, 11, 34n57; constructions of, 14; and heteronormativity, 30, 105

ableism, 31, 24–25, 27, 73, 88, 91, 157; ableist futures, 127; ableist language, 16–17; exclusionary principle of, 6–7; and gender, race, and class, 73; hierarchies of, 3, 5; ideology of ability, 6–7, 24, 73, 94, 97–98, 100n4; in Locke, 3–5, 8; logics of, 31; and Wollstonecraft, 139

accessibility, 7, 25, 27, 50, 92; in built environments, 24, 27, 106, 112; to education, 27, 49, 131

accommodation, 27, 71–72, 90–93

Æsop, 135–137, 139, 142, 147, 161n23

Age of Reform, 133, 138, 147, 151

aging, 29, 30, 62, 79, 85, 91, 105–106, 107, 115, 122, 125; and arbitrary bodily standards, 84; and crip theory, 123; and disease, 129n12; and impairment, 93, 98–99, 117; libertines, 110; old age undermines heteronormativity, 122; queerness of aged bodies, 122–124; social conditions for aging and disabled bodies, 112; spectacle of aging bodies, 128; vicissitudes of, 127

Ahmed, Sara, 50

amatory fiction, 26, 55–56, 59, 62, 66

Anderson, Misty, 122

Armstrong, Nancy, 4, 31n1, 72, 73, 100n10

audism (auditory normativity), 28, 65; in Locke, 47; viewing deafness and signing as unnatural, 37–38

Austen, Jane: health as imperative for marriage, 31, 165; *Mansfield Park*, 165; marriage, individual choice, class and economics, 165; *Northanger Abbey*, 166; *Persuasion*, 138, 165; *Pride and Prejudice*, 15, 165, 166; *Sense and Sensibility*, 165, 168; women and primogeniture, 15

Austen, Jane, *Sanditon*: and *aromantic* relationships, 31, 166; hypochondria as a malady of interpretation, 167; real and imaginary corporeal distress, 165; unheterosexuality, 168

Bacon, Francis: deformity aligned with gender mobility, 12; deformity produces ill-nature and transgression, 101n45, 135; empiricism of, 50; and eunuchism, 11–12; Hay on, 135; taxonomy of physical difference, 69n49, 101n45

Bakhtin, Mikhail, 111

Ballaster, Ros, 26, 55, 59

Bannet, Eve Tavor, 80, 95, 102n49

Bath: class and heteronormativity in, 111; environmental inconvenience for sick and disabled, 112; inaccessibility in, 27, 112; *Original Bath Guide*, 110; promise of health and pleasure, 110–111, 115; women and exposure in male domain, 113. See also Smollett, Tobias, *The Expedition of Humphry Clinker*

Bearden, Elizabeth, 48, 69n49, 101n37

Beaumont, John, 67n11

beauty, 7, 22, 135, 138; female, 90, 144–145, 156, 165; female, male overvaluing of, 146; physical and moral, 139. See also deformity

[185]

INDEX

Bedlam, 36
Bentham, Jeremy, 131
Berlant, Lauren, 32n4
Binhammer, Katherine, 141
Blackmore, Sir Richard, 108
blindness, 46, 91, 104, 117; and compensatory sensory perception, 47; and education, 48; empirical thought marginalizes, 5; feigned, 119
Bluestocking Circle, the, 85, 162n33
Bond, William, 67n11, 70n76
Borsay, Peter, 111
Boucé, Paul-Gabriel, 104, 105–106, 129n5
Boyle, Robert, 46
Brahmins, 44–45
Braidwood, Thomas, 52
Braidwood School for the Deaf (London), 44, 69n57
Branson, Jan, 67n6
Brown, Hilary, 86
Bulwer, John, 52, 57, 69n49; on bodily and sensory variation, 48; *Chirologia: or, the Natural Language of the Hand*, 47; community of senses, 49, 49–51, 68n38; compensatory sense perception, 48, 51; gesture as universal language, 47; impact on Duncan Campbell narratives, 47, 66; on the nation or tribe of the deaf, 44; *Philocophus: or, the Deaf and Dumb Man's Friend*, 44, 47, 49
Burgawer, Dominicus, 108
Burney, Frances: *Cecilia*, 142; *Evelina*, 25, 142; gender politics both feminist and conservative, 141; physicality of novels, 142; *Wanderer, The*, 142
Burney, Frances, *Camilla*: bodily erasure in, 159; disability, intellect, and morality, 139; female agency and vulnerability, 141, 144; female deformity as mark of genius, 30; impairment mediated through comedy, 142; and the male gaze, 30, 145–146; performance of genteel femininity, 133; and prescriptive gender roles, 141–142; privileges mind over body, 144; sexual terror, 14; starer and staree, 30, 128, 146; visibility of disfigurement in public space, 133, 139, 141, 146
Bute, Mary Stuart, Countess of, 134
Butler, Eleanor, 88

Cadogan, William, 111, 112; critique of bathing, 14; *A Dissertation on the Gout*, 108–109; on luxury, 109
Campbell, Duncan, 36, 43; authorship of works in the *Duncan Campbell Compendium*, 67n11, 70n76; cosmic queerness, 40–41, 45, 59, 66, 164; deafness and queerness of, 52–53, 55; deafness and second sight, 37–39, 45, 53, 56, 60; haptic experience of sound, 51–52; heroism of, 61–62; as impostor, 67n6; performance of identities, 57; queer phenomenology, 53, 66; site for projection of gendered and sexed values, 62, 64; source of paternalistic authority, 55. See also *The Friendly Daemon: or, the Generous Apparition*; Haywood, Eliza, *A Spy on the Conjurer*; *The History of the Life and Adventures of Mr. Duncan Campbell*; *The Supernatural Philosopher: or, the mysteries of magick, All exemplified in the history of the life and surprizing adventures of Mr. Duncan Campbell*
Carter, Elizabeth, 162n33
castrati, 34n67
Centlivre, Susannah, 36
Charles I, King, 37
Cheyne, George, 108, 111, 129n24
chronic disease, 8, 10, 13, 81, 90, 99, 103, 111, 121, 129n12; and disability, 29, 104, 117–119, 169; in *The Castle of Otranto*, 15–17, 19–20; in *Humphry Clinker*, 104–109, 111, 116, 124; treatments for, 106–107, 111, 118
Church of England, 71, 95, 121
class, 29, 45, 73; in *Humphry Clinker*, 110–111, 119, 120, 122, 124; impairment cuts across class system, 87; in *Millenium Hall*, 88, 91, 98
Clerc, Laurent, 44
complexion, 82, 90, 98, 102n55, 113, 114, 136, 146, 165; fluidity of, 31n2
compulsory heterosexuality, 11, 71–72, 88, 113; and able-bodiedness, 34n57; and compulsory reproductive futurity, 15, 17, 28; genteel, 84; and primogeniture, 15, 18
corporeality, 123–124, 136–137; the body as product of social forces, 3, 87–88; and intellect, 31; regularity, 87–88; and sexuality, 166. See also embodiment; physiognomy

[186]

INDEX

Crenshaw, Kimberlé, 10
crip theory, 8–9, 33n51; and aging bodies, 122–123; crip futurity, 9; to crip Georgian literature, 9, 14; supercrip heroism, 62–63
cross-dressing, 80–82, 100n17, 133, 148, 154
cross-sex. *See* heterosexuality
Croxall, Samuel, 136, 161n23
cruising, 132, 161n5
cultural production, 9, 13, 35n100, 111
Curll, Edward, 67n11

Dacre, Charlotte, 24
Davidson, Michael, 10, 33n51
Davis, Lennard, 2, 31n1, 33n18; on Duncan Campbell, 42, 67n6; on disability and identity in the novel, 35n99; on fascination with deafness, 46; on "normalcy," 87
deaf education, 66, 67n10, 69n54, 69n57, 164; and audism, 38; and fingerspelling, 46, 53, 54; oralist approach to, 52; perceived ineducability, 62; and signed language, 47, 53; speech exercises in, 52; written literacy in, 52–53, 58
deaf educators: Bonet, Juan Pablo, 52; Braidwood, Thomas, 52, 69n57; Green, Francis, 69n57; Ponce de León, Pedro, 52; Wallis, John, 52–53
deafness, 13; associated with disfigurement, 56; and bone conduction, 69n45; "Deaf-gain," 48; deaf soundscapes, 7, 47, 50–52; discourses of, 28; does not hinder communication, 48; and empirical theory of education, 4, 28; and language, 46; and sociability, 57
deaf people: accepting of auditory difference, 48; assimilation into hearing order, 37–38; containment and medicalization, 38, 66; deaf identity, 38; deaf subjectivity, 28, 44–45; and inheritance law, 52; and primacy of vocal interaction, 37; sharpening of other senses, 47–48; sociability of, 47; supernatural powers of, 37–38; as a transnational tribe, 44. *See also* audism (auditory normativity)
Defoe, Daniel, 25, 26, 67n11
deformity, 2, 6, 33n43; as aesthetic judgment, 7; "deformed" birth as procreative failure, 22; heterosexual eradication of (proto-eugenics), 22, 164; and intellect, 135–137, 147; as mark or enabler of genius, 7, 134; and moral philosophy, 7–8; as non-white and non-European, 161n23; and queer genders, 8. *See also* physiognomy
degeneracy: fear of heritable infirmities, 52; theories of, 14
Descartes, Rene, Cartesian duality, 5, 27
desire: and embodiment, 1, 9, 23, 74; excessive, 56, 82; female, 41, 55–56, 71, 112, 115, 138, 140, 162n39; heterosexual, 17, 50; homosocial, 126; libertine, 73, 79; male, 107, 132; monstrous, 23; non-normative, 85, 164, 169; non-procreative, 31n3; normative, 9, 11, 14, 17, 34n57, 169; and novels, 4; queer, 3, 8, 27, 29, 31n3, 32n10, 34n61, 83, 85; repressed, 19; same-sex, 67, 77, 88, 132; sapphic, 80–81, 88; of the subaltern, 112; traces of (desire lines), 50–51
Deutsch, Helen, 2, 7, 8, 12; on deformity, 2, 7, 8, 12, 33n43; on the disability-genius dichotomy, 134–135
Dickie, Simon, 7, 8
Digby, Kenelm, 47
disability: and aging, 116–120, 123; and the capacity for labor, 93; as catalyst for improvement, 92; cultural uncertainty about, 147; disabled identity, 38; disabled sociability, 117–118; disabled subjectivity, 24; as embodied problem to be solved, 31n1, 105; emphasized for ludicrous effect, 115; fluidity of, 11; and gender mobility, 148; as human variation, 7, 8, 84; as lived reality, 1, 3, 9–10, 20, 27, 31, 84, 90–91, 98, 141; mapped on the individual body, 31; oversimplified concept of, 101n37; and pain, 35n92, 84, 105, 141; performance of, 118; relational approach to, 3, 19, 24–25, 27, 33n19, 37, 103, 128, 131, 159, 164, 170n5; and procreative heterosexuality, 20, 116; as social category, 7, 24–25; social model of, 24, 35n92, 84; social vs. individual responsibility for, 25; and transgender bodies, 149
disability, medical model of, 102n59; and containment, 38, 40; and deaf education, 66; medical interventions, 29–30, 99

[187]

INDEX

disease: ague, 116, 122, 127; contagion from foul air (miasma), 109; and cure for excess of city living, 109; and disability, 103, 116, 119–120; epidemiology and, 129n5; heart failure, 85; hereditary, 108; and heterosexual failure, 116; humoral theory of, 109; knowledge of eventual bodily failure, 123; and needless suffering, 140; normalizing wellness and illness, 140; plague, 111; pursuit of sensual pleasure and disease, 107–108; rheumatism, 105, 127; smallpox, 85, 90, 133, 140, 162n35. *See also* chronic disease; gout

disfigurement, 6–7, 12–13, 56, 91, 104, 116, 136, 140–143, 161n8; Bacon on, 101n45; feigned, 119; gendered, 131, 133, 156; and witchcraft, 36. *See also* deformity; impairment

doctors, 99, 107, 155, 169n3; in Bath, 130n38; and the clinical gaze, 132; doctor-patient dynamics, 31, 106–107, 132, 167; in *Humphry Clinker*, 106–107, 126, 132; quacks, 83, 99; and Scott, 99. *See also* Blackmore, Sir Richard; Burgawer, Dominicus; Cadogan, William; Cheyne, George; Hill, Sir John; Quillet, Claude

Dodsley, Robert, 161n23

domesticity, 23, 82, 157; and class, 22, 76, 100n1, 148; danger outside domestic sphere, 148; as enslavement, 83, 132; and surveillance, 17–18

domesticity, heteronormative, 83, 155; fictional quality of health in, 157

domesticity, heterosexual, 99, 148, 157, 160, 169; in *Belinda*, 133, 148–149, 155–157; disruption of, 14, 148; and health, 159; in *Pamela*, 29, 72–73, 77–79; as performance, 30, 156–157, 159; and transformation of libertinism, 77–78, 98

domesticity, sapphic, 82–83, 133

Doody, Margaret, 142, 162n47

Douglas, Aileen, 3, 104, 128

Dowglas, Janet, 46

Edelman, Lee, 31n3

Edgeworth, Maria, *Belinda*: consensual queer intimacy in, 30, 133, 147–148, 158; and disruption of heterosexual domesticity, 14, 147; gendered pronouns in, 153, 163n55; heteronormative ending of, 148, 157; normative embodiment vs. queer eroticism, 159; performance of queer gender and kinship, 133, 147–148; physical disability and gender mobility, 148; starer and staree, 30, 128, 149–151, 158

education: and corporeality, 30, 138; feminism and disability, 30; writing and fingerspelling, 46. *See also* deaf education

education of women, 30; body-intelligence analogy, 134, 138; concealing learning, 134

embodiment: complex, 7, 32n5, 98; disabled, and education, 131; disabled, stereotypes of, 106; flexible, 28; gendered, 64, 135; healthy body and sound mind, 5–6, 139, 144; individual embodied subjectivity, 31; libertine, 23, 28; non-normative, 50–51, 118; normative, 14, 138, 159; queer and disabled, 14, 27, 50, 71, 159; sensational orientation of variable bodies, 51; spectacle of female, diseased, aging bodies, 128; transgender, 30, 149, 152–153, 156; variable, 41, 51, 64, 71, 91, 127, 131, 137

empiricism, 3, 5, 46, 50

epistle, epistolarity, 57–59, 106–107, 111–113; in *Camilla*, 142–144; in *Humphry Clinker*, 103–104, 106, 112–116, 120–121, 126–127; in *Millenium Hall*, 86, 89; as narrative frame, 86; in *Pamela*, 73–78

Erevelles, Nirmala, 10

Erickson, Paul, 104

eroticism, 31n3, 41, 56, 69n65, 72; absence of, 89; female, 71–72; gothic erotics of loss, 16; queer, 149, 159; in reading, 56; and scandal, 59; same-sex, 76, 81, 88, 100n17; woman-centered heterosexual, 55. *See also* homoeroticism

eugenics, 20–22

eunuchs and eunuchism, 11–12, 23, 24, 108

Farinelli (Carlo Broschi), 34n67

female husbands, 82–83

feminism: and achievement in typically male realm, 13; aligning "queer," "crip," and feminism, 34n57; antifeminist delicacy, 82; black feminist thought, 10; body-oriented, 99, 133; consent between starer and staree, 30, 128, 133; and disability, 1, 33n19; and education, 30, 141; and embodiment, 133, 147; gynocentric utopianism, 85; and intersectionality, 34; and mind-body connection, 134; and ocular relations, 128, 134; proto-feminism, 85, 137, 145; and Sarah

[188]

Scott, 79–80; and Mary Wollstonecraft, 139. *See also* ocular relations, oppressive
Fielding, Henry, 26, 82–83
Fielding, Sarah, 162n33
Fluornoy, John J., 44
Foucault, Michel, *Discipline and Punish*, 131; the clinical gaze, 132; surveillance, 131
Foucault, Michel, *History of Sexuality*, 2, 32n6; on "perverse" practices and degeneracy, 21
Fowke, Martha, 36
Frazer, John, 46
Freud, Sigmund, 12, 19, 21
Friendly Daemon: or, the Generous Apparition, The, 51–52
friendship, female, 85, 89, 153
friendship, male, 40, 117

Gallop, Jane, 123
Galton, Francis, 20, 21
Gamer, Michael, 157, 163n72
Garland-Thomson, Rosemarie: on baroque staring, 149–150; on the *normate*, 16, 34n73; and queerness, 155; on staring as conduit to knowledge, 132, 151; on staring back, 33n46
gender: agency and, 106; binary system of, 15, 151, 153, 164; categories, 8, 31n1, 32n6; crisis of, 147, 163n54; and deaf subjectivity, 45; and deformity, 12; and disability, 2, 7, 10, 11, 25, 71, 98; fixed, prescriptive renderings of, 29, 133, 141–142; flexibility of, 159; gendered embodiment not static, 64; heteronormative codes of, 77; identity, 133, 152; instability of, 151; and language, 153, 163n55; and medicine, 105; mobility, 12, 29, 40, 45, 52, 62, 64, 66, 80, 93, 131, 148, 151, 164; nonconformity, 132, 148, 148, 156, 158; normativity, 1, 20, 29, 83, 135, 148, 159; and ocular relations, 134–135, 148; performance of, 66, 83, 151, 158; queer gender, 1, 8, 34n61, 38, 40–41, 131, 133; and sensibility, 80, 147, 152; social regulation of, 81, 81; third (or "unsexed"), 152; variability of, 1, 73, 90, 169. *See also* eunuchs and eunuchism; transgender bodies
Glorious Revolution, the, 17, 34n74
Gonda, Caroline, 89, 100n20
Gothic, the, 15–16; *Castle of Otranto* as queer and crip, 14–16; unrestrained libido and power hunger, 24

Gottlieb, Evan, 111
gout, 105–108, 127–128, 129n19; Cadogan on, 108–109, 111; Cheyne on, 108–109; as a gentleman's disease, 107; Hippocrates on, 108; resulting from sexual indulgence, 106–107
Green, Francis, 69n57
Grinnell, George, 167
Grob, Gerald N., 129n12
Guy-Bray, Stephen, 40

Haggerty, George, 31n1, 85, 144; on Gothic fiction, 15–16
Hall, Stuart: on cultural production, 35n100; on representation, 37
Harlequin Skeleton, 125
Hay, William, 138; compares himself with famous men, 135–136; deformity promotes character and intellect, 135; opposes Bacon on deformity and malice, 101n45, 135; on shame felt about bodily difference, 118
Haywood, Eliza, 25, 36; *The British Recluse*, 59; *Love in Excess*, 59
Haywood, Eliza, *A Spy on the Conjurer*, 28; Campbell as vehicle for scandal fiction, 55, 58–59; Campbell's honesty, 60–61; Campbell's masculinity, 59, 61; Campbell and supercrip heroism, 62–63; deafness and polite society, 55–56; and the erotic imagination, 56; and educability of deaf people, 38; moral authority and second sight, 60; and witchcraft, 60–61
health, 2, 82, 108, 114, 158–159, 166–167; attainment of as fantasy, 29, 106, 111, 127, 164; bodily, 6, 104; and country retirement, 109, 120–121, 126–127; and disfigurement, 140; as emerging concept, 11, 99; and fictions of embodiment, 128; healthy body and sound mind, 6; and heteronormativity, 157–158; and heterosexuality, 13, 17–18, 30, 105–106, 116, 158–159, 164; and impairment, 14, 104, 142; and libertinism, 24; and marriage, 31, 105, 116, 116, 120, 122, 126, 126, 160, 165, 168; and masculinity, 118; and old age, 66, 126; performance of, 158; and reproductive futurity, 15–18, 20–22, 157; restorative treatments for, 80, 85, 99, 104, 109, 121; and sexuality, 99–100. *See also* Bath; chronic disease; disease; gout; hypochondria; impairment

[189]

INDEX

heteronormativity, 13, 30; in *Belinda*, 148, 154, 157; in *The Castle of Otranto*, 17; constructions of, 14, 164; in *Humphry Clinker*, 105; monogamy and, 155; "naturalness" of, 2; old age undermines, 122–123

heterosexuality, 1, 9; amatory fiction and heterosexual eroticism, 55; bodies in pain and, 390; bourgeois, 29; chronic illness and marriage at Bath, 111; and courtship rituals, 20; cross-sex courtship, 104; and eradication of deformity, 22; failure of, linked to disability and illness, 116; linked to health and ability, 2, 13, 30, 116, 127; logic of heterosexual desire, 50; and queerness, legibility of, 99; performance of, 158–159; romantic fulfillment, 127, 129. *See also* compulsory heterosexuality; unheterosexuality

Hill, Sir John, 108

Hippocrates, 108

Hirschmann, Nancy J., 6

History of the Life and Adventures of Mr. Duncan Campbell, The, 13; authorship of, 67n11; Campbell as queer angel, 28, 39–41, 45, 56, 62; circle of women as harem, 41–42; cosmic queerness, 28, 40–41, 45, 59; and deaf education, 27, 38, 52–53; deafness and second sight, 37–39, 45, 53; and deaf people as savage or mad, 37; and deaf subjectivity, 28; genteel masculinity, 45; hypervisibility vs. illegibility, 41, 45; feminized angelic beauty, 39–40, 68n22; Laplandish-Highland origins, 39, 45; and libertine indulgence, 45; queer and normative masculinities, 28, 38; queered and exoticized body, 38, 45; and stringed instruments, 28; as travel narrative, 40, 42, 44–45, 66; and Wallis's methods of deaf education, 53

Holder, William, 69n54

homoeroticism, 39, 40, 50, 66, 85, 101n38

homophobia, 150

homosexuality, 21; emergent notions of, 2; and heterosexuality, 11; and impairment, 40. *See also* queerness

homosocial bonding: among the aged and disabled, 116–117; and libertine traffic in women, 23; and Milton's *Paradise Lost*, 40–41; and women's companionship, 71

Humphrey, James, *The Real Man of Sensibility: Or the History of Sir George Ellison*, 102n49

hypochondria: and Austen, 31, 165–168, 170n5; as a malady of interpretation, 167

ideology of ability. *See* ableism

illness. *See* disease

impairment: and bitterness, 91, 101n45; and class system, 87; and illness as disorder, 104; as embodied, lived reality, 31, 72; as obstacle to be overcome, 106; as physical or cognitive condition, 24; representations of, 30; resulting from disease, 103; source of physical and social pain, 72–73; stigmatizing, 3. *See also* disability; disfigurement

Inchbald, Elizabeth, 163n71

individualism, 31n1, 33n21

Ingram, Allen, 104

intersectionality, 10, 34n57

intimacy, 128, 169; and aging and variable bodies, 30, 105, 127; between musician and deaf listener, 50; communal, 88; conjugal, 30, 88; female, 82; heterosexual, 67; immoderate, 130n44; norms of, 88, 169; queer, 30, 48, 147–148, 160, 164; same-sex, 67, 88, 90, 151. *See also* friendship, female; friendship, male; homosocial bonding; ocular relations; sapphism

invalid/invalidism, 106, 110, 167–168; in Bath, 110, 114, 118; and hypochondria, 166, 168. *See also* disease; health

Jamaica, 29, 73, 94–98

James II, King, 17

Johns, Alessa, 84–85

Johnson, Claudia, 141, 143, 163n54

Johnson, Samuel, 2, 162n33; on deafness, 57; deformity as mark and enabler of genius, 7, 30; monster-genius dichotomy, 134–135

Joshua, Essaka, 7, 8, 67n11

Juvenal, 5, 6

Kafer, Alison, 8–9, 11, 13, 33n19; aligning "queer," "crip", and feminism, 34n57

Kelleher, Paul, 7, 8, 32n10; on sentiment and morality in *Pamela*, 74

Kelly, Gary, 80, 112

King, Kathryn, 59

[190]

INDEX

Kirk, Robert, 46
Klein, Ula, 34n61, 80, 100n17, 154
Krentz, Christopher, 37

Ladies of Llangollen, the, 88
Lane, Harlan, 67n6
Lanser, Susan, 31n3, 85, 88, 101n38
lesbianism and sapphism, 101n38
L'Estrange, Sir Roger, 161n23
Lewis, G. M., 125
Lewis, Matthew G., 24
libertinism, 14, 35n86, 72–73; aging libertines, marriage, or bachelorhood, 110; despotic sexuality, 76; and disease, 105, 124; gothic unrestrained libido and power hunger, 24; homosociality and, 23; reformed and unreformed, 20–21, 64, 107; political and sexual ascendancy and able-bodiedness, 23–24; sensibility and the reformed rake, 64, 164
Linker, Beth, 103, 128n1
lip reading, 39, 51–52, 68n38
Lister, Ann, 31n3
Locke, John: ableism of, 3, 5; and mind-body duality, 27; educational barriers for disabled people, 5, 6; emergence of the individual, 4; on language and reason, 46–47; and literary emphasis on subjective experience, 4; and sensory impairment, 5, 68n33; sensory perception and subjectivity, 4–5; on signing, 68n33; sound body as gauge of educability, 6
Lubey, Kathleen, 56, 69n65
Luxembourg, François Henri de Montmorency-Bouteville, duc de, 136

Mallory-Kani, Amy, 169n3
Mary II, Queen, 17
masculinity: and aging, 125; and authority, 59; in *The Castle of Otranto*, 16, 18–20, 23; classed standards of, 122, 151–152; and education, 137, 139; female assumption of, 74, 81, 151; and friendship, 40; and gender mobility, 41, 64, 66; genteel, 45, 118; hypermasculinity, 61, 64; ideal, 62; markers of, 64, 80; normative, 28, 38, 55–56; performance of, 45; queer, 28, 38; and sensibility, 64; sentimental, 72, 147
McKeon, Michael, 26, 73
McRuer, Robert, 8, 11, 13, 34n57

medicine, eighteenth-century: bodies in pain, 29, 106; the clinical gaze, 132; doctor-patient dynamics, 31, 106–107; fantasy of achieving health, 106; illness and impairment as disorder, 104; and medical authority, 169n3; and medical intervention, 29, 104; popularized, 140. *See also* disease; doctors; health
melancholy, 20, 116, 121, 142–143
Methodism, 115, 121–122, 130n50, 155, 163n58
Miller, D. A., 108, 168, 170n5
Miller, Don, 67n11
Milton, John, 40
Minear, Andrea, 10
Mitchell, David T., 11, 13, 75
monstrosity: hypersexuality and, 115; monster-genius, cultural construction of, 30; physical difference as, 31n1, 56; shocking body as monstrosity, 137–138
Montagu, Elizabeth, 85, 162n33
Montagu, Lady Barbara, 85–86
Mounsey, Chris, 32n5

narrative prosthesis, 29, 72, 75–76, 78, 98, 159. *See also* Mitchell, David T.; Snyder, Sharon L.
"normalcy," the idea of, 87
normate, the, 16, 34n73
Norton, Rictor, 161n5
novel, the: and disability in narrative structure, 27; discursive mediation of ableism, 24; embodiment in, 27; epistolary form, 106–107, 111–113; heteroglossia in, 111; hybridity of form, 27, 106; novel and romance, 25–27, 157; novels as histories, 25, 37; polymorphous nature of, 159; readers' sympathetic imagination, 26; and realism, 26–27, 157; and travel literature, 44. *See also* Armstrong, Nancy; Ballaster, Ros; McKeon, Michael; Watt, Ian; Warner, William
Nussbaum, Felicity, 41, 61, 85, 143, 161n8

ocular relations, 131–132; baroque staring, 149–150, 152, 154–155; and performance of relationships, 158; queer, 132, 155, 158; reader as ultimate privileged starer, 158; staree's intention to provoke wonder, 152; staring as potentially transformative act, 131–132, 149, 151, 155, 160; visual engagement, 132, 154; a "wanton eye," 149; warnings against, 161n11

[191]

ocular relations, oppressive: clinical gaze, 131, 133; male gaze, 30, 132, 133, 145, 153; panoptical gaze (surveillance), 131, 133, 159
Ottoman Empire, 42–44
Ottaway, Susannah R., 129n15

patients, 109; at Bath, 112–113, 130n38; doctor-patient dynamics, 31, 106–107, 132, 167. *See also* disease; doctors; health; hypochondria
patriarchal society, 13, 80, 164; and class, 100n1; destructive effects of, 80, 141, 145, 164; domination and power, 17; genteel, 91; and heterosexuality, 151; and insensible men, 71; and the male gaze, 30, 132, 133, 145, 153; and markers of masculinity, 64; mastering the subaltern, 112; negotiating with, 73; objectification of women, 132; righting the wrongs of, 13, 71, 81; subversion and disruption of, 85, 88, 161n30
Pepys, Samuel, 46
physiognomy, 39, 74, 84, 93, 115, 123; deaf people expert in, 68n38; marks of villainy, 72; physical and moral beauty linked, 139
Ponsonby, Sarah, 88
Pope, Alexander, 2, 82; deformity as mark and enabler of genius, 7, 30; and the monster-genius dichotomy, 134–135
Popham, Alexander, 52, 69n54
Port, Cynthia, 122–123
Porter, Roy, 105
primogeniture, 14–15, 17, 108; compulsory heterosexuality and, 15, 18; and reproductive futurity, 15–17; women and, 15

queer family and kinship, 31n3, 86, 89, 93, 122, 147
queerness: cosmically queer, 28, 39–41, 45, 59, 66, 164; and heterosexuality, legibility of, 99; involuntary disfigurement and queer ways of being, 12; and lived experience of disability and, 1; nonreproductive and ungendered sexuality, 40; queer and disabled/variable bodies, 15, 74, 76–79, 98, 99; queer relations, 131, 160; reconceptualizes temporality, 122; resistance to categories, 31n3; same-sex desire, 31n3, 132; and sapphism, 31n3
queer ocular relations, 30, 132

queer pastoralism, 71
queer phenomenology, 51, 53, 66
Quillet, Claude, 22

race, 29, 73; blackness and physical ability, 94, 96–97, 99; blackness as social disability, 94; fluid understanding of, 95, 102n55; white paternalism and black bodies, 29
Radcliffe, Ann, 24, 25
Reeve, Clara, *The Progress of Romance*, 25–26
Reid, B. L., 104
reproductive futurity, 1, 13, 22; aged and queer insurgency against, 123, 126–127; "deformed" birth as procreative failure, 22
Rich, Adrienne, 11
Richard III, King, 136
Richardson, Samuel, 26; and bourgeois heterosexuality, 29; and reform of heterosexual relations, 78
Richardson, Samuel, *Pamela*, 67; character overcoming adversity in, 25; deformity as sign of uninhibited desire, 74, 76–77; Mrs. Jewkes and heteronormative gender codes, 75–77; Mrs. Jewkes as surrogate for Mr. B., 76–78; Mrs. Jewkes's queer deformity, 74, 76–79, 98, 164; and heterosexual domesticity, 29, 72–73, 76, 78; impairment as metaphor, 71–72; and the libertine reformed, 22, 28, 64, 73, 76–77, 164; narrative prosthesis (deformity enabling narrative), 75, 78, 98; negotiating marriage contract, 73; and sentimental masculinity, 72, 78
Richman, Jared S., 102n59
Rizzo, Betty, 95, 100n20, 102n54, 162n33
Robinson, Terry F., 157, 163n58, 163n71
Rochester, John Wilmot, Earl of, 23, 35n86
Romantic era, medical shifts in, 31, 167
Rousseau, Jean-Jacques, 46–47
Royal Society, 52, 69n54

Salisbury, Robert Cecil, First Earl of, 136
Sanchez, Melissa, 68n21
Sancho, Ignatius, 95
Sandahl, Carrie, 8
sapphism, 88; and the Bluestockings, 85; and class, 101n38; and compensatory conservatism, 85, 88; healthy sapphic domesticity, 82; monstrous, 164; same-sex eroticism, 88; sapphic conjugality, 85; sapphic desire and labor, 80

Scarron, Paul, 136
Scott, Sarah: conservatism of, 85, 88; disability as a natural physical state, 29, 72; and entrenched class hierarchies, 85, 93, 94; female desire and deformity, 162–163; feminism of, 79–80, 99; gender mobility, 80, 83; marriage of, 100n20; partnership with Lady Barbara Montagu, 85–86; physical ability, 80; queer disabled bonds vs. heterosexual union, 72; reformist vision, 29, 67, 71, 73, 79, 84–85, 88, 94, 96, 98; sapphism vs. patriarchal rule, 81, 86; on slavery, 94, 102n54; theories of embodiment, 73
Scott, Sarah, *Agreeable Ugliness*, 102n47, 146, 161n30; female desire to be celebrated, 138; plain looks enable virtue and intellect, 137; "shocking" body as monstrosity, 137–138
Scott, Sarah, *A Journey through Every Stage of Life*, 72; cross-dressing in, 81–82; female performance of maleness, 79, 81, 83; and Fielding's *The Female Husband*, 83; heteronormative conclusion of, 83; queer and disabled bodies and reform, 29; sapphic desire in, 80–81, 83; separates queerness and disability, 79
Scott, Sarah, *Millenium Hall*: against cruelty to women and the disabled, 93; aged, disabled, queer bodies and reform, 29, 67, 79, 84, 88; and class, 85, 88, 92; conjugal and group sapphism, 88–89; labor and community, 92; male point of view in, 89; the normative body, 87; physical marks and sapphic orientation, 13; queer and disabled characters accommodate, 27, 71; redefining family by choice and love, 86, 89, 93; utopian retreat from patriarchal cruelty and ableism, 71, 84–86; women's ideal Christian practice in, 84–85, 89; and women's variable embodiment, 90–91
Scott, Sarah, *The History of Sir George Ellison*, 72; extent of criticism of slavery, 95; global reform, 29; Humphrey's *The Real Man of Sensibility: Or the History of Sir George Ellison*, 102n49; lived experience of enslaved black people, 94; paternalistic sensibility and the slave owner, 95–97
second sight, 61; Duncan Campbell and, 13, 28, 36–37, 39, 41, 44–46, 53, 59, 60, 64;

Janet Dowglas, 46; and Scotland, 36, 46; sensory impairment and, 46
Secret Memoirs of the Late Duncan Campbell, The: Campbell as sentimental reformed libertine, 63–64; Campbell's second sight, 63–65
Sedgwick, Eve, 23
sensibility: cross-sex sentimental romance, 72; and gender, 80, 147; models of decency in, 2, 74; patriarchy and unsentimental men, 71; reform in the Age of Sensibility, 94, 98; sentimentalized masculinity, 147; sentiment and heterosexuality, 20; and slavery, 95–96
sex and sexuality: binary thinking about, 151; dysfunction, 23; emergence of peripheral sexualities, 2; pursuit of sensual pleasure and disease, 107; and the repressive hypothesis, 2, 13. *See also* libertinism
Siebers, Tobin: on complex embodiment, 7, 32n5, 84, 100n4; on disability and intersectionality, 34n57; the ideology of ability, 6–7
sight impairment, and empirical theory of education, 5. *See also* blindness
signing and signed language: Bulwer on gesture as universal language, 47; and Campbell, 68n33; debates about, 38; demonstrates rationality among the deaf, 47; Locke on expressing ideas by signs, 68n33; and Ottoman culture, 43; as viable form of expression, 47; vs. fingerspelling, 53
slavery: and ability to labor, 95–96, 99; barbaric cruelty, 96; paternalistic sensibility and the slave-owner, 95–97; Scott and chattel slavery, 99, 102n54
Smith, Adam, 7–8
Smollett, Tobias, *Expedition of Humphry Clinker, The*, 13, 100; the body in pain and medical intervention, 29, 104; corporeal satire in, 106, 111, 112, 117, 130n38; critique of Bath in other works, 130n38; disability-medical reading of, 103; on display of diseased and deformed bodies, 114, 117; fantasy of healthy closure, 29, 106, 111, 127, 164; inaccessibility in Bath, 27; lady-lapdog convention, 130n44; patriarchal mastery of the subaltern, 112; physiognomic indication of character, 115, 123; social causes of corporeal vulnerability unquestioned, 127; spectacle of variable bodies, 128; and Steele's ugly club, 117. *See also* gout

[193]

INDEX

Snyder, Sharon L., 11, 13, 75–76
Spectator, The, 161n11
Stanback, Emily B., 103
staring. *See* ocular relations
Steele, Sir Richard, 36, 67n2, 145, 161n11; and ugly club, 117, 162n50
Sterne, Laurence, 95
Stoler, Ann Laura, 22
Straub, Kristina, 93, 141, 162n40
supercrip, the, 62, 125
Supernatural Philosopher: or, the mysteries of magick, All exemplified in the history of the life and surprizing adventures of Mr. Duncan Campbell, The, 42, 43
Sutherland, Alex, 46
synesthesia, 48

Tatler, The, 36
Taylor, Gary, 12
theater, 37, 110, 157
Thersites, 136
Thrale, Hester, 162n33
transgender bodies, 149, 152; female husbands, 82–83, 163n66; misgendering, 153; mollies, 163n66
transphobia, 150, 152
Traub, Valerie, 34n61
travel, 83, 103, 110; and exoticism, 45, 66; and the picaresque, 80; and restoration of health, 29, 106, 120, 124, 127; and sensibility, 44; travel narratives and the novel, 40, 42, 44
Turner, David, 2, 32n4, 124–125

ugly clubs, 118; Richard Steele and, 117, 130n45, 162n50; *The Ugly Club Manuscript*, 100n19
unheterosexuality, 168
utopia, female, 13, 71, 84–86, 88–90, 92, 93

vagrancy and fraud, 100n19
Vermeule, Blakey, 3
Volz, Jessica A., 160n4

Wallis, John, 52, 69n54
Walpole, Horace, *Castle of Otranto*, 3, 14; chronic illness, melancholy, and primogeniture, 20; critique of libertinism, 22–23; Conrad as queer and disabled, 16–17; Conrad's crip haunting of heteronormativity, 18; the erotics of loss, 16; gothic terror as infection, 19; libertine sexuality and domination, 23; Manfred's ableism and heteronormativity, 16–18; Manfred's moral deformity, 17, 24; normative embodiment and heterosexual desire, 17; primogeniture and reproductive futurity, 15–17
Warner, William, 26–27, 32n4
Watt, Ian, 26, 73
West, William, 104, 129n5
Wheeler, Roxann, 31n2, 102n55
Wiehe, Jarred, 34n68
William of Orange, 136
Williams, Raymond, 4, 33n21
Wiltshire, John, 169n1
Wollock, Jeffrey, 69n49
Wollstonecraft, Mary, 85; links education and normative body, 138; *Vindication of the Rights of Women*, 138, 154
women: anti-feminist delicacy, 83; body shaming, 113; and curiosity, 49, 133; homosocial companionship, 41, 71–72; physical variability and superior intellect and morality, 137; resistance to sexual violence, 72; and sensibility, 80, 83; sexual desire beyond reproductive years, 115; sociability, contradictions in, 113; social outlets for, 160; subversive female sexuality, 72; vulnerability in public spaces, 112–113; and widowhood, 162n51. *See also* education of women; feminism; ocular relations, oppressive; sapphism
Woolley, Hannah, 149
Wortley Montagu, Lady Mary, 140; on the danger of women's hypervisibility, 134, 158
Wycherly, William, *The Country Wife*: negotiating ability and disability in, 24; performance of disease, 23–24

ABOUT THE AUTHOR

JASON S. FARR is assistant professor of English at Marquette University. His articles on the topics of eighteenth-century British fiction, disability studies, queer studies, and women writers have appeared in the journals *Eighteenth-Century Fiction*, *Journal for Early Modern Cultural Studies*, and *The Eighteenth Century: Theory and Interpretation*, as well as in the edited collection *The Idea of Disability in the Eighteenth Century* (Bucknell University Press, 2014).

Printed in the United States
By Bookmasters